M000266461

Site Furnishings

Site Furnishings

A Complete Guide to the Planning, Selection and Use of Landscape Furniture and Amenities

Bill Main and Gail Greet Hannah

WILEY

John Wiley & Sons, Inc.

Dedications

Bill Main: To Kathy and our sons Brian, Matt, and Justin. Mom and Dad, too.

Gail Greet Hannah: In memory of Rowena Reed Kostellow and Christine Rae.

This book is printed on acid-free paper. ♾

Copyright © 2010 by John Wiley & Sons, Inc. All rights reserved

Published by John Wiley & Sons, Inc., Hoboken, New Jersey

Published simultaneously in Canada

No part of this publication may be reproduced, stored in a retrieval system, or transmitted in any form or by any means, electronic, mechanical, photocopying, recording, scanning, or otherwise, except as permitted under Section 107 or 108 of the 1976 United States Copyright Act, without either the prior written permission of the Publisher, or authorization through payment of the appropriate per-copy fee to the Copyright Clearance Center, 222 Rosewood Drive, Danvers, MA 01923, (978) 750-8400, fax (978) 646-8600, or on the web at www.copyright.com. Requests to the Publisher for permission should be addressed to the Permissions Department, John Wiley & Sons, Inc., 111 River Street, Hoboken, NJ 07030, (201) 748-6011, fax (201) 748-6008, or online at www.wiley.com/go/permissions.

Limit of Liability/Disclaimer of Warranty: While the publisher and the author have used their best efforts in preparing this book, they make no representations or warranties with respect to the accuracy or completeness of the contents of this book and specifically disclaim any implied warranties of merchantability or fitness for a particular purpose. No warranty may be created or extended by sales representatives or written sales materials. The advice and strategies contained herein may not be suitable for your situation. You should consult with a professional where appropriate. Neither the publisher nor the author shall be liable for any loss of profit or any other commercial damages, including but not limited to special, incidental, consequential, or other damages.

For general information about our other products and services, please contact our Customer Care Department within the United States at (800) 762-2974, outside the United States at (317) 572-3993 or fax (317) 572-4002.

Wiley also publishes its books in a variety of electronic formats. Some content that appears in print may not be available in electronic books. For more information about Wiley products, visit our web site at www.wiley.com.

Library of Congress Cataloging-in-Publication Data:

Main, Bill, 1953-
   Site furnishings : a complete guide to the planning, selection, and use of landscape furniture and amenities / authors, Bill Main and Gail Greet Hannah.
      p. cm.
   Includes index.
   ISBN 978-0-470-39183-9 (cloth)
      1. Urban beautification.   2. Streets—Accessories.   3. Outdoor furniture.
   I. Hannah, Gail Greet.   II. Title.
NA9052.M25 2009
717—dc22
                                                                    2009011986

Printed in the United States of America
10 9 8 7 6 5 4 3 2 1

CONTENTS

FOREWORD

When Does Furniture Work in Outdoor Spaces?

Kathryn Gustafson (KG):   A dialog about the relationship of furniture and landscape has to begin by asking, "What is the landscape?" If we consider this question from the perspective of public exterior space, I think about the variety of roles the landscape plays, from social and political to aesthetic and experiential. Early models came out of communal forests which were productive and spiritual domains, not for leisure. There were no furnishings that didn't have direct functional uses, like fencing or way marking. Another model was the private lands of the royalty. Their gardens, fields and woodlands contained objects that weren't necessarily purely utilitarian, ways of framing and adding cultural information to the landscape such as arbors, walks, statuary. Neither model was about furnishing outdoor space for public occupation, but was more for uses such as harvesting timber, cultivation or displaying wealth.

Today so much of what we do with outdoor space is about solving problems such as remediation. We try to make things whole, shape it to allow people to connect so they'll want to take care of it. Furniture works when it connects people to landscape, and opens up someone's psyche to experience space more fully. Furniture acts as a set of tools, or sets of elements that heighten and reveal.

Jane Amidon (JA):   It seems there are many objects that equip outdoor space functionally which we wouldn't consider to be furnishing, but are fundamental to spatial identity because these objects amplify experiential aspects of the landscape. For example, bicycles and cars create transitory effects, completely altering how we perceive our surroundings. Is a basic definition of furnishing simple awareness, or must it invite mental or physical participation?

KG: When we're least consciously "aware" and acting intuitively, the body responds to how a space is furnished and how objects equip the user for living. Eero Saarinen's chairs are sensual, sensorial; you participate ergonomically and it changes the meaning of the landscape around you at that moment. Each of his pieces gives the user a sense of newness. Josef Albers said that designers should strive to do better, not just different—I'm inspired by this and believe that furniture works when it excites our perceptions in a fresh way each time we encounter it.

André Le Nôtre's mastery of perspective using topography, water and formal plantings furnished the royal gardens of Versailles for the display of power and wealth. Credit: photographs by Kathryn Gustafson.

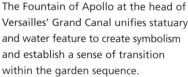

The Fountain of Apollo at the head of Versailles' Grand Canal unifies statuary and water feature to create symbolism and establish a sense of transition within the garden sequence.

Why do we have certain furniture in our lives? Like our attitudes toward clothing, how we use furniture has shifted through history. Some roles are constant: furniture constructs certain ways of using the landscape, like socializing, gathering. Newer roles include more active uses of site and increased security concerns.

JA: Over time we've become more informed and informal toward our bodies, scientifically and, are contemporary etiquettes that certain furniture and site configurations communicate. If you extend that idea to the question of outdoor spaces that for reasons of budget, program or maintenance require standardized furnishings, one might say it's the designer's responsibility to encourage responsivity to unique site qualities. The interaction between user, site and objects is a phenomenon we can anticipate, but not predict. It's about using furnishing to suggest experience rather than using it to reinforce consistency.

KG: Design, and experience of what's been designed, is about discovery. Any recipes for the design of landscape or public places are inappropriate. Formulas can dumb things down. Good furniture isn't about predictable decorating of exterior space for public consumption, but for building on *genus loci,* revealing, introducing circumstances for discovering the landscape.

On a recent visit to London I found a wonderful garden I'd never seen before. It's fully enclosed on four sides, you approach through what used to be the service entrance. I came upon a chair that through its placement and shape magically focused the entire space within itself and outward along the central

In the Victorian-era garden, chaise-longues and writing tables composed a social setting out of the natural surrounds. Credit: Austrian National Library Vienna, Picture Archive.

Eero Saarinen's *Womb Chair* series for Knoll defined the mid century modern life style and reflected advances in fabrication technologies. Credit: photograph is courtesy of Yale Archives, photographer was Harvey Croze.

sight line. This single piece established the meaning of the garden for me. It was about contemplation, intensification.

If you have the right material in the best configuration placed sensitively into the landscape, furniture is inseparable from its space and place. The café chairs at Jardin du Luxembourg can be arranged and re-arranged, but their visual language remains the same and defines the park's character because it's in tune with all the other site elements such as the ground plane, the vegetation, the water. Although most site furniture isn't made from animate matter and thus doesn't evolve the way plants do, it's capable of reflecting and bringing forth ambient qualities of the environment. For me it comes back to sensory perception—by taking in intuitive information about how something sits within the landscape, we discover ways of imagining ourselves in the site.

In the 1970s, designer Luigi Colani imagined an integrated, "biodynamic" living environment furnished with sensuous forms derived from the interplay of anatomy and technology. Credit: photograph courtesy of Bangert verlag.

JA: The range of materials today suggests furniture as an activated object that mediates between human perception and site performance.

KG: There are many new manufacturing processes that take advantage of contemporary material technologies. But there's also prevalence of historic techniques that we've rediscovered in the age of sustainability. Getting back to the comment on how etiquettes shift over time, this generation's concern for the environment is driving greater interest in "green" design practices. So we're moving from global sourcing and manufacturing to regional contexts. When we're working on a project in Asia, for example, we use a different palette than for projects in Europe or North America. We look at local woods and stone, vernacular fabrication and preservation methods.

The sequence of movement through the garden at St. John's Lodge, Regent's Park, London is guided by a language of furnishing and its relationship to vegetation: leafy arbor as gate and visual frame for the central axis, edged turf surface as path, statuary as focal point, memorial chair and benches as destination. Credit: photographs by Kathryn Gustafson, May 2009.

The public's expectation is that designed sites and their furnishing respond to environmental ethics. Although once we solve the energy conundrum and have unlimited access to renewable energy resources, I think we're going to see an immediate return to globalized design approaches.

JA: Cultural adaptation is a fluid but profound influence on how we think about furnishing and occupying outdoor spaces. You've already adjusted your practices to more local ranges. In what other ways do you see the relationship shifting between furnishing and landscape.

KG: I like to think that in the near future we'll be designing furniture that produces positive environmental effects, like arbors that capture and store solar energy. Already many public projects attempt to balance their energy budget by including site features that "pay" for themselves through life cycle performance. Also durability is a big question for furniture in the landscape; not only do we try to minimize fabrication and transportation costs and therefore environmental impacts, but we're also thinking about how a particular material will hold up over time. Designers have to consider long term maintenance as much as how a piece looks and works. Are there changes in how long we expect things to last? Yes. Instead of making a bench from non renewable hard woods preserved to last twenty years, should we use less durable, recycled materials that are cheaper and quicker to produce and wear out more quickly? Perhaps. Reclaimed materials have become more current—many public landscapes integrate fragments from past use to construct a new identity. How we re-imagine, re-purpose and re-situate objects within a site is a fascinating design exercise. Bill Main and Gail Greet Hannah's book covers both practical and creative aspects of the role furniture plays in bringing outdoor space to life. The writers explore this subject at length, providing a level of attention that reveals its importance in the design of landscapes.

Kathryn Gustafson
Gustafson Guthrie Nichol Ltd, Seattle
Gustafson Porter Ltd, London

Jane Amidon
Associate Professor of Landscape Architecture
Ohio State University

ACKNOWLEDGMENTS

Many people contributed to this book in ways large and small, direct and indirect. Some of the subject matter was quite familiar to us and was written from our own experience. But much was collected from others who generously offered their experiences and insights. The book would have been impossible without their contributions and we are grateful for their time, energy and interest. We offer special thanks to the following people: Thomas Balsley, Jerome Barth, Marc Boddewyn, Paul Broadhead, Steve Cancian, Ted Crabb, Susan Goltsman, Astrid Haryati, Walter Hood Jr., Kevin Jensen, Deb Kinney, James Koth, Laura Lawson, Kathy Madden, Clare Cooper Marcus, Charles McKinney, Bob O'Boyle, Tom Oslund, Jaume Plensa, Peter Schaudt, Robert Schultz, Mark Sexton, Jerry Smith, William Sullivan, Kent Sundberg, and James Urban.

We'd also like to thank those people who provided materials and information or helped us find needed resources: Jeanne Ernst, Kathy Garcia, Our friends at Santa & Cole, Leslie Saxman, Ken Smith, Neal Speers, Ed Uhlir, and Cliff Welch.

Many people at Landscape Forms have helped by allowing Bill the time to pursue this book project. Some who contributed content or helped with particular tasks deserve special thanks: Janis Etzcorn, Todd Halstead, Richard Heriford, Mark Kramer, Don Lavender, Peter Rohrer, Denise Smith, Rick Utting, Mardi White, Tammie Winfield, LuAnn Woodhouse, and Arno Yurk.

Thanks to Margaret Cummins, our editor, who was always supportive and enthusiastic.

Thanks to Norm Lee, of Design Tower in Chicago, for his design expertise and valuable suggestions.

Thanks to Bob Chipman, ASLA, for his wonderful sketches.

Finally, thanks to all of the people who provided the photos and images used throughout the book. They are named in the photo credits.

INTRODUCTION

Furniture matters—outdoors as well as in. No one would think of asking an interior designer if furniture is important to a space. It's understood that in order to design any space, the designer needs detailed information about how the space is to be used, who will use it, and the feeling or identity it is intended to impart. And it goes without saying that the designer will use this information in the design process to select and plan furniture that will fulfill the functional, aesthetic, social or emotional, and bottom-line objectives of the project. In contrast, furniture in outdoor spaces is sometimes an afterthought. The relationship between the design of a site and the furniture elements that support desired activities and help define character of place is not always fully understood. As a result, the selection and planning of furniture may be left to the end of a project and the furniture not as well applied as it might be. Understanding the connections between site and site furniture enhances the creative opportunities for designers of outdoor spaces and increases their ability to influence the long-term success of the spaces they design.

Site furniture matters because it's good to be outdoors. Sitting in the sun on a cool day, resting in the shade on a warm one, strolling on a breezy beach are deeply pleasurable experiences. They might also be good medicine. Numerous scientific studies document a variety of ways in which humans function better when they have contact with nature. The sun is an important source of vitamin D, which is essential for healthy metabolism and growth. Outdoor exercise, including simply walking, can help control weight, improve circulation and heart function, and build muscles and bone.

Social science research supports the mental and physiological benefits of contact with the natural environment. William Sullivan is a landscape architect who teaches in the Department of Landscape Architecture at the University of Illinois in Urbana-Champaign and directs the university's Environmental Council. He conducts research that asks, in part, if having everyday contact with green spaces helps people function more effectively. A study of the effects of green neighborhood landscapes on individuals and communities, conducted at Chicago's Robert Taylor and Ida B. Wells public housing developments, showed that higher levels of greenness in neighborhood landscapes yielded stronger ties among neighbors and less aggressive behavior. He concludes, "The surprising connections between neighborhood green spaces and the strength of neighborhood social ties, lower levels of aggression and violence and lower levels of reported crimes provides compelling evidence that nearby nature is a necessary component of a healthy human habitat."[1]

Citing numerous supporting studies, Sullivan further concludes, "There are compelling arguments that regular contact with nearby nature is a requirement for mental health. . . . A large number of studies now show that settings that contain nearby nature, even urban environments that have trees and grass, foster recovery from mental fatigue and restore mental functioning. And, exposure to nearby nature enhances the ability to cope with and recover from physiological stress, cope with subsequent stress, and even recover from surgery."[2]

The Therapeutic Garden Design Professional Practice Network of The American Society of Landscape Architects (ASLA) documents research and best practices in the design, programming and application of therapeutic gardens that support physical, mental and spiritual healing and nurture quality of life. The United States Department of Veterans Affairs (VA), the largest not-for-profit healthcare system in the nation, includes therapeutic gardens among the complimentary treatments provided within its restructured systems.

There are practical reasons for going outdoors as well. For people in many parts of the world living in marginal, overcrowded quarters, the out-of-doors is the last refuge of physical and psychic space. For people working in cities like New York, having lunch outdoors is often cheaper and faster than eating in restaurants.

Furniture enhances the opportunities to reap the benefits. It creates the settings for resting, eating, socializing, meeting. This can be especially important for the elderly, people with limited mobility, and families with small children. We believe that the right furniture thoughtfully and appropriately placed can attract people to outdoor spaces and add to their enjoyment once they get there. Getting people outdoors is the challenge. Helping them feel welcome, comfortable and engaged is the goal.

Design professionals, urbanists, and social scientists have written about the importance of furniture in outdoor public spaces since William H. Whyte did his groundbreaking observational research in the 1960s and 1970s. However, this information is scattered throughout numerous sources, making it difficult to access. In this book we take a fresh look at the subject, bringing together current thinking about the role of furniture in outdoor space and the practical information required to implement ideas. This is the first book to focus exclusively on site furniture: principles, processes, and best practices. It provides a single source for conceptual approaches, technical information, and examples of applications that succeed and, sometimes, fail.

Experience in the site furniture business and with the landscape architecture profession leads us to the conviction that there is a strong connection between the furniture installed in outdoor spaces and the success of those spaces in achieving the goals of designers and clients. In our day-to-day work we have an opportunity to experience outdoor spaces around the United States and in other countries, and to talk with some of the most creative, successful designers of outdoor spaces working today. They have a great deal to tell us about successful practices. In interviews for this book, many of these design professionals shared their experiences of what works, what doesn't, and why.

Talking to experts on the ground and studying a broad cross-section of designed spaces has helped us identify patterns and formulate guidelines for using outdoor furniture to achieve quality spaces that work for the people who own them, use them, and manage them. We cite best practices in the use of outdoor furniture and related site elements to achieve functional, responsive, and supportable outdoor spaces. We aspire to give landscape architects and other designers of outdoor spaces the defensible information they need to make furniture an integral part of their projects' scope and budget. We offer corporate, university, and government decision makers investing in costly, long-term projects useful information for making decisions that can help maximize their investments. In the process, we provide a technical reference for site furniture functional requirements, materials, installation methods, and maintenance. Our goal is to elevate the importance of site furniture by showing how it can be used to further the mission, purpose, and program of outdoor public space.

Chapter 1, "The Role of Furniture in Outdoor Spaces," looks at what some influential experts and commentators have to say about the importance of furniture to these spaces. It discusses measures of success and the many ways in which furniture contributes to the quality of outdoor space. It identifies the various constituencies for furniture in public spaces and cites current social, cultural, and economic trends that impact outdoor spaces and the furniture within them. It concludes with a case study of Crown Fountain at Chicago's Millennium Park, focusing on the role furniture plays in the success of the space.

Chapter 2, "The Furniture Plan," proposes that furniture planning is an essential step in the overall project process. It provides some useful conceptual tools and a step-by-step process for developing a furniture plan. It includes a case study of Capitol Plaza, a Thomas Balsley project in New York City in which the furniture planning and site planning were intimately intertwined.

Chapter 3, "Types of Spaces," identifies the major categories of outdoor spaces in the public realm. It enumerates their unique furniture and amenity requirements, identifies special issues for each, and offers guidelines for furniture selection and placement. A chart for quick reference is included.

Chapters 4, 5, and 6 provide detailed information on furniture elements by type. Chapter 4, "Seating," deals with the full spectrum of seating, from benches and chairs to leaning rails and modular systems. It describes attributes, discusses user needs, and proposes appropriate applications. This chapter includes a case study of a movable chair with a long history and icon status at the University of Wisconsin, Madison, Memorial Union Terrace.

Chapter 5, "Receptacles," provides more information on receptacles than one expects would exist on the subject. As it turns out, this common, essential site furniture element is not quite as simple as it looks. This chapter lays out what, how, why, where, how many, and how big, with variations on the theme.

Chapter 6, "Other Site Furniture Elements and Accessories," deals with other prominent site furniture elements and accessories, including tables (with and without attached seating), umbrellas, planters, bike racks, and transit shelters. It describes what they are and how they are used, and provides useful information for successful applications.

Chapter 7, "Selecting Site Furniture," defines the issues that inform site furniture decisions, identifies the concerns that various constituencies bring to the decision-making process, and describes the characteristics and differences between standard, special, and custom furniture.

Chapter 8, "Accessible Design," outlines and defines principles and practices for creating universal outdoor spaces that are accessible to a broad range of people. It includes detailed information on American Disabilities Act Accessibility Guidelines (ADAAG) applicable to site furniture in public spaces.

Chapter 9, "Management," explores a subject whose relationship to site design is not always clearly understood. The fact is, management has a huge impact on the success of public spaces, and managing site furniture is a big part of the story. This chapter concludes with a detailed case study of how site and furniture management is carried out at Bryant Park, one of the world's most successful, and successfully managed, public spaces.

Chapter 10, "Materials and Finishes," lays out the key factors that drive material choices for site furniture, identifies what makes a material suitable for a particular application, and discusses in detail the most commonly used site furniture materials and finishes.

Chapter 11, "Installation and Maintenance," addresses two critical issues. The first can literally make or break the site furniture on a project. The second can wield huge influence on how long site furniture serves its purpose and how good it continues to look in the process. Recommended guidelines and regular maintenance protocols are provided.

Chapter 12, "Sustainability," presents the major issues involved in making sustainable site furniture choices, identifies areas where information is available and where it is lacking, alerts the professional to areas in which questions should be asked and trade-offs may have to be made, and outlines industry and professional initiatives that will influence sustainability going forward.

As authors, we recommend reading, or at least scanning, the entire book to gain an overview of the subject and the perspective from which we write. However, readers may skip around and tap individual chapters as reference sources for specific types of information. The case studies and photographs speak for themselves.

Endnotes

1. William Sullivan, "Nature at Home: An Evolutionary Perspective," in *Urban Place: Reconnecting with the Natural World*, ed. P. Bartlett (Cambridge, MA: MIT Press, 2005), 246.
2. Ibid., 248.

1. The Role of Furniture in Outdoor Spaces

What do we mean when we talk about site and street furniture? For the purposes of this book we mean elements introduced into outdoor spaces to provide comfort and convenience for the people who use them. In general, we do not include elements more properly considered aspects of infrastructure. In cases where there's a fine line between the two, we come down on the side of what we know. So we will talk about seating in its many forms—benches, chairs, stools, and lounges, both primary and secondary (the latter being additional built-in or movable seating for peak times)—as well as tables, both with and without attached seating. We will consider litter receptacles and ash urns, shade structures, bollards and bike racks, and planters. We will touch on lighting and signage. We will not include elements such as fire hydrants and water features. In our discussion of spaces, we include streets, plazas, parks, courtyards, campuses (both corporate and institutional), trails, retail centers, health care settings, rooftops, and education. We do not include pool and patio or residential.

How Do We Measure the Success of a Space?

William H. ("Holly") Whyte assumed the number of people using a space to be the first measure of its success. Many design professionals and owners of public spaces agree. Whyte began the research that culminated in his watershed book, *The Social Life of Small Urban Spaces*, in order to understand "why some [city spaces] work for people, and some do not."[1] He noted that "the tightest-knit CBD (central business district) anywhere contained a surprising amount of open space that was relatively empty and unused."[2] His assumption was that a better understanding of how and why people use outdoor spaces would lead to more densely used, and thus more successful, spaces.

Whyte's assessment of use as the major determinant of success has been endorsed by other thinkers and practitioners. Landscape architect Mark Francis writes: "Recently it has become more commonly understood that successful parks and open spaces such as plazas, streets, and public gardens are ones that are lively and well-used by people." He notes that the works of William Whyte, Clare Cooper Marcus, Kevin Lynch, Jan Gehl, Louise Mozingo, and Lyn Lofland, among others, "have shown definitely that use is a requirement for good public landscapes."[3]

1.1 A comfortable bench provides the perfect place for ladies who lunch. Photo: Mark Bugnaski, used with permission of the *Kalamazoo Gazette*, copyright 2008, all rights reserved

1.2 What makes a great place? Furniture can contribute to many of the intangibles supporting all of the key attributes. Credit: copyright 2002 Project for Public Spaces

The Project for Public Spaces is renowned for its insistence upon use as the key measure of success, and for its programming and advocacy designed to increase public use of outdoor spaces. "In evaluating thousands of public spaces around the world, Project for Public Spaces (PPS) has found that successful ones have four key qualities: they are *accessible*; people are engaged in *activities* there; the space is *comfortable* and has a good image; and finally, it is a *sociable* place: one where people meet each other and take people when they come to visit."[4]

Density of use is not the only yardstick for measuring the success of outdoor public spaces. The people who design, commission, or enjoy those spaces often have other expectations and goals. Designers typically put a high value on aesthetics in furniture and site design.

- The furniture itself may be conceived as art.

1.3 Above: Atwater Place, South Waterfront District, Portland, Oregon. This private courtyard of a housing and retail complex contains a series of reflecting pools. A small plaza enjoyed by residents creates a seamless transition from the courtyard to surrounding public spaces. Copyright 2008. Photo credit: Mayer/Reed and C. Bruce Forster

1.4a, 1.4b "Two Too Large Tables" by Allan and Ellen Wexler at Hudson River Park, in New York City, are designed to encourage interaction (and perhaps bemused smiles). Chair backs hold up the tall table which is at roof height. Chairs form the legs of the lower table, which is at normal height. Photo credit: Bill Main

1.4c The seating designed by Martha Schwartz for Jacob Javits Plaza in New York City filled the void left when Richard Serra's controversial sculpture was removed. The dominant element in the new plaza design, which reanimates the space and reconnects the plaza to its surrounding context, it offers innumerable seating opportunities provided on back-to-back twisting strands of New York City park benches. Photo credit: Martha Schwartz Partners

1.5 Ping Tom Park employs Chinese cultural and historic motifs in this popular riverside park serving Chicago's Chinatown neighborhood. Photo: copyright © Jim Powell

- Sometimes the aesthetic of the furniture defines the character of the space. (See figure 1.4c)
- Communities may find the success of a place in the pride it engenders or in its expression of cultural heritage. (See figure 1.5)
- Special features such as fountains or sculpture can make spaces successful. (See figure 1.6)

1.6 British artist Anish Kapoor's "Cloud Gate," aka "The Bean," reflects images of the city and the hordes of visitors it draws to the AT&T Plaza in Chicago's Millennium Park. Photo credit: Bill Main

1.7 A beautiful space, beautifully maintained, beckons at Norman Leventhal Park in Boston's Post Office Square. Photo credit: Bill Main

- The ability of a space to conjure or enable experiences such as hearing the sounds of wind or water or watching the play of light is an important measure of success. (See Figure 1.7)

- The ability to manage and maintain a space can determine (or undermine) success. (See Figure 1.8)

1.8 An object lesson in poorly maintained public space. Photo credit: Bill Main

1.9 Bryant Park provides spaces for a wide range of people and activities—some work, some play. Credit: Bryant Park Corporation, photo: Ethan Lercher

- The extent to which a space supports multiple constituencies and allows people to work and play together can be critical to its success. (See Figure 1.9)

Why Does Furniture Matter?

All that said, our focus is not on outdoor space itself but on what's in the space. So why does furniture in these spaces matter? Furniture is vital to the

1.10 Rain or shine, people can't stay away from New York City's Paley Park. Photo credit: Bill Main

1.11 Signature seating at the Luxembourg Gardens, Paris. Photo credit: Jardins du Luxembourg, Paris, Mia Serra 1995

way people respond to outdoor space and to the duration and quality of their experience there. It has numerous roles.

- Furniture in outdoor spaces may embody and convey powerful symbolic meanings. Seating and tables in outdoor spaces say, "This place is for you." They extend a friendly gesture that attracts and welcomes. Sociable tables and chairs in New York's Paley Park were a magnet for passersby three decades ago when William H. Whyte observed activity there, and the same furniture in the same configurations still draws people into this enduringly successful public space today. (See Figure 1.10)
- Furniture in outdoor spaces can communicate identity and project image. Family-friendly? Hip? Traditional and enduring? Nothing says Paris like the iconic chairs of the Luxembourg Gardens. (See Figure 1.11)

1.12 The sunburst chair welcomes visitors to Memorial Union Terrace, University of Wisconsin, Madison. Photo credit: Bill Main

- The signature yellow and red sunburst chairs at the University of Wisconsin's Memorial Terrace have become so synonymous with the school and its culture, they've been trademarked. (See figure 1.12)
- In its type and arrangement, furniture can communicate social messages. By enabling community activity and group interaction, it expresses support for civil society. And by providing opportunities for underserved populations, such as the elderly or disabled, it signals commitment to inclusiveness. In its style, furniture may embody and convey historical connections to a specific time or event, or to the architectural heritage of a place. In its materials and the way it physically connects to the natural world, outdoor furniture may embody and express environmental values and aspirations. It may be upscale and contemporary or rustic and down-home, to complement sophisticated urban settings or evoke rural woodsy environments. New or unusual styles, materials, colors, and configurations can be a vehicle for expressing local identity or rebellion against sameness and the mundane.

- Furniture in outdoor spaces also has important functional roles. It adds to the overall usefulness of spaces by supporting multiple options for activities, both active and passive.
  - Well-designed seating provides ergonomic support and comfort, enabling many people to enjoy outdoor spaces and to spend more time in them. (See Figure 1.14)
  - Litter receptacles and ash urns support cleanliness and hygiene. (See Figure 1.15)
  - Furniture renders outdoor spaces more convenient by punctuating distances with places for people to rest, meet, and dispose of trash. (See Figure 1.16)
  - Bike racks and bollards provide security and safety. (See Figure 1.17)

1.13 Chicago's Daley Plaza hosts a festival in its multifunctional space. Photo credit: Bill Main

1.14 Give them a good place to sit, as here in Spain. Photo credit: Bancos Neoromantico. Barcelona, Julio Cunill 2001

1.15 Receptacles help keep it clean. Photo credit: Bryant Park Corporation

- Furniture can be used very effectively to create visual order, provide space definition, delineate functional areas, and provide orientation. A good example is Daley Plaza in Chicago, a big, flat open space in which the furniture around the perimeter provides a border for and defines the space in the center, which is used for activities and social events. (See figures 1.13, 1.14)

1.16 Walkways, well-placed benches, shade, and views. It's all there in Hudson River Park, New York City. Photo credit: Bill Main

1.17 An orderly procession of bike racks enhances the streetscape in Ann Arbor, Michigan. Photo credit: Bill Main

The importance of furniture to the viability and vitality of outdoor spaces is supported by research. The observations of William H. Whyte, based on time-lapse photography and participant-observation techniques and documented in *The Social Life of Small Urban Spaces*, have influenced

1.18 Furniture around the perimeter provides lively settings and defines central open space in Chicago's Daley Park. Photo credit: Bill Main

decades of public space design and policy. In New York City many of his recommendations for seating in public spaces have been encoded into law.

Whyte was interested in why, in their use of plazas, New Yorkers consistently gravitated to some and bypassed others. He looked at likely causes: the sun, the aesthetics of the space, and the shape of the space. All of these factors were found to be important but not sufficient to explain the differences in use. When he looked at the amount of space in a plaza, he discovered that sheer space alone does not draw people and may have the opposite effect. Then he asked, "What about the amount of sittable space?" Indeed, his charts plotting usage over time showed that the most popular plazas had considerably more space for sitting than the less frequented ones. He tried weighting for variables such as backrests, armrests, and physical comfort. "No matter how many variables we checked," he wrote, "one point kept coming through . . . : *People tend to sit most where there are places to sit.*" Whyte was quick to admit that this was not an "intellectual bombshell." But it was a critical piece of information that led to a basic guideline for the design of public spaces. "Sitting space, to be sure, is only one of the many variables. . . . But sitting space is most certainly prerequisite. The most attractive fountains, the most striking designs, cannot induce people to come and sit if there is no place to sit."[5]

Whyte was also interested in the quality of the sitting experience. He acknowledged the importance of physical comfort but after much study concluded, "It's more important . . . [that sitting] be *socially* comfortable. This means choice: sitting up front, in back, to the side, in the sun, in the shade, in groups, off alone."[6] Another guideline for the design of successful public spaces was laid down.

Research on the role of furniture in public spaces has been done in other cultures as well. Jan Gehl is an urban designer, a professor of urban design at the School of Architecture in Copenhagen, Denmark, and director of its Center for Public Space Research. For more than three decades he has been a student and theorist of urban spaces and what makes them work. Gehl was instrumental in helping to transform Copenhagen from a car-dominated city to what *Metropolis* magazine rates as "one of the world's great pedestrian cities." He recently consulted on the transformation of New York City's Broadway between 42nd Street and Herald Square from a four-lane thoroughfare to a two-lane street with lanes set aside for bicycles and a pedestrian walkway with cafe tables and chairs. In Gehl's seminal book *Life Between Buildings*, he posited conclusions, based on systematic study and recording of people in the city, that underscore and expand on Whyte's contribution:

> It is of particular importance to emphasize what good sitting arrangements mean in all types of public spaces. . . . Only when opportunities for sitting exist can there be stays of any duration. If these opportunities are few or bad, people just walk on by. This means not only that stays in public are brief, but also that many attractive and worthwhile outdoor activities are precluded.
>
> The existence of good opportunities for sitting paves the way for the numerous activities that are the prime attractions in public spaces: eating, reading, sleeping, knitting, playing chess, sunbathing, watching people, talking, and so on.
>
> These activities are so vital to the quality of public spaces that the availability or lack of good sitting opportunities must be considered an all-important factor in evaluating the quality of the public environment in a given area. To improve the quality of the outdoor environment in an area by simple means, it is almost always a good idea to create more and better opportunities for sitting.[7]

The Project for Public Spaces has studied and improved thousands of public spaces around the world as it carries out its mission: "connecting people to ideas, expertise, and partners who share a passion for creating vital places." In "A Primer on Seating," PPS declares, "Seating that is accessible, comfortable, well-maintained, and located in the right places is critical to successful placemaking."[8]

Jay Walljasper writes in *The Great Neighborhood Book*: "A key ingredient of lively, safe, fun neighborhoods is public spaces where people will spontaneously gather. People out on the streets bring a community magically alive. You get to know your neighbors, you feel secure, and you have a place to hang out. And there's one simple way to do this: Give everyone a spot where they can sit down. A bench or chairs can transform a lonely space into a lively place."[9]

In *How to Turn a Place Around*, PPS analyzes why many public spaces fail and concludes:

> Today, many public spaces seem to be intentionally designed to be looked at but not touched. They are neat, clean and empty—as if to say, "no people, no problem!" But when a public space is empty, vandalized

1.19 A well-designed, well-maintained, busy, and welcoming space. Photo credit: Capitol Plaza, New York City, Thomas Balsley Associates.

1.20 No good place to sit in a sad space. Photo credit: Bill Main

1.21 The value of absence: unoccupied chairs in the Luxembourg Gardens, Paris. Photo credit: Jardins du Luxembourg, Paris, Mia Serra 1995

or used chiefly by undesirables, this is generally an indication that something is very wrong with its design, or its management, or both. . . . Some problems are related to the design of a space . . . [including] lack of good places to sit.[10]

Clare Cooper Marcus and Carolyn Francis, editors of *People Places: Design Guidelines for Urban Open Space*, write: "Site furniture makes the space usable. Without it, people's choices are limited, and they are likely only to look around or walk through a space and then leave. Site furniture should enable the space to be used by as many people as possible throughout the year."[11]

Even when good places to sit are unoccupied, they can convey powerful meanings about a space. "The value of absence is another good keynote for urban elements," writes Marius Quintana Creus. He goes on to explain:

> The image of the empty chairs in the Jardin des Tuileries and the Jardin du Luxembourg in Paris is perhaps what best sums (this) up. We can still feel the presence of the people who have just used them. The positions in which the chairs have been left allow us to guess at the number of people who gathered and the arrangement in which they sat. The place and orientation they occupy help us to seek out the spot's finest views. These are chairs so simple and almost natural in design. But this simple and natural design is fruit of the mobility and adaptation they allow the user, their long presence in these places and the lengthy tradition lying behind these urban spaces. They are the elements which lend these places their definitive content, once places of contemplation and dramatism, now become places of tranquility and relaxation in the midst of the great metropolis.[12]

Furniture Is for People

The foundation for all of the discussion in this book is the conviction that furniture in outdoor spaces is for people. Its primary role is to provide utility and comfort. It may play a secondary role in accessorizing, but if it is no more than an object to pretty the plan or occupy a void, it isn't doing what it can do. Furniture is a key touch point of outdoor spaces. It's where people stop and make a physical connection with a space. It is direct evidence that a space was designed with people in mind.

The number of people using a space drives furniture demand. The more people in the space, the more furniture required. (It's not rocket science. When you give a party, you borrow or rent more chairs.) Too much furniture can make a space appear overprogrammed. Too little furniture can discourage people from frequenting the space. How much and what kind of furniture is needed in any given space should be the subject of careful research and planning. Just as every landscape architecture project includes a site analysis, every outdoor space intended to attract people and support their activities should include a furniture plan. The plan should address who is expected to use the space, why, how, and when it will be used. User input can be invaluable in getting a plan off the ground and avoiding misunderstandings and missteps down the line. The furniture plan should—by design—leave some room for surprise. Planning to the last detail can dampen the spirit of a space. Learning through the process and observing people actually using a space can lead to inspired evolution. (For detailed information on furniture planning, see Chapter 2.)

Whose Furniture Is It?

Furniture in public spaces has multiple constituencies, each with its own expectations and agendas. Whom does the furniture serve? Owners, for example, are typically concerned with how furniture looks and how it complements the larger project or site. As the people who write the checks, they also have a healthy interest in the bottom line. Some owners use their authority to achieve amazing things. Others have been known to opt for the easy choices: lesser-quality furniture in limited quantities to save on first costs; fixed, rather than movable, furniture to reduce maintenance and limit loss; multiples of a single type instead of a variety of furnishings, to simplify purchasing and management; furniture lined up in repetitive rows to systematize installation and cleaning. None of these choices necessarily considers the impact on spaces and the people who use them. W. H. Whyte's work in New York City was targeted at (and culminated in) establishing a body of regulations to ensure that owners who were granted bonuses to build public plazas were forced to consider the needs of the public and do the right thing.

The users of outdoor public spaces come from many different groups with potentially conflicting interests. Moms with toddlers don't have the same furniture or space needs as solitary elders. Teenagers looking for a space to hang out have different needs than do office workers looking for a place to set up a laptop. People from different ethnic and cultural groups have different expectations about acceptable levels of density and noise in public space. All will promote their own needs and defend their own choices. Selecting and arranging furniture that accommodates all of them is a formidable task.

The maintenance staff in a public outdoor space is critical to its success. It, too, has interests to defend. Complexity in furniture types and configurations is more difficult to deal with than simplicity and repetition. Certain types and sizes of litter receptacles may be judged easier to handle; certain materials are considered easier to clean and maintain. These preferences are often independent of the convenience or comfort of the people who use the space.

The designer is faced with the difficult challenge of reconciling needs and differences. But designers don't stand outside the realm of conflicting interests, either. They have their own agendas. Although professional practice is certainly trending toward a user-based approach to outdoor spaces, critics still charge designers with pursuing purely visual or aesthetic solutions to the detriment of other concerns. Often the critique is leveled at budget expenditures for elaborate infrastructure or special features that do not enhance amenity for users and leave no funds for activities and management over time. Aesthetic integrity is entirely compatible with people- and activity-based solutions—look at Bryant Park. It just takes a commitment to make it happen.

While public furniture has many constituencies, sometimes it's left on its own: an orphan, with no one looking out for it or taking care of it. Once it is set out and the ribbon is cut, it may have to rely its individual fortitude to survive and serve in the public domain. Site furniture sometimes has to be its own best friend.

In general, we suggest that an appropriate mind-set for addressing furniture in outdoor spaces might be the hospitality model. Pay attention to everyone. Aim for the satisfaction and comfort of all. Focus on first impressions. (If they won't walk in, you've lost the game.) Follow through with substance. Keep all the balls in the air.

Trends Worth Tracking

Social, cultural, and economic trends influence the importance of public spaces, how they are used, and how they are furnished. Among those influences having tangible impacts today we note:

- *Reurbanization.* The revitalization of American cities has led to a rethinking and revaluing of public space. Density, diversity, walkability, a live/work ethic, the return of young couples with children, and a 24/7 social scene are drawing people into public spaces and upping the ante for quality and amenity. Investment in outdoor public space is a vital aspect of reurbanization initiatives.

- *The use of outdoor space as a choice, rather than a necessity.* This puts the focus on the importance of quality. The Danish urbanist and researcher Jan Gehl writes: "In a society where public life is dominated by necessary activities the quality of the public spaces is not an all-important issue. People will use the city spaces regardless of quality because they have to. This pattern can be seen all over the world in countries with less developed economies. In a society situation where use of public space becomes more and more a matter of interest and choice, the quality of the spaces becomes a crucial factor for the death or life of modern cities. . . . Protection, comfort and enjoyment are essential for open space design."[13]

- *The Starbucks effect.* The proliferation of sidewalk cafes and al fresco dining has energized life along the streetscape. It's a virtuous cycle in which people are drawn out into public spaces and in turn draw others in their wake.

- *Fluctuating fuel costs and other economic bad news.* Sticker shock at the gas pump is reflected in rising numbers of people using public transportation, placing greater importance on bus stops, light rail stations, and transit hubs. More people are riding bikes—and looking for places to park and lock. There is anecdotal evidence that as people are driving less, they are making more use of outdoor parks and other leisure spaces close to home. In a sagging economy, sit-down restaurants are reporting declines in business, and analysts see a trending down to fast-food venues. An increase in takeout and brown-bagging increases attendance, especially during lunch hours, in plazas and parks.

- *The 100 percent corner.* In many cities around the world, investment in public spaces has had the positive effect of encouraging real estate development and driving up neighborhood occupancy rates. The demonstration that public projects, including parks, plazas, transit systems, and high-profile streetscapes, often draw significant private investment is helping justify funding for these projects and spurring the proliferation of business improvement districts to ensure their maintenance and vitality.

- *The importance of place.* Richard Florida, in his critically acclaimed book *The Rise of the Creative Class*, posited that the successful cities of the future will be those that provide the three T's: technology, talent, and the tolerance required to attract the young creatives who are driving emerging economies. In laying out what he calls his "creative capital theory," Florida notes the importance of opportunities for outdoor recreation in the places that win the high-stakes competition for this dynamic, influential group of movers and shakers.[14]

- *Wi-Fi in the wide outdoors.* Public spaces are more than places for rest, recreation, and recuperation. They're extensions of the workplace. You can take it with you, as the growing presence of laptops, BlackBerry devices, and cell phones in outdoor spaces testifies. More things to do in outdoor spaces means increased demand for spaces in which to do them and amenities, including furniture, to support them.

- *The "undesirables."* From spikes and moats to strategic management, we've been here before. After the winos it was the hippies, and today it's the skateboarders and the homeless. But before all that it was someone else. In 1857, when the debate on funding New York's Central Park was raging, the *New York Herald* came out in strong opposition to the plan. The newspaper saw no way that Olmsted's democratic notions of a park for all the people could work. Referring to a fictitious composite character called "Sam the Five Pointer," a resident of the city's notorious Five Point slum, it opined: "He will run races with his new horse in the carriageway. He will knock any better-dressed man down who remonstrates with him. He will talk and sing, and fill his share of the bench, and flirt with the nursery girls in his own coarse way. Now, we ask what chance have William B. Astor and Edward Everett against this fellow-citizen of theirs? Can they and he enjoy the same place?"[15] Today, the answer is "of course." After generations of inspired but mostly unsuccessful deterrents, many of them inflicted on furniture, a more nuanced approach to "undesirables" in public spaces has emerged. It is now clear that if the furniture in outdoor spaces is designed to discourage certain people, it will discourage everyone. Ensuring spaces that are open and inviting to all has become a matter of management, rather than interdiction or medieval intervention.

CROWN FOUNTAIN CASE STUDY

Crown Fountain, Millennium Park, Chicago, Illinois
Jaume Plensa, artist, Barcelona, Spain
Krueck + Sexton, architects, Chicago, Illinois

In Jaume Plensa's Crown Fountain, two 50-foot-tall glass towers separated by a long shallow pool literally face off. Projected images of humankind in all its diversity and eccentricity engage in wordless dialogue punctuated by sudden spouts. Kids splashing in the water below catch the spray, and the milling crowd mostly grins. The fountain, which opened on July 16, 2004, is a hugely successful public attraction and a prime example of how compelling art and inspired site furniture can work together to create a truly great space.

The 42-by-222-foot pool is set into a black granite platform 276 feet long by 84 feet wide. Hewn log benches set about 17 feet from the edge of the pool line both sides. The benches, although installed a year after the fountain, were always part of the plan. "My intention was to create a space in itself," Jaume Plensa explains. "The towers were an excuse for me to create an emptiness that draws people in and, with the reflecting pool, makes a place for gathering. The two lines, one on each side, enclose this space and the benches delimit the perimeter of the project. The benches are the same length as the reflecting pool, and it is really nice to walk between them and feel that you are inside a place. Many times in public spaces the benches are a problem. It's a complicated element in the urban design. But in this case the whole project has been created as one idea."

"The bench as a huge log was Jaume's inspiration," says Mark Sexton, principal of Krueck + Sexton, who collaborated with the artist to turn his vision into physical reality. Plensa and the project architects went to Vancouver to source the Canadian red cedar trees and watch them being milled. The choice of material was calculated. Plensa explains, "My project has a lot of technology and hard surfaces—glass, stainless steel, LED. I wanted to introduce something warm and natural. Something coming from the most basic thing, which is wood, and which is always warm. So I looked for this kind of big, big timber. The benches are simple in just the way that, when you are walking in the mountains and you are tired, you sit on a log."

The 18-inch-high,18-inch-deep wood benches are constructed of long pieces joined end to end to create the expanses Plensa had in mind. The benches are

CROWN FOUNTAIN CASE STUDY

(Continued)

1.22 Crown Fountain, Millennium Park, Chicago, Illinois. Photo credit: Bill Main

1.23 Crown Fountain, Millennium Park, Chicago, Illinois. Photo credit: Bill Main

set on 2-inch-high stainless-steel legs, so splashed water washes under them, creating the illusion that they are afloat. "The pool becomes like a stage," Plensa explains. "When you decide to walk in the pool you decide to play. And the rest of the people, just like in the theater, are sitting and looking up at what the players are doing. People are smiling and enjoying and suddenly one decides to be part of the theater—and it's in and out and in and out. The bench is where you rest a little bit. It's a kind of transition."

1.24 Crown Fountain, Millennium Park, Chicago, Illinois. Photo credit: Bill Main

1.25 Crown Fountain, Millennium Park, Chicago, Illinois. Photo credit: Bill Main

"It's miraculous what happens there every summer day," Mark Sexton adds. "It's as if that bench is at Malibu Beach. People sit for hours watching the waves come in and out, but it's more alive because they're watching a flow of people, not water."

CROWN FOUNTAIN CASE STUDY

(Continued)

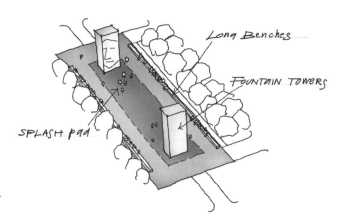

1.26 Crown Fountain, Millennium Park, Chicago, Illinois. Credit: Robert G. Chipman, ASLA

Indeed, the magnetic pull that Crown Fountain exerts on visitors to the park necessitated some changes to the adjacent landscape. The Boeing Gallery, a terrace elevated 6 feet above the fountain, originally did not offer direct access to the fountain space. But so many people watching the scene below began climbing over the terrace rail and down the planted slope that a stairway was built and an opening was cut in the bench nearest to it to provide access and promote safety. The overflow of people also required widening the pavement behind the benches to allow people to circulate in the area between the bench and the shrubbery border.

The Crown Fountain project was awarded after a competition. "Plenty of people in the city were against the project because they said it had too much technology, it was too intellectual," Plensa recalls. "They were afraid that it was something more for the museum than for the street. But when we unveiled the project, there was an extraordinary response. Kids really saved it—they just went boom. And I remember the parents were a little disappointed with me that day because all the kids were completely wet. The next day they did the same thing, but they brought towels. And everybody was happy. So probably the most intellectual piece I ever did in the public space has become the most physical one. People use the space as an experience."

The benches are integral to that experience. It's an instance of Whyte's triangulation made manifest.

"The bench supports conversation," Mark Sexton explains. "You turn to the person next to you and laugh at the crawling toddler at the edge of the pool. The very long bench is democratic. It welcomes everyone. It's nonhierarchical. It makes no distinctions among people. And it's nonprescriptive. Because of its length, you can sit anywhere. The bench ultimately connects the whole experience."

Endnotes

1. William H. Whyte, *The Social Life of Small Urban Spaces* (New York: Project for Public Spaces, 1980), 10.

2. Ibid., 15

3. Mark Francis, *Urban Open Space: Designing for User Needs*, Landscape and Community Design Case Study Series (Washington, DC: Island Press, 2003), 1.

4. Project for Public Spaces, "What Makes a Successful Place?" www.pps.org/ topics/gps/gr_place_feat.

5. Whyte, *The Social Life of Small Urban Spaces*, 28.

6. Ibid.

7. Jan Gehl, *Life Between Buildings*, 6th ed. (Copenhagen: Danish Architectural Press, 2006), 155.

8. Project for Public Spaces, "A Primer on Seating," www.pps.org/civic_centers/ info/how_to/amenities_bb/general_seating.

9. Jay Walljasper, *The Great Neighborhood Book* (Gabriola Island, BC: New Society Publishing, 2007), 38.

10. Project for Public Spaces, *How to Turn a Place Around* (New York: Project for Public Spaces, 2005), 20–21.

11. C. Cooper Marcus and C. Francis, eds., *People Places: Design Guidelines for Urban Open Space*, 2nd ed. (New York: John Wiley & Sons, 1998), 328.

12. Marius Quintana Creus, "Space, Furniture and Urban Elements," in *Elementos Urbanos/Urban elements*, 4th ed., ed. Josep Ma Serra and Jaume Tutzo Gomila (Barcelona: Editorial Gustavo Gilli, 2000), 14.

13. Jan Gehl, "Public Spaces for a Changing Public Life," *Topos* 61 (2007): 15.

14. Richard Florida, *The Rise of the Creative Class* (New York: Basic Books, 2002), 249–50.

15. David Schuyler, "Central Park at 150: Celebrating Olmstead and Vaux's Greensward Plan," *Hudson River Valley Review*, Spring 2008, 14–15.

2. The Furniture Plan

Furniture planning is a step in overall project programming, planning, and design. A furniture planning process guides designers of outdoor spaces in selecting and configuring furnishings that support the people and activities in the spaces they create. Isolating furniture planning within the overall process enables designers to highlight and address furniture issues early and to optimize the value and utility of furnishings for the users of a space.

The furniture plan begins with programming and defining the type of space: park, street, urban plaza, waterfront, recreational area, mall, transit hub, and so on. It asks the basic questions: who will use the space, why and when will they use it, and what will they do when they are there? And, following the typical project process model, it proceeds through analysis, concept development, detailed design, implementation, and maintenance. The furniture plan draws on the intelligence gathered in the overall programming and analysis and drills down to the micro level to discover more detailed information relevant to the selection and placement of furniture. It is not a separate document analogous to a structural or electrical plan, but a body of detailed information on furniture requirements incorporated into the macro plan. The process involves continual back-and-forth between the macro dimension and the micro dimension to fine-tune plans to achieve desired goals. For example, a detailed furniture plan may reveal the need to allocate additional hard space for furnishings to accommodate proposed activities and the number of people expected to use a space.

First, some conceptual tools could be useful.

Conceptual Tools for Furniture Planning

Social scientists and design professionals have developed concepts and language describing human behavior in public spaces that have proven applicable in creating successful spaces. Four of these conceptual models seem to us particularly useful in thinking about how furniture is located and configured in outdoor spaces.

The Hidden Dimension: Proxemics or Measures of Distance

In his 1966 book *The Hidden Dimension*, the anthropologist Edward T. Hall introduced the term *proxemics* to describe different types of spaces and set measurable distances between people

2.1 Intimate distance: 6 to 18 inches.

2.2 Personal distance: 1.5 to 4 feet.

2.3 Social distance: 4 to 12 feet.

Credit, Figures 2.1 through 2.6: Robert G.
Chipman, ASLA.

as they interact. Hall's three space types and four measures of distance in interaction are still used by social scientists and architects today. They offer helpful guidelines for defining spheres of interaction and comfort zones for a range of behaviors within the outdoor realm.[1]

The three types of space are:

- Fixed-feature space: comprising things that are immobile (walls, territorial boundaries, fixed furniture)
- Semi-fixed-feature space: comprising movable objects such as furniture that is not fixed
- Informal space: the personal space around the body that travels around with a person and determines distance among people

The four measures of distance are:

- Intimate distance: for embracing, touching, or whispering (6–18 inches)
- Personal distance: for interactions among good friends (1.5–4 feet)
- Social distance: for interactions among acquaintances (4 to 12 feet)
- Public distance: for impersonal observation (12+ feet)

Different cultures have different standards of personal space. In Latin cultures, relative distances are smaller and people are more comfortable getting close to each other. In northern European cultures, the opposite is true and people typically put more distance between themselves and nonintimate others. In addition to culture, comfortable personal distances are dependent on situation, gender, and individual preference. In densely populated areas the social and public distances may be condensed. The behaviors deemed acceptable within the three types of space also differ by culture and custom, and variations can lead to confusion and discomfort. For example, while in some situations it is permissible to move furniture that is part of semi-fixed-feature space, in others that might be seen as overstepping one's bounds and an intrusion on others.

2.4 Public distance: 12+ feet.

Sociopetal and Sociofugal Space

Humphrey Osmond, a Canadian-born psychiatrist interested in how social environments influenced welfare or recovery within mental institutions, identified two major systems for patterning space that proved to have a significant effect on the interactions of patients. Sociopetal space tends to bring people together and encourage communication and interaction. In spatial terms it is described as radial, with merging and overlapping routes and interconnected rings and spirals. Sociofugal space tends to keep people apart and suppress communication. Spatially it is described as boxlike or gridlike. Designers can influence the amount of interaction within a space or within a setting by the way they configure the space itself and the furniture elements within it.

Like outdoor space, furniture may be sociopetal or sociofugal in its arrangement and effects. Sociopetal furniture configurations orient people toward one another, encouraging face-to-face interaction. Sociofugal furniture

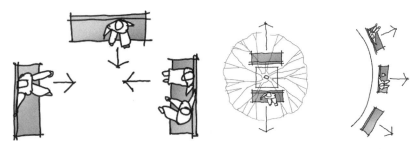

2.5 Sociopetal seating (inward-facing).   2.6 Sociofugal seating (outward-facing).

arrangements orient people away from one another, discouraging face-to-face encounters and promoting individual isolation within public spaces.

Prospect and Refuge

In 1975 the English geographer Jay Appleton proposed the theory of "prospect and refuge," a theory of human aesthetics that states that humans are attracted to art and circumstances that satisfy inborn desires and replicate conditions that have proven historically optimal for human survival. The theory predicts that humans will prefer broad vistas; visible places for easy refuge; positioning at the edge of spaces, where the back is protected, rather than in the middle, where it is exposed; and spaces that provide cover, rather than open exposure to the sky.[2]

While the theory is controversial among aesthetes and scientists, observations of how people choose to position themselves in public spaces appear to support its precepts and landscape architects have used prospect-refuge theory in the design of public spaces with positive results.

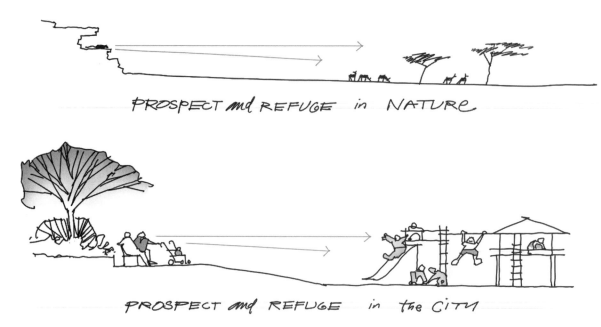

2.7 Prospect and refuge (view forward, back protected). Credit: Robert G. Chipman, ASLA.

A Hierarchy of Space

In their seminal book *A Pattern Language*, Christopher Alexander and coauthors propose an organization of spaces in which smaller spaces look out into larger ones and work together to form hierarchies. "Outdoors, people always try to find a spot where they can have their backs protected, looking out toward some larger opening, beyond the space immediately in front of them. . . . [T]here is almost no more basic statement to make about the way people place themselves in space. And this observation has enormous implications for the spaces in which people can feel comfortable." These comfortable places have both a back and a view into a larger space.[3] This permits users to migrate to their desired scale of place much as they would migrate to shady or sunny places as they wish.

These concepts will be useful throughout the furniture planning process.

A Step-by-Step Process for Making Furniture Decisions

Programming

Programming is the crucial stage that sets the direction of the project. Initially, the designer works with the client to define the project, determine the type of space needed, and establish the most critical goals. During furniture planning, the program should be reviewed with special attention to those aspects that should drive furniture decisions.

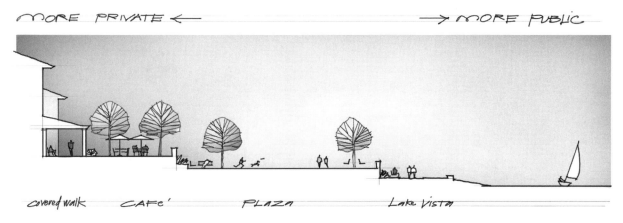

2.8 A hierarchy of space (looking to an opening beyond the space immediately in front). Credit: Robert G. Chipman, ASLA.

This includes:

- *Who will use the space?* Will it be young children, teenagers, older adults, men, women, singles, couples, small and large groups, pets? What are the local ethnic groups and their preferences? Different people will choose different types of furniture, and will use what is provided in different ways. For example, kids may use a bench as a climber, while the elderly will sit in it and appreciate a back and an armrest.

- *What will those people want to do while they're there?* Some of the many possibilities include rest, read, eat, make out, watch people, work on a laptop, meet friends, sleep, meditate, feed the birds, monitor children at play, exercise, listen to music, or participate in programmed activities such as markets, festivals, and political events. With the exception of dedicated spaces such as bus stops, this will typically constitute a rich mix of humanity and activity in a dynamic environment in which the players change and the action evolves. Groups will appreciate social seating configurations, while others may be looking for a quiet spot or Wi-Fi access.

- *When will they use it?* The time of day in which spaces are used and by whom, weekday or weekend use, and variations in use based on seasons and the weather add to the complexity. Midday users may appreciate shade, while evening users may need lighting; weekends may bring more groups and families.

- *Where will people want to be?* What are the prime locations, special views, active pathways, and interesting activities that will attract people? Fountains and water features, for example, are often people magnets. People near food vendors may be on the lookout for seating or a trash receptacle.

The more complete the view of people and activities in the space, the more likely it is that the furniture plan will adequately address needs, expectations, and opportunities.

Site Analysis and Beyond

The analysis phase for the furniture plan should address all aspects of the locale, including its natural features and conditions and its social, cultural, and historical context.

Natural Features, Climate, and Environment

Outdoor spaces are subject to unique conditions. Natural features such as site elevations and water, as well as conditions including temperature, precipitation, sun, wind, noise, and smells, all impact the quality of experience. Unlike interior spaces, where people can adjust lights and thermostats to achieve desired comfort levels, the ability to control the external environment is limited. The sun can be glaring on a hot day, the lack of sun can make spaces inhospitable on a cool day, and the wind can blow away papers and food cartons. By and large, outdoor spaces are used primarily when the seasons and weather permit. In general, people will flock to a great space when conditions are favorable and will stay away when the snow and rain set in. But there are exceptions. Bus stops and walking thoroughfares are used regardless of the weather. And certain activities, such as dog walking, go on regardless of the temperature or precipitation. Although seating in these areas will remain largely unoccupied under negative conditions, litter receptacles and ash urns will still be used.

That said, we have observed that furnished outdoor spaces even in harsh climates are highly valued and intensively used. Though (or perhaps because) the time spent in outdoor spaces by people living in places with seriously cold winters, hot summers, or rainy seasons is limited, it is also precious. A space is not a failure if it's not packed in inclement weather. The designer's task is to make sure that when the weather permits, the spaces they've designed are filled with people enjoying the experience of being outside. We are of the conviction, arguably influenced by a bias toward furniture, that sites should have all the furnishings they need for the best days, if not in fixed arrangement, then in stored portable pieces that can be brought out on demand. An outdoor space with furniture left unused because of rain isn't forlorn. It's just waiting for a nice day. After all, theaters are empty until movie time.

Some natural features can be leveraged in productive ways. Site elevations requiring stairs or ramps may offer opportunities to provide seating on steps or ledges. Features such as water or rock outcroppings can provide focal points or backdrops for furniture in a space.

Microclimate

Perhaps the most important environmental factor designers must address is sun. Patterns of sun and shade will play a critical role in how furniture is placed. The furniture plan should include mapping of sun and shade over the course of the day and the season. In an environment such as a suburban or rural park, this will involve mapping the sun's path as well as the location and density of trees and other features of the environment, such as rock outcroppings, that might block direct sunlight. In a city plaza, it will require mapping shade from trees and adjacent buildings as well as massive structures such as bridges and overpasses that limit sun exposure.

The site analysis should incorporate typical wind direction and velocity. For cities it's important to remember that the dense alignment of tall buildings can create wind tunnels, and winds sweeping down the sides of skyscrapers can achieve gale force (a problem confronted by people who tried to walk across the former World Trade Center plaza on a windy day).

Local precipitation and temperature patterns should be considered on both daily and seasonal bases.

Significant ambient sights, sounds, smells, or other sensations that would affect people's experience should also be noted, including information about their timing, frequency, and potential impact.

Social, Cultural, and Historical Context

The information and insights gained through this aspect of analysis can help designers make furniture choices that effectively address functional and aesthetic criteria, resonate on an emotional level with the people for whom the space is intended, and anticipate changing uses and constituencies.

Relevant social and cultural factors to explore include the demographics of the neighborhood, the cultural heritage and practices of the population, the expectations of people who will use the space, and competing interests among existing constituencies. Information on historical background should include the history of the neighborhood, former uses of the site, and patterns of change over time, including projections for the future.

Surrounding population density is immensely important, as are patterns of use. Dense populations represent a strong latent opportunity for a base of users. Enriching these potential visitors' experience becomes critical, as does understanding their alternative venues and activities. Lack of density of surrounding populations tends to make attracting visitors the priority. Patterns of use such as running, parents with strollers, dog walking, lunching, and tourism should be noted and considered.

Determining key constituencies and gathering their input is an important aspect of analysis. This may require a public input process. Underestimating the importance of public input or misunderstanding its message can derail any project.

Assessing the surrounding built environment provides information on architectural styles and planning schemes that might be integrated into a space. Looking at other outdoor spaces in the area helps designers recognize what is already provided, what is lacking, and what services and opportunities can be offered by a new or reimagined space. Understanding the identity of a site (city or town, district or neighborhood, campus, organization, or facility) enables designers to capitalize on a sense of ownership and the references, symbols, or signature elements associated with these places.

Reconciliation

If the analysis reveals information that conflicts with the program, go back to the program and reconcile before moving on to the next step.

Concept Development

Concept development is the stage in which the program and analysis information is synthesized and expressed in a physical plan. There are multiple factors to consider during this process.

Seating is the key element. The primary goal of furniture planning is to create and facilitate places for people. To maximize seating quality, plan the furniture from the seating perspective and add other elements later.

People in outdoor spaces choose their seating carefully and strategically. They select seats that, from their personal perspective, offer the best comfort, security, functionality, and view of the action. These options are unlikely to be available if the seating was located randomly or solely on aesthetic principles rather than on user preferences.

Seating preferences are quite universal. Finding a comfortable level of sun or shade for the moment is an important seating criterion for users of an outdoor space regardless of the type of space they are in or where in the world they may be. The strong interest in people watching on the part of most users of outdoor spaces is not dependent on the type of space or geography. Jan Gehl observes:

> A summary of observations and investigations shows that people and human activity are the greatest object of attention and interest. Even the modest form of contact of merely seeing and hearing or being near others is apparently more rewarding and more in demand than the majority of other attractions offered in the public spaces of cities and residential areas.[4]

It's a bottom-up process. Because seating preferences are fairly predictable and universal, furniture planning starts by addressing those preferences at the micro level and then rolling out those opportunities across the site to

Figures 2.9a-g Credit: Robert G. Chipman, ASLA

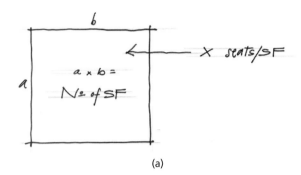

(a)

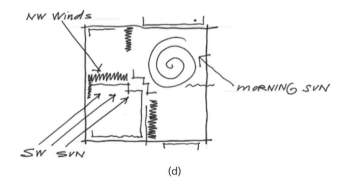

(b)

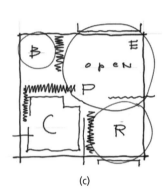

(c)

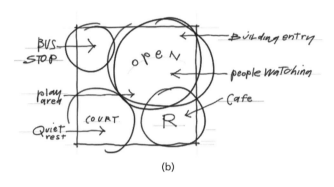

(d)

ADA compliant
walkway clearance
edge protection
Lighting
CPTED

(e)

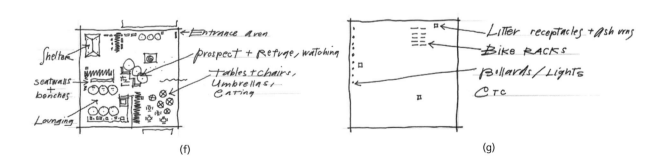

(f)

(g)

achieve the macro level. Approaching the furniture planning process this way mimics users' process of entering a space and looking for the seating that best fits their needs at the moment.

It's an iterative process. Decisions at one level may suggest or require revisiting prior steps. Build on lessons learned as you develop a variety of vignettes to support the range of people and activities in the space.

Concept development has seven basic steps (though they don't necessarily go in this order):

1. Determine how much seating is needed.
2. Identify the best seating opportunities schematically.
3. Provide hierarchy, structure, scale and framing for seating and standing spaces.
4. Address the seating and standing microclimates.
5. Address CPTED (crime prevention through environmental design), ADA (Americans with Disabilities Act), and safety issues.
6. Create choices.
7. Add other furnishing elements.

During this process, thought should also be given to appropriate aesthetic and material choices. These choices won't be finalized until the detailed design step.

How Much Seating Is Needed?

The quantity of seating offered establishes the maximum number of seated people that the space can serve. The availability of seating is a critical factor in the extent to which people use spaces, especially if they want to eat, rest, work, read, or enjoy the space for a period of time that is too long to comfortably stand. (See Figure 2.9a.)

Some projects have a specific number of required seats, for example, an outdoor café designed to serve a targeted number of customers or a privately owned public space that is required to offer a certain amount of seating to qualify for development benefits.

Most spaces, however, do not have such a clear mandate and the amount of seating needed is unclear. Facilities that have the opportunity to adjust the quantity of seating to see what works best in various situations have an advantage. Both Bryant Park and the University of Wisconsin Memorial Union Terrace (see case studies) added many additional seats over time and, in doing so, also added to their popularity and success.

Unfortunately, the available budget often ends up determining the seating quantity provided even though it may have little to do with the quantity needed. When this is the case, guidelines and procedures should be established for future additions as the budget permits in order to maintain a continuity of design and spirit.

Projects on which the one good opportunity to put in seating is at the time of construction may want to maximize this initial opportunity by offering a large quantity of good seating.

New York City, one of the few places to quantify seating requirements, requires 1 linear foot of seating per 30 square feet of plaza space to qualify for developer incentive bonuses stemming from privately owned public spaces. (NYC Planning Commission regulations can be viewed at www.nyc. gov/html/dcp/pdf/priv/101707_final_approved_text.pdf.) One linear foot of seating per foot of perimeter has also been suggested as a seating quantity guideline for urban spaces.

As a rule of thumb for city or residential environments, Jan Gehl suggests that "suitable places to sit should be located at regular intervals, for example, every 100 meters."[5]

Consider occasional spikes in demand such as lunch times, festivals, or a visit from a busload of school children. These peak loads may be addressed with secondary or temporary seating.

To estimate average capacity of prime sitting space at peak times, Clare Cooper Marcus and Carolyn Francis suggest dividing the number of linear feet of seating provided by three.[6]

Ultimately, the quantity of seating needed may be a judgment call. If possible, keep open the opportunity to add more seating over time as the need becomes clearer. If that's impossible, err on the side of "more" at the very beginning. Use the needed seating quantity as a guide through the furniture planning process.

Identify the Seating Opportunities Schematically

> Where outdoor seats are set down without regard for view and climate, they will almost certainly be useless.
>
> —*Christopher Alexander*[7]

The key for identifying seating opportunities is the old saying "Location, location, location." (See Figure 2.9b.)

People Watching

People love to watch people, and it is clearly one of the top attractions of public spaces. The best people-watching opportunities are often found around entrances, sidewalks, cafés, water features, kids, and pets.

2.10 People watching in Columbus Circle, New York City. Credit: OLIN

2.11 Seating in Honolulu: a lot to look at. Photo credit: Bill Main

The distance from seating to the viewing opportunity will vary based on who is watching whom. Hall's proxemic measures are useful here. People watching other people in a park or plaza have a comfortable vantage point within the 12-to-25+-foot "public" range (or less if the people are in motion, as when walking by on a sidewalk. See Figure 2.25).

Attractive Activities

Optimize seating near attractive activities such as eating, dog walking, playgrounds, transit access, biking, walking, waiting, meeting, shopping, programs and special events, fountains, vistas (especially water), and so on.

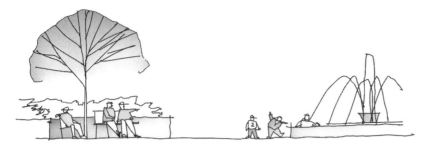

2.12 Compelling visual elements influence furniture placement. Credit: Robert G. Chipman, ASLA

Benches that provide a good view of surrounding activities are used more than benches with less or no view of others. . . . When benches do not face activities, either they will not be used—or they will be used in nontraditional ways.

—*Jan Gehl*[8]

Key Characteristics and Highlights

Note natural terrain and views and man-made elements such as water features, sculptures, and surrounding architecture. Consider neighborhood characteristics, urban density, the quantity and quality of pedestrian traffic—that is, the whole constellation of physical and visual elements that will impact furniture placement.

> In situations where we have benches on both sides of a wide promenade, we typically don't make them face each other. They are offset, so I can look ahead without having another person in view: I have a landscape in front of me and they have a landscape in front of them. Visual order leads you to think that we ought to dance them on down. But visual order is less important than the social dynamic and the views.
> —*Charles McKinney, Chief of Design, City of New York Department of Parks and Recreation*

Object Watching

Popular objects of attention include water, scenic views, landmarks, sculpture and other artworks, and urban architecture. Water is a magnet for people in public spaces. They seem to love watching it almost as much as they love watching other people. In general, the distance from seating to the object of the view will vary with the size of the object. Determine how far away from the object the viewer needs to be to take in the whole thing. If this distance becomes very large, because the object being viewed is very large, the seating space may seem monumental and impersonal. This may be acceptable if one is viewing the Washington Monument, but in situations where the grand effect is not desired, it can be mitigated with framing and structuring. (See the next section, "Provide Structure, Scale, and Framing.") If you don't have a waterfront, an elegant water feature, or a truly grand monument—there is only one Eiffel Tower, after all—you should probably

2.13 Chicago's Buckingham Fountain is large and imposing. Seating placed at a distance enables viewers to take it all in. Photo credit: Bill Main

build your seating plan around people watching and other activities rather than object watching, as they have more assured appeal.

Transit Access and Waiting

People waiting and watching for cars, buses, or trains want to sit, stand, or lean with a good view of incoming traffic. They do not want nontransit activity (e.g., a hot dog stand) between them and the loading point. Seating needs to be close enough to the loading point to enable people to get aboard quickly, but far enough away to avoid congestion or getting splashed on a wet day.

2.14 A vista in British Columbia: seating that's right at home in the great outdoors. Photo credit: Bill Main

2.15 Waiting for the bus at a transit stop in San Francisco: good placement, clear views. Photo credit: Bill Main

Entering and Exiting Buildings

The entrances to buildings are busy spaces that offer prime opportunities for people watching, meeting, and waiting. If there's room, provide a bench or two. Keep them clear of doorways and walkways.

2.16 A downtown Chicago building with clearly delineated zones for seating, walking, and entering the building. Photo credit: Bill Main

2.17 Al fresco dining enlivens a downtown Chicago streetscape. Photo credit: Bill Main

Outdoor Dining

Restaurants and bistros with outdoor spaces liven up outdoor spaces. They require chairs, tables, and usually umbrellas, which are typically owned and maintained by the establishment.

Brown-Bagging/Food Vending

Lunchtime and fine weather create demand for good places to sit and eat informally. It can be a formidable task to eat lunch while sitting on a bench

2.18 Brown- bagging it along the Chicago River: a planter ledge will do. Photo credit: Bill Main

2.19 Seating with overhead cover provides a well-defined core for this play area. Photo credit: Bill Main

or ledge without getting food on your clothes or leaving some on the seat. Tables, "tablets," and movable stools can help.

Play Areas

Parents and others supervising children in play areas appreciate a nearby place to sit and use as a "base of operations" for jackets, snacks, and so on. (See Figure 2.19)

2.20 Seating located at the edge of the action provides a perfect vantage point for special events in Daley Plaza, Chicago. Photo credit: Bill Main

2.21 An occasional bench provides a welcome resting place along the trail. Photo credit: Bill Main

Special Events and Programs

These are often conducted in the open center of a large plaza. Provide places to sit and watch from the perimeter. Do not place fixed seating in areas that might be used for events. (See Figure 2.20)

Resting

Seating spaced regularly along linear parks, walkways, and bikeways provides periodic opportunities for rest. (See Figure 2.21)

2.22 Movable chairs encourage socializing in outdoor public spaces. Photo credit: Bill Main

2.23 It's too bad this interesting sculptural seating is so close to the fence, curb, and vehicle exhaust. Roppongi Hills, Japan. Photo credit: Bill Main

Socializing

The emphasis on linear seating in many spaces makes it difficult for couples or groups to sit comfortably facing each other. Movable seats or fixed seating configured with groups in mind (in face-to-face or angled configurations, also known as sociopetal) make it easier to interact. (See Figure 2.22)

Negative Activities

Avoid or mitigate seating near negative activities such as sources of noise and smell, loading docks, parking lots, objectionable views, and the like. (See Figure 2.23)

Provide Structure, Framing, and Scale

Good seating spaces are anchored within their setting by natural or man-made elements and are designed to human scale. They don't just float in a large space or stand stark against an expansive backdrop. (See Figure 2.24 and 2.26) Once seating opportunities have been identified, they need to be appropriately structured or framed and given scale and context. The conceptual tools of proxemics, prospect and refuge, and hierarchy of space introduced at the beginning of this chapter can be useful in this process.

As prospect-refuge theory posits, people typically prefer to have their backs protected when they are seated. Mitigate feelings of vulnerability and exposure by providing sitting space against walls or dividers. For structure and scale consider using walls, ledges, trees, planters, umbrellas, trellises, and other elements and structures to help create microspaces for seating. To achieve human scale, avoid placing seating next to monumental walls, streets, or expanses that invariably make people feel small and inconsequential unless mitigated by more intimate elements.

> Places for sitting along facades and spatial boundaries are preferred to sitting areas in the middle of a space, and, as in standing, people tend to seek support from the details of physical environment. Sitting places in niches, at the end of benches, or at other well defined spots and sitting places where one's back is protected are preferred to less precisely defined places.
>
> —*Jan Gehl*[9]

Consider pedestrian flows through the space and provide seating around the edges, where viewing opportunities and action abound.

> Where pedestrian flows bisect a sittable place, that is where people will most likely sit.
>
> —*William H. Whyte*[10]

2.24 A structure with seating in Gustafson Guthrie Nichols's Lurie Garden at Millennium Park provides a protected niche with views of the city garden. Photo credit: Bill Main

2.25 Where pedestrian flows bisect a sittable place: Planting, lighting, and seating set back from the pedestrian flow create the structure for these well-used benches at the entry to Millennium Park. Photo credit: Bill Main

Establish Environmental Comfort by Addressing the Microclimate

Provide access to sun or shade as the site conditions demand. Although it's not possible to completely control the conditions of climate and

2.26 A lonely bench placed against a monumental wall is dwarfed in scale. Who would happily sit in this inhospitable space? Photo credit: Bill Main

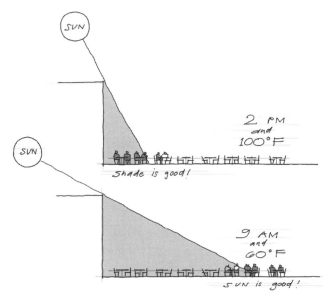

2.27 Provide places to sit in the sun when it's cool and in the shade when it's hot. Credit: Robert G. Chipman, ASLA

environment, they can be mitigated by furniture location, tree canopies, screening, and shade structures. (See Figure 2.9d.)

Sun and Temperature

People in outdoor environments move to the place that has the temperature and light they prefer. As people have different reasons for being in spaces and divergent preferences and tolerances, a negative for one person may constitute a positive for another. To mitigate the effects of sun and temperature, create a number of different "environments" that provide

2.28 Locate seating on the wind-protected side of plantings or structures. Credit: Robert G. Chipman, ASLA

choice. Create places to sit in the sun during peak lunch hours on cool days and places to lunch in the shade when the weather is hot. The ideal solution, site permitting, is to create opportunities to sit and eat in both sun and shade. Provide umbrellas or other sunshades in areas without natural shade or to augment naturally shaded options.

Wind

People will generally choose to sit in areas protected from wind. Locate seating on the protected side of a wall, hedge, or building.

Noise

Ambient noise is difficult to moderate. Locate seating as far as possible from the source. If possible, place seating in areas protected by walls or plantings.

Smells

Locate seating away from likely sources, such as dumpsters, litter receptacles, and smoking areas.

Identify Safety, Accessible Design, and Crime Prevention Issues

See Figure 2.9e.

General safety rules include:

- Set seating back from sidewalks a sufficient distance so that sitters' feet don't protrude into the walkway (30 inches is optimal).

- Do not place benches where they might be used as aids for climbing over railings or barriers.

Universal design and ADA guidelines related to furniture are covered in Chapter 8, "Accessible Design."

CPTED recommends:

- Locate furniture so that sitters can see and be seen, away from dark and isolated areas.
- Provide adequate lighting in seating areas.
- Bollards, benches, planters, bus shelters, and so on may be used to visually "harden" the site and discourage vehicle intrusions.

For a detailed discussion of CPTED principles, see *Landscape Architectural Graphic Standards.*[11]

Create Choices

A range of furniture options is key to successful spaces (see Figure 2.9f). People tend to self-select on the basis of their preferences of the moment, and the more choices they have, the more likely they are to enter a space and to remain once they are there.

Consider physical comfort. Provide seating in sun and shade, and ergonomic comfort through attention to back heights, armrests, and rolled edges where the chair seat meets the back of the legs. Address age-related preferences: more support and comfort for older sitters, one-piece seat-and-back styles for young children so they can't slip through the cracks. Where possible, include both primary seating (chairs, benches, stools) and secondary seating (built-in ledges, steps, planter edges) for overflow crowds. (See Chapter 4 for a more detailed discussion of seating types and features, including ergonomics and seating comfort.)

Consider social comfort. If possible, provide fixed and movable seating, some with tables or tablets. Arrange seating in linear and interactive (angled, curved, or opposed) configurations that offer sociofugal and sociopetal seating choices. Consider openness and privacy and appropriate proxemic distances. Provide a choice of seating and tables that meet ADA requirements.

Placement of seating must be guided by a thorough analysis of the spatial and functional qualities of the location. Each bench or seating area should preferably have an individual local quality and should be placed where there is, for example, a small space within the space, a niche, a corner, a place that offers intimacy and security and, as a rule, a good microclimate as well.

—Jan Gehl[12]

Add Other Furnishing Elements

Identify the need and appropriate locations for litter receptacles, ash urns, bike racks, bollards, and other accessories—see Chapters 4 and 5 for details. (See Figure 2.9g.)

Pay particular attention to litter receptacles. Too few can result in increased littering. Remember, the first rule of litter receptacle placement is *don't put the trash next to the bench*. While receptacles should be placed close enough to seating to encourage use, they must be placed far enough away to avoid unpleasant sights, smells, and bugs. The optimal distance is somewhere between 12 feet and 40 feet, depending on the space.

Get Public Feedback

The conceptual presentation to this point should be descriptive enough to clearly communicate the designer's vision and flexible enough to adapt to public response.

Detailed Design

Make selections, issue specifications. Choose furniture materials, designs, special features and options, and colors. Select manufacturers for standard products and custom designs, fabricators for built-in furniture elements. Specify configurations, locations, and anchoring systems. (See Chapters 4, 5, 6, and 10 for details.)

Installation

Monitor the process. Furniture is extremely vulnerable in this phase of the process. Staging, assembling, and installing offer ripe opportunities for things to go wrong. Good execution by the contractor is critical to avoid common pitfalls, such as careless handling on the site, improper assembly, improper installation, and loss of parts. Getting implementation right has serious implications for the project schedule in the short term and for the performance of the furniture over time. (See Chapter 11.)

Maintenance

Keep up appearances. Well-maintained outdoor spaces are inviting places that appeal and attract. Poorly maintained spaces are breeding places for vandalism and abuse. Furniture maintenance is a key aspect of the overall care of a site. The process includes ongoing inspection, cleaning, repair, and touch-up. It calls for regularly emptying and removing trash, as well as raising and lowering umbrellas in response to the weather. It may require taking furniture in at night, putting it out in the morning, and storing it during the off-season.

Management

Pursue continuous improvement. Ideally, the furniture plan shouldn't end when the furniture is in place. Some of the most successful projects we've seen have become processes in which the plan is repeatedly revisited and fine-tuned to meet evolving conditions. Fortunately, unlike buildings or parking lots, furniture can be relatively easily added, taken away, reconfigured, and sometimes retrofitted, and the positive benefits to the space can be significant.

There is a model for this process. W. Edwards Deming's plan-do-check-act (PDCA) cycle is used in manufacturing to promote continuous improvement and implement change. We believe it can be productively applied to the furniture plan.

- *Plan.* Recognize an opportunity and plan a change.
- *Do.* Test the change. Carry out a small-scale study.

2.29 W. Edwards Deming's PDCA cycle is a useful tool for promoting continuous improvement and implementing change. Credit: Robert G. Chipman, ASLA

2.30 The Memorial Union Terrace at the University of Wisconsin, Madison, has pursued continuous improvement in site and site furniture over decades of service. Credit: Wisconsin Department of Tourism, 2007

- *Check*. Review the test, analyze the results, and identify what you've learned.
- *Act*. Take action based on what you learned in the study step. If the change did not work, go through the cycle again with a different plan. If you were successful, incorporate what you learned from the test into wider changes. Use what you learned to plan new improvements.

A postoccupancy evaluation (POE) is an ideal tool for assessing how well furniture in outdoor spaces is meeting programming expectations and user needs. We recommend conducting such an evaluation to identify opportunities for improvement and to initiate change.

This outline of a process for furniture planning is intended for use in conjunction with the information provided in Chapters 3–6. Together they offer a resource for identifying and implementing appropriate site furniture applications in a variety of public spaces.

FURNITURE PLANNING BEST PRACTICE

Capitol Plaza, New York, New York
Designer: Thomas Balsley Associates, New York City

Background

Capitol Plaza, designed by Thomas Balsley Associates, is a privately owned public space completed in 2000 as part of the Capitol at Chelsea, a 39-story building containing apartments atop retail and office space at the corner of 26th Street and Sixth Avenue. The new structure replaced a commercial building demolished after zoning changes opened opportunities for residential development in the area. Under a program administered by the New York City Planning Commission, the owner of the lot and building was granted a floor area bonus as an incentive for creating public space on the undeveloped portion of the property. The 50-by-200-foot site was a gritty parcel, last used as a flea market, connecting two blocks lined by older commercial buildings.

Programming

Balsley started his research by walking the local streets within a four-to-five-block radius, casting a keen eye on street-level business and types of pedestrians. "Retail tells you everything in an urban neighborhood," he says. "Retailers succeed or fail based on the people on the street, so what you see there is what you've got." The small downmarket shops and food sellers in the neighborhood served employees in local businesses. There was foot traffic through the area, but little to draw people or keep them there. Almost no families and few older people were to be seen. The expected users of the plaza appeared to be clerical and industrial workers who came from elsewhere and left at the end of the day. But there were signs of change. Attracted by reasonable rents, design and high-tech companies were creating a growing community that Balsley calls a "design ghetto." Young website designers and workers in the hip-hop shops were arriving in the neighborhood, and they didn't all work from nine to five. Artists and designers were creating live/work lofts in vacated commercial space. And plans were being floated for more high-rise residential construction nearby. So while the established constituency for a public space in the neighborhood was limited, Balsley saw that "the handwriting was on the wall. We knew that Capitol Plaza should be a space that didn't just target what was here right now, but anticipated what was to come."

FURNITURE PLANNING BEST PRACTICE

(Continued)

Site Analysis

At the proposed plaza site, Balsley and his team looked at patterns of sun and shade. There were no existing trees or other plant materials on site. The entire 200-foot length of the space was bounded on both sides by multistory structures, and the cross streets at the south and north entrances to the plaza were similarly developed. The sun would be blocked for long periods of the day by the rising walls of the surrounding city. During the middle of the day, the overhead sun would flood the plaza with light. The space would be subject to traffic noise.

The team investigated other public spaces within a half-mile radius to determine what was currently available. They found two. One was a small triangle with few amenities sandwiched into an island at a busy intersection; the other was Madison Square Park, a beautifully maintained formal park with a children's playground, a dog run, and benches lined up along fenced lawns with signs warning people to keep off the grass. Neither of them addressed the needs of the constituencies the designer believed would use the new space. "I wanted Capitol Plaza to be an alternative," he says, "a relaxed place where there would be plenty of space for people to meet friends for lunch and socialize over coffee, have outdoor meetings, sit alone in a sheltered area and read a book, or perch out in the open and watch people go by."

To make this happen, the designer believed the plaza needed to be a "through space" rather than a pocket enclosed on three sides. He conceived of it as a place with a promenade passing through it and convinced the New York City Planning Commission to agree to his plan (despite concerns that through spaces in the city can become refuges for "undesirables"). As part of his plan to encourage foot traffic in the plaza, he negotiated with the owner of the Capitol to provide an entry door midway into the plaza for use by residents walking to the subway.

Balsley looked at the key points where the plaza intersected the street. On the southwest corner a planned café with outside tables and an entrance facing the plaza would provide a welcoming niche. On the northeast, a long, narrow (8 by 100 feet) strip of vacant property running along half the length of the plaza posed a potential problem. The owner planned to build parking stackers in the dead space. Balsley convinced him he could make more money building retail space that opened onto the plaza. "I saw that space as the ultimate coffee or martini bar," he says, his first incentive being another active edge for the plaza.

Although the building constructed by the plaza's owner was renter-occupied at the time the plaza was designed, Balsley ascertained that a conversion to condos was part of the long-term plan. This critical piece of intelligence was to influence his furniture decisions.

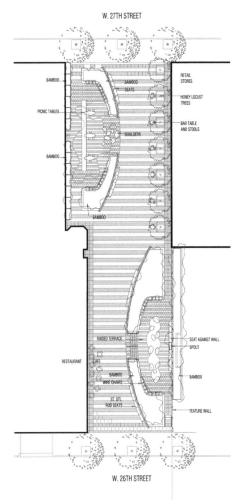

W. 27TH STREET

BAMBOO

BAMBOO SEATS

PICNIC TABLES

BOULDERS

BAMBOO

BAMBOO

RETAIL STORES

HONEY LOCUST TREES

BAR TABLE AND STOOLS

RAISED TERRACE

RESTAURANT

CAFE

BAMBOO

WIRE CHAIRS

ST. STL. ROD SEATS

SEAT AGAINST WALL

SPOUT

BAMBOO

FEATURE WALL

W. 26TH STREET

2.31 Capitol Plaza: plan drawing.
Drawing credit: Thomas Balsley
Associates

Concept Development

As Balsley and his design team talked and sketched though the process,
they defined several different areas or precincts within the plaza where
people could sit, each one supporting a specific type or range of activity:
eating, meeting, resting, reading, watching, working. They laid out the
promenade through the space to not only offer connections to the streets
of the city but also provide space delineation, boundaries for the various
settings within the plaza, and a prime vantage point for people watching.
Choice emerged as the dominant theme of the space—choice in types of
settings, furniture types, the way the furniture is configured, the furniture's
location within the larger space, exposure or seclusion, form, and materials.

One choice not included was movable furniture. Balsley reasoned that
when the developer, who had received a financial incentive for putting

FURNITURE PLANNING BEST PRACTICE

(Continued)

2.32 Capitol Plaza: overview. Photo credit: Thomas Balsley Associates, photo by Michael Koontz

in the plaza, later turned over the building to a condo board, which had a financial stake in the space, maintenance would become an issue. The likelihood that the board would manage, maintain, and replace movable furniture was slim. Better to provide flexibility through a wide range of fixed options, he decided, than to provide movable furniture that, once damaged or disappeared, would never be replaced. (Movable tables and chairs in the café are the province of the concessionaire.)

Balsley envisioned an aesthetic for the space and furniture that would resonate with the hip sensibility of the young, creative types who were establishing their presence in the neighborhood. He proposed using strong, muscular materials that would reflect the industrial history of the neighborhood, withstand heavy use, and survive with minimal maintenance.

Public input was solicited from and final approval granted by the New York City Planning Commission and the local community board. Under the city's "bonus plaza" regulations, which were enacted as a result of the work of William H. Whyte, Capitol Plaza was required to meet a number of detailed furniture mandates, among them:

- A broad variety of seating types and configurations

- Ample seating placed in close proximity and at angles to one another or in facing configurations that facilitate social interaction

- A minimum of 1 linear foot of seating for each 30 square feet of public plaza area

- At least three different types of seating (required for public plazas greater than 5,000 square feet)

- A prohibition against devices such as spikes or deliberately uncomfortable materials or forms on horizontal surfaces, such as ledges and steps, otherwise suitable for seating

- A requirement that seats facing walls be a minimum of 6 feet from such wall.

Detailed Design

The plaza is designed as a series of vignettes. For the bamboo-sheltered raised garden on the southeast corner, conceived as quiet, contemplative space, the designer chose steel wire benches with individual contoured seats. Balsley explains that the seats "were intended for a comfortable extended stay, but were chosen for their curve-framed profile, which discourages lying down." Along the plaza's colorful corrugated metal east wall he placed custom-designed stainless-steel wall-mounted benches with "tablets," multipurpose elements for holding a book, laptop, or snack.

The at-grade garden on the northwest corner, bordered by a seating wall, is intended as a social setting to provide places for groups to meet and eat. For this area, Balsley designed furniture he describes as an "urban picnic table." The elliptical brushed stainless-steel tables and precast concrete stools are "a much-loved seating arrangement that allows for co-worker lunches and, who knows, maybe a chance social encounter."

2.33 Custom-designed stainless-steel wall-mounted benches with "tablets" provide a place for a laptop, a latte, or a book. Photo credit: Thomas Balsley Associates, photo by Michael Koontz

FURNITURE PLANNING BEST PRACTICE

(Continued)

2.34 Elliptical brushed stainless-steel tables and precast concrete stools create social settings for small groups. Photo credit: Thomas Balsley Associates, photo by Michael Koontz

2.35 Bar-height tables with swivel stools provide seating with an elevated perspective and couples in mind. Photo credit: Thomas Balsley Associates, photo by Bruce Katz

For the vignette on the northeast corner, Balsley designed a custom stainless-steel bar table with swivel stools. He explains, "Placed along the retail food and beverage area, these tables and stools provide a slightly elevated perspective to satisfy the desire to perch and provide flexibility in seating proximity for shared kisses or shared work."

Battered concrete walls line the promenade, which runs north to south through the heart of the plaza. Balsley designed a custom stainless-steel bench that is mounted along the walls. He says, "These seats provide an ideal

2.36 Concrete walls with attached benches line the promenade through the heart of the plaza and provide front-row seats. Photo credit: Thomas Balsley Associates, photo by Michael Koontz

meet-and-greet opportunity. The solid bar construction resists skateboard abuse and is always dry. The battered wall angle is perfect for comfort."

Short-term overflow seating is provided by precast concrete seat walls, and, he notes, "visitors can be predictably found sitting on the stairs facing the promenade as well as on top of the battered wall, which was kept low enough to encourage the inevitable desire to perch."

Bamboo screens were planned to provide shelter for quiet areas and act as buffers along the street. A row of locust trees was planted along the northeast quadrant, providing shade for the bar table/stool vignette. (Balsley is not an advocate of intensive tree planting in urban spaces. He believes people in the shadow of skyscrapers welcome the sun, especially in the spring and fall.) Seating at street entrances was oriented inward, away from street noise. Steel bollards at north and south entrances allow free passage and also support low, railed panels that are installed at night (the plaza closes at 10:00 p.m.) and put away again in the morning. The barrier discourages trespassing while avoiding the use of less friendly fences.

Balsley's selection of furniture and materials makes for a lively space and resonates with the community the plaza serves. "The type of furniture sends a message of invitation and seating convenience," he says. "There's more to it than a place to sit." And the way the furniture is configured is quite successful in supporting the social interaction that was a goal of the space. "There's a bit of social engineering we do," Balsley explains. "Understanding the dynamics and setting up synergies and interrelationships."

Thomas Balsley loves designing urban spaces. His approach to the furniture, as in Capitol Plaza, can be whimsical. But there's a deeply philosophical

FURNITURE PLANNING BEST PRACTICE

(Continued)

vision driving the design. "You can judge the success of the plaza by the number of people in the seats," he says. "I try to fill spaces as if I were a retailer. I want the stuff to fly off the shelves."

Implementation and Management

Balsley anticipated some key implementation and management issues early in the furniture planning process. He selected robust materials and specified that most furniture be embedded and wall-mounted. He opted for a wide variety of fixed furniture types in lieu of maintenance-intensive movable tables and chairs for an environment that would not be able to sustain them. He designed for a broad constituency of users by creating distinctly different areas within the space and furnishing them with visually and functionally distinct elements. His experience tells him that neighborhoods and the public spaces within them inevitably change over time. So he tries to provide enough variety to weather the changes. "You can't put all your eggs in one basket," he says. "You have to provide for a broad constituency, so if one group goes, the space is still viable and able to sustain itself." He negotiated with building owners on either side of the plaza to secure features (retail, a café, building entry) that would encourage people to enter and use the space.

As a public space owned and maintained by private parties, Capitol Plaza is unlikely to be reevaluated for its success in serving the public at large unless present conditions were to change radically and the property were to become a liability. That seems unlikely in the foreseeable future, as this former vacant lot in an upward-trending neighborhood hosts a steady stream of workers, residents, and tourists pleased to enjoy a small oasis in the big city.

Endnotes

1. Edward T. Hall, *The Hidden Dimension* (New York: Anchor Books, 1990).
2. Jay Appleton, *The Experience of Landscape* (London: John Wiley, 1975).
3. Christopher Alexander et al., *A Pattern Language* (New York: Oxford University Press, 1977), 558.
4. Jan Gehl, *Life Between Buildings*, 6th ed. (Copenhagen: Danish Architectural Press, 2006), 29.
5. Ibid., 162.
6. C. Cooper Marcus and C. Francis, eds., *People Places: Design Guidelines for Urban Open Space*, 2nd ed. (New York: John Wiley & Sons, 1998), 44.
7. Alexander et al., *A Pattern Language*, 1119.
8. Gehl, *Life Between Buildings*, 27.
9. Ibid., 157.
10. William H. Whyte, *The Social Life of Small Urban Spaces* (New York: Project for Public Spaces, 1980), 33.
11. Leonard J. Hopper, ed., *Landscape Architectural Graphic Standards* (Hoboken, NJ: John Wiley & Sons, 2007), 158–74.
12. Gehl, *Life Between Buildings*, 157–58.

3. Types of Spaces

Different kinds of spaces have different furniture and amenity requirements. The configuration of spaces, who uses them, and how they are used should all be taken into account in specifying and laying out furniture elements to support typical and desired activities. Table 3.1 defines some major spaces by type, with special issues and recommended furniture guidelines for each.

Pedestrian Mall

A pedestrian mall is an urban street on which vehicle traffic has been eliminated or severely limited and pedestrian space and amenities have been added is a pedestrian mall. It may have a bus or light rail line along its length. It may include several blocks and numerous types of spaces in search of a common identity for purposes of improvement, development, and promotion. Pedestrian malls are typically mixed-use, including retail, business, and transit.

Special issues:

- Fostering a strong, district identity

  Guidelines: Establish a portfolio of standard products including benches, litter receptacles, bike racks, signage, and lighting to be used throughout the mall.

- Supporting transit and retail activity

  Guidelines: Provide seating for shoppers in social clusters; provide benches at bus or rail stops; provide litter receptacles near benches (but not too near) and at regular intervals along the street.

Urban Sidewalk Streetscape

An urban sidewalk streetscape is defined as the pedestrian area between buildings or storefronts and the curb.

Special issues:

- Visual clutter when multiple constituencies introduce individual elements

  Guidelines: Establish "decluttering" protocols that specify the type and number of elements that can be introduced to the space; establish a portfolio of standard products, including benches, litter receptacles, bike racks, signage, and lighting; limit the color palette.

Table 3.1: Typical Furnishing Needs for Major Space Types

TYPE OF SPACE	BENCHES	SEAT WALL	MOVABLE CHAIRS	LEANING RAIL	LITTER RECEPTACLES	SMOKING RECEPTACLES	RECYCLING RECEPTACLES	PET WASTE RECEPTACLES	EATING TABLES	LOW TABLES	TABLES WITH ATTACHED SEATS
Pedestrian mall	X	X	X		X	X	X		X		X
Urban streetscape	X				X		X		X		X
Plazas	X	X	X		X	X	X		X		X
Urban parks	X	X	X		X	X	X	X	X		X
Recreational park	X				X		X	X			X
Trails and linear parks	X				X		X	X			
Theme parks	X	X	X		X	X	X		X		X
Children's park	X	X	X		X		X				X
Retail centers	X		X		X	X	X		X		X
Healthcare	X		X		X	X	X		X	X	X
Corporate campuses	X		X		X	X	X		X	X	X
Transit and transportation centers	X			X	X	X	X				
Transit stops	X			X	X	X	X				
Cafés and outdoor food courts			X		X	X	X		X		X
College campuses	X	X			X	X	X				X
K-12 schools	X				X		X				X
Office entries	X				X	X	X				
Roof tops	X										X

PICNIC TABLES	UMBRELLAS OR SHADE STRUCTURE	BIKE RACKS	BIKE GARAGES AND LOCKERS	PLANTERS	TRANSIT SHELTERS	BOLLARDS	NEWSPAPER BOXES	DRINKING FOUNTAINS	GRILLS	SIGNAGE AND WAYFINDING ELEMENTS	TREE GRATES AND GUARDS
	X	X		X	X	X	X	X		X	X
	X	X		X	X		X			X	X
	X	X	X	X		X				X	
X	X	X				X		X		X	
X	X	X				X		X	X	X	
		X				X		X	X	X	
	X			X	X	X		X		X	
X	X	X		X		X		X			
	X	X		X	X	X	X	X		X	
	X	X	X	X	X	X				X	
	X	X	X	X	X	X					
		X		X	X	X	X	X		X	
		X			X					X	
	X			X							
	X	X		X	X	X	X				
X		X				X					
		X	X	X		X					
X				X							

3.1 Pedestrian Mall, Rio de Janeiro, Brazil. A major avenue converted to a lively public space: mixed-use retail, restaurants, and business on a pedestrian scale. Photo credit: copyright © 2003 Project for Public Spaces

3.2 In this Ann Arbor, Michigan, streetscape, standard site elements are neatly organized in zones to reduce visual clutter. Photo credit: Bill Main

- Heavy pedestrian traffic

  Guidelines: Create zones for furniture and other elements that separate them from walkways and allow unobstructed pedestrian circulation.

- Strong opinions by individual business operators about the placement of particular elements at their location

  Guidelines: Work with local merchant associations or business districts to educate on benefits of street amenities for business; gain consensus/ trade-offs among constituencies

3.3 Daley Plaza, Chicago. A classic example of the urban plaza combines open space, art, trees, water, and people-friendly amenities. Photo credit: Bill Main

- Growing popularity of outdoor eating venues in urban settings

  Guidelines: Provide spaces in front of cafés, restaurants, and coffee shops to accommodate tables and chairs; provide litter receptacles nearby.

Plaza

Plazas are outdoor spaces, mostly in urban areas, designed for heavy use by local residents and workers and in some cases as a destination. Most are hard-surfaced, and they are often located adjacent to a major building. They may be publicly or privately owned but are open for public use. Plazas may include services such as food, beverage, and newsstand sales, and focal points such as water features or sculpture.

Special issues:

- Located in areas with dense populations, affording a ready and varied constituency over the course of a day

  Guidelines: Determine areas of sun and shade; provide seating and location choices for individuals and groups of varied ages, interests, and needs.
- Potential for crowding on nice days, especially at midday if the space attracts a lunch crowd

  Guidelines: Consider providing tables for brown bag lunches (eating on a bench can be awkward); provide ample litter receptacles; offer overflow or secondary seating for busy days in the form of seat walls or movable chairs.

- Often used for civic and seasonal events

  Guidelines: Provide flexible, open space to accommodate special events; offer secondary seating for large crowds.

- Have great visibility and represent an important opportunity to make a statement about the community and the place

  Guidelines: Choose furniture elements that complement local architecture, reflect historical heritage, and/or include symbols of community identity; provide accessible furnishings that enable all members of the community to use the space.

Urban Park

Urban parks are outdoor spaces providing soft-surface green amenities, including grass, shrubs, and trees; they are almost always public and may be designed to provide a sense of refuge. Furniture and services may be dispersed through the park, with green space in between. Urban parks may include focal points such as gardens, water features, or sculpture. They often occupy an entire block or more.

Special issues:

- May be more leisurely than plazas, encouraging longer stays; greater need for comfort

  Guidelines: Provide benches with backs for comfort and support.

- Attract people who come to walk as well as sit

  Guidelines: Provide benches at regular intervals along pathways.

3.4 Palisades Park, Santa Monica, California. A picnic grove with tables and seating provides refuge in an urban park. Photo credit: Wallace Roberts & Todd

- May be used more on weekends and in the evenings

  Guidelines: Provide secondary seating in the form of seat walls, planter ledges, and so forth to accommodate fluctuations in density; provide adequate lighting.

- Litter may be an issue

  Guidelines: Provide waste receptacles near entries and areas of congregation.

- May attract dog walkers

  Guidelines: Provide receptacles for dog waste bags at entrances/exits.

A Tale of Two Parks

Within types, spaces can embody great diversity. Consider two parks located in close proximity in downtown Chicago: Connors Park and Mariano Park. Almost identical in size and shape, both are very small triangular spaces created by intersections with Rush Street as it angles across the vertical grid, and they are within blocks of each other. However, the two parks are quite different in design and function.

Connors Park reflects the residential history of its immediate neighborhood and borrows design details from an adjacent landmark church. Surrounded by a low fence, graced by a pergola, and anchored by a fountain, it is described by landscape architect Astrid Haryarti, a member of the Teng & Associates design team that redesigned it, as "romantic" and "an urban oasis." Connors Park is furnished with formal benches and attracts solitary individuals and moms with small children who play at the edge of the

3.5 Connors Park, Chicago. Photo credit: Bill Main

3.6 Mariano Park, Chicago. Photo
credit: Bill Main

fountain. Haryarti says, "It was designed to be an internal room. People
can walk along the fence at the edges and look into the park, but they need
to go through an entryway to get into the space, where there is a more
intimate scale."

Mariano Park, on the other hand, is a lively, "external" space, located
in a commercial neighborhood with many food establishments nearby.
Originally a private park donated to the city in 1848 and transferred to
the Chicago Park District in 1959, it is a bustling little place that is open
to the street and is furnished with whimsical benches, small tables, and
movable chairs. A coffee kiosk serves a steady stream of visitors, many
of them workers in the immediate area, who gather in social groups.
"The different flavors and activities of these spaces are determined not by
mandate or intention," Haryarti explains, "but by context." The furnishings
support and enhance the character and function of each.

Recreational Park

Recreational parks are designed for recreational activities such as tennis,
softball, soccer, children's play on structures and equipment, walking,
running, swimming, and so on. They may also have picnic facilities.

Special issues:

- Places needed for walkers and runners to rest

  Guidelines: Provide benches at rest stops spaced out along walkways
  and trails.

3.7 Millennium Park, in Grand Rapids, Michigan, provides a place for recreation and welcomes families with its picnic-style seating and umbrellas. Photo credit: Trevor Bosworth, Landscape Architect, OCBA photo

- Parents' need to observe children at play

  Guidelines: Provide benches close to play structures for parents and kids; consider wide, flat surfaces and other flexible solutions to accommodate stuff (bottles, jackets, toys, strollers, etc.).

- May generate a lot of litter

  Guidelines: Provide large-capacity litter receptacles to reduce overflows and frequency of emptying.

Trails and Linear Parks

Trails and linear parks, designed for walking, running, biking, and in-line skating, are often located on property formerly or currently used for roads, railroads, industrial waterfronts, power lines, and the like.

Special issues:

- Spaces often used for intense physical activities

  Guidelines: Provide benches at rest stops spaced along walkways and trails; provide bike racks at major stopping points and attractions.

- Typically used by individuals or couples rather than whole families or larger groups

  Guidelines: Provide benches of medium length; long benches not required.

- Typically have clear entry and exit points

  Guidelines: Provide benches at entries for tying shoes, waiting; provide litter receptacles at entry and exit points to discourage littering.

- May offer features and services at nodes and crossroads

  Guidelines: Provide benches, litter receptacles, and bike racks in areas where people are likely to gather.

3.8 A simple bench and table along a walking trail in Australia provide a place to rest, snack, and enjoy the views. Photo credit: Bill Main

3.9 A theme park seat wall with a view of the water and the Ferris wheel. Photo credit: Cathy Comeaux-Wright

Theme Parks

Theme parks are private for-profit entertainment parks operated as destinations for day trips or longer. These are usually large areas oriented to families and young adults.

Special issues:

- Experience involves a great deal of walking, waiting, and sensory overload

    Guidelines: Provide a lot of seating along walkways to rest tired backs and feet; provide benches with backs in areas where people are likely to linger.

- Groups of families and friends as visitors

    Guidelines: Provide long benches and social seating configurations to accommodate families and groups.

- Relatively high level of maintenance and security

    Guidelines: Freestanding and movable furniture may be feasible.

Children's Park

Children's parks are spaces designed with play structures and activities targeted specifically at young children.

3.10 A children's play area in the Park at Lakeshore East, Chicago, includes benches in a shaded area where parents and kids can set up base camp. Photo credit: Bill Main

Special issues:

- Parents watching children and guarding stuff while children go back and forth between them and the play area
  Guidelines: Provide benches or other wide flat surfaces as "base camps" for family groups.
- Play structures often in open, sunny sites
  Guidelines: Consider providing shaded benches or tables with fixed umbrellas and attached seats for extended stays.

Retail Centers

Outdoor common areas of shopping centers and strip malls, often with a walkway along the front to facilitate access to multiple stores.

Special issues:

- Strip malls: facilitate quick "get in and get out" shopping
  Guidelines: Provide litter receptacles at entry points, which may be virtually every store in a strip center. Few other amenities may be needed.
- Upscale: need to differentiate from other centers
  Guidelines: Use furnishings and planters to create attractive focal points at key places throughout the center.

3.11 This retail center common area includes seating, a water feature, and greenery to soften the space. Photo credit: copyright © Jim Powell

- Larger centers: defined seating areas, services, and other amenities, often including food vendors

  Guidelines: For the longer stays in such larger centers, provide benches and litter receptacles in common spaces, in waiting areas, and near services and activities; provide tables, chairs, and umbrellas outside food venues.

- Larger centers: may lack intuitive orientation or be difficult to navigate

  Guidelines: Provide a wayfinding system and directories.

- Access by public transit as well as automobiles

  Guidelines: Provide benches at pickup and drop-off nodes and at transit stops.

- Arid and uninviting hardscapes

  Guidelines: Consider providing planters for colorful accents.

Hospitals

Entries, gardens, and courtyards at hospitals providing acute, short-term care may present particular challenges.

Special issues:

- Creating a warmer, friendlier first impression with garden areas

  Guidelines: Provide comfortable benches and other furnishings (tables and umbrellas as appropriate) in outdoor social spaces. Consider planters for warm and colorful accents.

- Use of garden areas by employees and families of patients for breaks, to rest, to relieve stress

  Guidelines: Provide benches and chairs for individuals and social seating configurations for groups.

3.12 The environment and experience of this garden at an urban hospital is vastly different from what is inside just a few feet away. Photo credit: Peter Rohrer

- Smoking areas

  Guidelines: Provide ash urns in clearly designated areas outside the direct path to entries and at a distance from seating areas.

- Patient and visitor pickups and drop-offs outside doors

  Guidelines: Provide benches at entries for people arriving or waiting for rides.

Residential Care Facilities

Residential care facilities (assisted living facilities and nursing homes) frequently feature entries, gardens, and courtyards.

Special issues:

- Front entries of assisted living and nursing facilities are often preferred by residents who like to sit where there are people and activities

  Guidelines: Provide benches and chairs designed for the elderly and infirm (backs, armrests with hand grips, no bucket seats).

- Outdoor garden areas often used by employees and the families of patients for breaks, to rest, and to relieve stress

  Guidelines: Provide benches and chairs for individuals and social seating configurations for groups.

- Wheelchair access and clearances for walkers

  Guidelines: Carefully consider placement of outdoor furniture. For example, use corner tables instead of coffee tables to avoid blocking benches and chairs.

3.13 Wood benches in the plaza of the Center for the Intrepid, a Department of Veterans Affairs rehabilitation center, are configured to provide space for wheelchair access. Credit: JJR, LLC

3.14 This courtyard at the Novartis headquarters in Basel, Switzerland, is a corporate space with a birch grove, sculptural furniture forms, and a play of reflection and shadow that gives it visual lightness and a distinctly noncorporate feel. Credit: PWP Landscape Architecture

- Elderly and infirm require protection from the sun

  Guidelines: Provide umbrellas or other shade structures for protection in sunny seating areas used for extended periods of time.

Office Courtyards

Outdoor areas adjacent to office buildings are used by employees for breaks and lunches and sometimes for working. Courtyards are often provided at suburban corporate facilities where employees would otherwise have to drive off-site to find restaurants and related services.

Special issues:

- Difficult for suburban employees to go off-site during short lunch or break periods

  Guidelines: Provide benches and tables with attached seating or movable chairs. It is not necessary to provide outdoor seating for every employee, as break times are often staggered and not everyone will use the space.

- Courtyards often adjacent to indoor cafeteria or break areas

  Guidelines: Specify outdoor furniture that complements interior furniture and is perhaps interchangeable with it.

- Smoking areas populated by "regulars"

  Guidelines: Provide ash urns (and perhaps seating) at a distance from entrances and eating areas for this social subset.

3.15 A remote parking area at Los Angeles International Airport provides light, airy shelters with benches and off-the-grid solar lighting for the comfort and safety of travelers waiting for shuttles to the terminal. Photo credit: copyright © Jim Powell

- Courtyards considered as an employment benefit, sending a positive message to employees even when they are not using it

  Guidelines: Make it beautiful; choose furnishings that complement the architecture and express corporate identity.

Transportation Hubs

Transportation hubs, such as bus and train stations and airports, often feature exterior waiting areas used by people waiting for cars, taxis, and shuttles, as well as by smokers. At train and bus stations, exterior waiting areas may be provided near departure gates as well.

Special issues:

- Passengers' need to monitor arrivals and departures

  Guidelines: Orient seating to provide clear visual access to traffic and activities.

- Heavy public use, sometimes for extended periods

  Guidelines: Provide sociofugal (outward-facing, nonsocial) seating to maximize seating density. A high percentage of visitors will use the seating, some for extended periods, so focus on seating quantity and comfort.

- Travelers who are tired, stressed, anxious, hungry, bored, confused, and/ or distracted

  Guidelines: Provide plentiful seating and litter receptacles; provide information kiosks and other services nearby.

- Damage to finishes from baggage

  Guidelines: Specify furniture materials and finishes that will stand up to impacts and scrapes.

- Weather

  Guidelines: Provide protection from the sun, rain, snow, and other elements.

- Homeland security requirements

  Guidelines: Affected sites, including some rail stations, may need blastproof or clear receptacles (or none at all).

Transit Stops

Bus stops and light rail and commuter train stops have their own furnishing requirements.

Special issues:

- Number of riders

  Guidelines: Provide shelters of appropriate size for the location, and benches, litter receptacles, and amenities in quantities sufficient to serve the ridership, which may vary from stop to stop.

- Weather

  Guidelines: Provide protection from the sun, rain, snow, and other elements.

3.16 A transit stop in New York City provides protection from the elements, good visibility, a bench, and advertising space to help pay for it all. Photo credit: Bill Main

- May attract loiterers

  Guidelines: In areas where this is an issue, consider using leaning rails and narrow benches to discourage use by nonriders.

- Visibility, both for drivers to see people waiting at stops and for travelers to see the vehicle coming.

  Guidelines: Place shelters and benches near the curb; avoid placing other elements (e.g., newspaper boxes or signage) between the waiting area and the point of boarding.

- Advertising may be a major funding source because of the captive audience

  Guidelines: Provide structures and protocols for signs and digital displays.

Cafés and Restaurants

Outdoor seating at cafés, coffee shops, and restaurants adds vitality and choice to urban streetscapes.

Special issues:

- Often located in space borrowed from the sidewalk

  Guidelines: Use narrow planters or railings to demarcate the café space from the sidewalk.

- Tables and chairs usually privately owned, and taken in or locked up at night

3.17 Café seating at Mariano Park in Chicago. Movable chairs offer maximum flexibility. Photo credit: Bill Main

3.18 Students are flexible when it comes to seating. Seat walls create well-used resting and gathering places on the University of California, Berkeley, campus. Photo credit: Bill Main

Guidelines: Consider lighter-scale furnishings (made possible by ownership attention and oversight); specify small tables and chairs to increase density in these typically limited spaces.

- May be seasonal

Guidelines: Provide stacking chairs and folding tables to facilitate overnight and seasonal storage; consider umbrellas and propane heaters, operated by staff, to protect customers from the elements and extend the time outdoor spaces can be used.

College Campuses

Large campuses typically have a variety of types of outdoor spaces, including many described in this chapter.

Special issues:

- Campuses are key factors in school identity. An attractive campus can be a major recruiting tool.

Guidelines: Establish standards for campus furnishings to reinforce identity and ensure consistency.

- Colleges have a large, captive population of mostly young people, who are works in progress.

Guidelines: Anchor or embed furnishings on campus to reduce migration, vandalism, and theft.

3.19 This waiting area near the entry to Eaglecrest High School in Denver, Colorado, provides benches and receptacles for students awaiting rides. Photo credit: Vivian Kovacs

- Automobile use severely limited on most campuses; walking and bicycle riding more common

  Guidelines: Provide a large quantity of bike racks; consider the simple inverted U embedded in concrete to save space and cost.

- Ergonomic comfort and support needs different for young people

  Guidelines: Provide basic, flexible, sturdy furnishings. Be prepared for unconventional use, such as sitting on the backs of benches and the edges of tables.

- Studying and using laptops outdoors

  Guidelines: Consider tables with attached seating to support these activities.

Schools (K-12)

Elementary, middle, and high schools usually have entries and playgrounds; they may also have outdoor (patio) eating areas near the cafeteria, a large front entry courtyard, and outdoor classroom space.

Special issues:

- Close supervision required for children in lower grades

  Guidelines: Provide benches near play structures so parents and teachers can keep an eye on young children.

- Students waiting for parents or guardians to pick them up after school

  Guidelines: Provide a bench or two at identified pickup points near entries ("I'll pick you up at the red bench"); bollards may be useful to separate vechicle and pedestrian traffic.

3.20 First impressions matter. Low seating walls at the entry to Caltrans's District 11 Regional Headquarters on the edge of historic downtown San Diego reflect the architecture of the old town and the archway of the building. Credit: Wallace Roberts & Todd

• May have patios for outdoor eating

Guidelines: Provide sturdy tables with attached seating.

Building Entries

Outdoor areas near significant entries to large buildings have the potential to make a positive first impression.

Special issues:

• Initial impressions are imporant

Guidelines: Where space permits, provide a bench or two as a welcoming gesture and a convenient place to wait for a ride.

• Litter receptacles required

Guidelines: Select attractive litter receptacles that don't detract from the architecture or spoil the sense of entry.

• Smokers

Guidelines: Locate smoking receptacles to balance visitors' need to dispose of cigarettes prior to entering the building with the desirability of keeping smokers at a distance from paths of entry.

Roof Gardens

Gardens and courtyards may be developed on urban rooftops.

3.21 A roof garden designed by Hoerr Schaudt located on Michigan Avenue in Chicago,. Photo credit: copyright © Scott Shigley

Special issues:

- Roof membrane must be protected.

  Guidelines: Coordinate roof contact points and anchoring methods with roofing requirements.

- Weight important

  Guidelines: Coordinate weights, especially of planters, with structural engineers.

- Unusually strong winds and updrafts at roof level

  Guidelines: Avoid freestanding tables, umbrellas, and lightweight chairs if there is any chance that they can be blown off the roof.

Coda

These categories are not exhaustive. They may not even be sufficient. Landscape architect Walter Hood cautions against allowing terminology to stifle ingenuity. He explains:

> Perhaps old terms have lost meaning. Reinventing outdoor spaces may require using a new nomenclature. If I call it a "bio-field," or a "rain garden," or a "paseo," I will design it differently. But if I keep calling it a park the expectation is that it will smell like a park, taste like a park, and work like a park. In the urban environment we have only a few typologies at work. And they are not diverse enough to do all the kinds of things we need them to do.

4. Seating

Outdoor seating comes in many forms. Benches, chairs, stools, built-in seats, seat walls, leaning rails, modular beam systems, and amphitheater seats are the most common, and these are the types we will discuss here. In addition, other objects or elements are often used as seats, whether or not intended by the designer for such purpose. It's common to see people in public spaces perched on boulders, logs, railings, steps, walls, planters, fire hydrants, and almost any other handy surface that allows them to get off their feet. We will not discuss these seating options in detail, but we encourage designers to remain open to the rich possibilities they offer, especially for secondary or overflow seating.

The seating types we will discuss in this chapter vary widely in structure, design, materials, dimensions, and applications. Before we examine their individual characteristics, let's consider the overriding factors that apply to all.

Seating Really Matters

Seating is the most important furniture in most outdoor spaces. It's also the most personal.

Sitting is a close encounter of a special kind. It's an immediate, tactile experience. When you sit, you place yourself directly in or on the seat. If the seat is wet or hot or cold, you feel it. Ditto if it is comfortable or uncomfortable, slippery or scratchy, in the sun or in the shade, clean or dirty, stable or broken. Seating materials, location, design, and maintenance all have very direct personal impacts on the user.

Seating is controlling or empowering. It either directs you and orients you or allows you to direct and orient yourself to face what you will and present yourself to your group and to passersby as you choose. Seating can either help you or hinder you in your chosen activity—for example, eating, resting, waiting, or watching—depending on how it is configured, located, and ergonomically designed.

Providing seating is an act of hospitality, and the quality and condition of the seating is a clear indication of the level of hospitality on offer. The seating in an outdoor space often is a good indication of the concerns and priorities of the people responsible for the space. Thoughtful, well-cared-for seating indicates a desire to enrich the space and provide for its users. Uninviting or

4.1 Seating in outdoor spaces is social and personal. The chairs in the Luxembourg Gardens are symbols of welcome and hospitality that contribute to the success of this world-renowned space. Photo credit: Jardins du Luxembourg, Paris, Mia Serra, 1995

visibly deteriorating seating is an indication that no one much cares about the space or the people who use it.

More than any other kind of furniture, and perhaps more than many aspects of the space design, seating sends a message about what is considered important and appropriate in a space. It's not always a matter of money, although in some cases it may be. There are usually more and less expensive options for accomplishing the same mission. Successful seating solutions are an expression of welcome and hospitality that can almost always be achieved on a budget as well as with high-concept design and execution.

Choice Is Critical

Users of outdoor seating may be of different ages, sexes, sizes, shapes, physical abilities, and preferences. They may be alone, in pairs, or in groups. They may be there to eat, watch, rest, socialize, read, and/or engage in any number of other activities. While they will probably be willing to use and make the best of whatever seating is offered, it is highly unlikely that they all actually want or need the same thing. Providing choices allows people to self-select the seating that suits their current needs and preferences. Older people may select seats with backs and arms. Kids may prefer the steps or a cluster of boulders. Lunchers will seek enough space to spread out their fare and eat without getting food on their clothing. Groups will look for seating in which members can face each other without twisting their bodies or necks. Movable seating allows users to configure their own seating, but carries with it the additional burdens of managing and tracking. If movable chairs are not practical for the site, consider using both benches and circular tables with fixed or attached seats. These offer convenient places to eat and the social value of sitting around a table.

Hudson River Park provides a variety of bench types, depending on location.

4.2a "On the piers, where there is an almost 270-degree vista, we use backless benches because we don't want to spoil the views," explains James G. Koth, vice president of operations, Hudson River Park Trust. Photo credit: Bill Main

4.2b "Along the linear north-south walk where there are benches under trees, I insist on benches with backs," says Marc Boddewyn, vice president of design and construction, Hudson River Park Trust. "If you don't have a back, you lessen the duration of the visit. People are just not going to be comfortable." Photo credit: Bill Main

The Users' Needs Come First: Location and Configuration

Where seating is located and how it is configured are key to addressing the needs of users in outdoor spaces. Seating positions people in the space, determining what they see and by whom they are seen. Seating locations and configurations influence the degree and ease of social interaction. Seating, especially benches, sometimes seems to be located without regard to where people really want to sit. In parks, for instance, the benches facing play structures and fountains tend to be in high demand, whereas benches out in the open often have few users, mostly those looking for rest and solitude.

Comfort

Attitudes about the need for comfort in public outdoor seating are changing. Not so long ago it was commonly believed that people in outdoor spaces shouldn't get "too comfortable" or should be made comfortable for only brief intervals before they went on their way. Today, that attitude is giving way to the belief that better seating attracts more people and gets them to stay longer in public spaces—and that this is a thing to be encouraged.

Seating comfort is a function of seat design and individual body characteristics. While indoor furniture has the luxury of using soft padding to cradle almost any body shape, outdoor site furniture is typically, of necessity, made of hard materials with little or no padding or adjustments. As every body is different, any given seat may evoke different levels of comfort in different users, depending on their height, weight, shape, and sensitivities. Nonetheless, it is quite possible to find site furniture seating that most people regard as reasonably comfortable. Starting from the front of the bench, here are the most critical comfort factors.

Dimensions, Angles, and Slopes

The typical seat with a back is about 17–18 inches above the ground near the front and slopes down toward the back 3 to 10 degrees. This slope and a corresponding backward tilt of the backrest help position the user comfortably in the seat and counteract the tendency for the butt to slip forward as the user leans back. The low spot of the seat bottom is sometimes called the bucket. A deep bucket (more than 3 or 4 inches) starts to feel "lounge-y" as the knees get positioned higher than the hips. (A deep bucket in the seat bottom can make the seat more comfortable but can also make it harder to get up; see Figure 4.3. For elderly or infirm users a flat seat bottom will be easier to get up from than a seat with a bucket.) If the

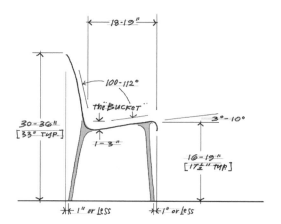

4.3 Typical seat profile. Credit: Robert G. Chipman, ASLA

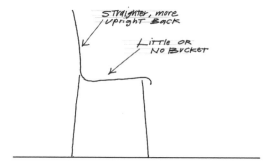

4.4 Dining seat profile. Credit: Robert G. Chipman, ASLA

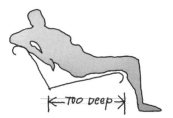

4.5 Too deep for comfort. Credit:
Robert G. Chipman, ASLA

high point of the lip of the seat is situated more than about 18 inches off
the ground, the feet of many adults won't easily touch the ground, a position
that can be uncomfortable and awkward. Rounding or easing the front
edge of the seat (i.e., creating a chamfered edge) so that it doesn't create
a pressure point on the back of the knees enhances comfort, especially for
shorter people whose legs may hang or press against the edge of the seat
to reach the ground. The seat can be from 15 to 20 inches deep (front lip
to the back), with 18 inches being typical. An angle of 100 to 110 degrees
between seat bottom and back is typical.

A backed seat is more comfortable than a backless seat, especially for older
people, for long periods of sitting, or for resting after a long day or a lot of
walking. By providing back support, a backed bench allows users to relax
more of their muscles than is possible with a backless bench. (The same
might be said of a chair with a back versus a stool.) Young users with lots
of kinetic energy and little interest in sitting still may not fully appreciate
a backed bench. But for elders the resting experience may be incomplete
unless they have a back to lean against and can more fully "take a load off."

The back of the seat should reach at least 30 inches above the ground, and
can be higher. Because people's backs usually have less padding than their
behinds, they can be quite sensitive to a seat back that hits them in the
wrong place. While this is an individual thing, a common comfort problem
is caused when the seat is too deep and/or the back is too low, making it
difficult to sit naturally with the spine resting against the seat back. Instead,
the back of the sitter angles toward the back of the seat, making contact
only with the top of the seat back instead of the full supporting back plane.

Exceptions to the Rule

Variations from the typical public seat profile described above are possible
and in some cases desirable. Chairs used for eating at a table should have a
smaller bucket and a closer-to-vertical back in order to position the body
higher and nearer to the food, making it easier to eat and less likely that
food will end up in the lap. Chairs designed for relaxing may have a deeper
bucket and a back angle that is further from vertical, as, for example, in

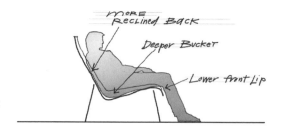

4.6 Lounge seat profile. Credit: Robert
G. Chipman, ASLA

4.7 This Adirondack chair is
constructed of recycled plastic. Photo
credit: Bill Main

the Adirondack chair. (See Figure 4.7.) Reclined seats should be a little
lower to the ground, to allow the feet to reach the ground while extended.
Wide armrests add comfort and assist sitters in getting up from the seated
position.

Drainage and Ventilation

Most outdoor chairs and benches are designed with holes, gaps, or
perforations in the seat to let rain and snow escape and to prevent heat
buildup from the sun. (Gaps have the added advantage of making the seat
less attractive to graffiti artists.) The size and spacing of openings and
the geometry of edges will affect comfort. Some early wire grid seats had
spacing of approximately two inches between wires, leading to discomfort
and complaints of "waffle butt." Most makers later closed the spacing and
the complaints disappeared. For comfort, keep wire spacing to ½ inch
or less. In metal or wood slat seating, slats placed too far apart can cause
discomfort also. In general, whatever the material, gaps, or holes in a seat

4.8 For comfort, wire grid spacing on seating should be ½ inch or less. Photo credit: Allen Wheeler

begin to be noticeable at about ¾ inch and become progressively more uncomfortable as they get larger.

Padding

Padding on the seats and backs of benches or chairs can increase comfort but is seldom practical in outdoor public areas. Pads get wet, trap dirt, get lost, and have a life span much shorter than that of the seat. Once wet, padding can act like a sponge. It may not appear wet on top, but until it is completely dry it will wick the last vestiges of trapped rainwater onto the clothing of unsuspecting sitters—a sure recipe for a spoiled afternoon. So pads, like movable chairs, come with a management factor. They need to be brought in before a rain, stored until it's over, dried thoroughly when they get wet, and cleaned when they get dirty. It is our experience that the stewards of outdoor public spaces are seldom willing or able to commit resources to these tasks.

Cleanliness

Outdoor seating routinely accumulates dust, pollution, leaves, bird droppings, and spills from beverages or food. The horizontal parts of the seat collect more than the vertical parts. While most public seating is never or rarely cleaned except by the natural forces of rain and wind, the seats in high-quality spaces, especially eating areas, may be wiped off at the start of the day. Users, of course, may also be cleaning the seats without realizing it. It's always best to look before sitting, and most people do.

Fortunately, the need for cleaning is minimal in most cases. The combined effect of wind, rain, and the occasional brushing off of debris by users is usually enough. If more is needed, smooth surfaces such as powder-coated metal can be easily wiped with a damp cloth, hosed down, or pressure-washed. Rough surfaces such as textured concrete, masonry, or stone will hold dirt and resist wiping, so pressure washing is a better solution. If washing is done with water, it's important to allow ample drying time before resuming use.

Ironically, seats under canopies that keep the rain off are more likely to need manual cleaning. Solid surfaces and colors will show dirt and debris more readily than patterned or textured surfaces.

A pressure washer should never be used on painted wood, as it may peel the paint. While most furniture finishes are resistant to most cleaning chemicals, there is no real need for harsh chemicals and water will usually be sufficient to do the job. (See Chapter 11 for more information.)

Safety

Generally, site furniture is pretty safe, but there are a few things to watch for.

Visible Damage

Broken or missing slats, loose bolts, cracked castings, and bent supports are common problems resulting from wear and tear, vandalism, accidents, and defects. While the user's perception of seating safety has a lot to do with location, it may also be driven by the condition of the seating and the appearance of strength and stability in the seat structure. Signs of damage and deterioration will discourage users, will undermine their confidence in the space, and can result in injury, so they need to be promptly identified and fixed. Seating should be regularly inspected for signs of damage *or wear*. Depending on the level of use, annual inspection may be sufficient for benches. Chairs and tables, which are typically constructed of much lighter materials and are less durable, should be checked more often. The lighter the chair and the heavier the use, the more often inspection is necessary. Chairs should be discarded if they show signs of bending or breakage, unless replacement parts are available. Bent legs should not be straightened, as metal fatigue will leave the leg weaker than its original designed strength.

Tipping

Tipping is a critical seating safety issue. If seating is not anchored to the ground, it may tip if placed on an unstable or uneven surface or loaded in a way that its design does not support. If the surface on which the seating

4.9 Oops! Lightweight seat with cantilever: a dangerous combination. Credit: Robert G. Chipman, ASLA

rests is soft (such as grass or gravel) or uneven (such as stone), a sled base may help spread the load to achieve stability. The structure of the seating element will influence the tipping point. For example, in cantilevered seating, in which an upper part of the seat projects beyond the points at which the seat legs contact the ground, it is particularly important to pay attention to the front lip of the seat relative to the front ground contact points and the top of the back relative to the rear ground contact points. People may sit on the extreme front edge of the seat, causing it to be very unbalanced toward the front. Or they may sit on the back with their feet on the seat or lean with their weight against the back, either of which will cause imbalance toward the rear. A heavy seat may remain stable in these situations even if there is some cantilever present. But a light seat, especially on a slippery surface, will tip quickly beneath the user if there is any cantilever present. Most freestanding seating designs today avoid cantilevers because of these concerns.

4.10 Sled bases spread the load to provide stability on softer ground. Photo credit: Allen Wheeler

Heat

Heat buildup is a common concern in outdoor seating. Can a seat ever heat up to the point where it is too hot to be safely touched by bare skin? Five conditions will determine the answer:

1. The intensity of the sun
2. The ambient temperature
3. The color of the seat
4. The material of which the seat is made
5. The geometry of the seat

If one considers the combined effects of sun and temperature, it is safe to say that, in general, heat buildup will be an issue of concern only when the sun is very bright and is shining directly on the seat and the air temperature is warm to hot. A cool day with bright sun or a hot day on which the seat is in shade may lead to a warm seat but will not create a really hot seat.

4.11 Spaces between metal parts on bench seats allow air circulation, reducing heat buildup. Photo credit: Allen Wheeler

When the day is hot and the sun is shining brightly on the seat, it may become too hot if other conditions are also present. Dark colors absorb heat and light colors reflect heat. Placed side by side under the same conditions, a black seat will be hotter than a white seat, and there is a corresponding range for the colors in between. Seat material plays a major role. Metals conduct heat better than wood, plastic, or masonry, so metal will feel hotter at any given temperature because the heat is conducted faster to the skin. Heat conducted more slowly may allow the user time to gradually get used to the warmth, much like a bather slowly immersing in a hot bath.

The final variable, and a very important one, is geometry. If the seat is flat, uninterrupted metal, it can become very hot. (Touch the hood of a black car on a hot sunny day to see just how hot.) On the other hand, if the seat is a black wire grid, the chances are that it will barely feel any warmer than the air, especially if there is a breeze, as the wind will help pull heat out of the seat. Air spaces that break up the expanse of metal both reduce the area exposed to the sun and allow the absorbed heat to radiate off the seat. The higher the ratio of air space to metal, the less likely the seat is to overheat to the point of being uncomfortable or dangerous.

In general, only dark-colored seats that allow skin contact with metal parts that are more than 1½ inches or so wide will become hot enough in full sun on a hot day to be a problem. Most metal seats are perforated or made up of many individual pieces that are spaced apart to reduce or eliminate this risk. Nevertheless, in places that can expect high heat and a lot of sun, it may be wise to avoid dark metal seats unless their geometry offers a lot of air space to dissipate the heat.

4.12a A beautiful bronze bench . . .
Photo credit: Bill Main

4.12b . . . but read before you sit.
Photo credit: Bill Main

Moisture

Moisture on seating is another issue of concern to users. In most cases it
is the result of rain, snow, washing, or spills. Seats are pretty much out of
service until they dry, so seats that dry quickly have more uptime, especially

in rainy areas or in spaces in which seats are regularly cleaned with water. Drying is affected by some controllable factors and some uncontrollable ones. Sun, wind, and temperature are the major uncontrollables. If the rain is followed by cloudy and cool weather, the drying time will be significantly extended. The primary controllable factors are drainage, texture, and absorption. Fast drainage is facilitated by sloped surfaces and by surfaces that have plenty of gaps or perforations for the water to escape through. Smooth surfaces will drain faster than textured surfaces. Impermeable materials such as metal or plastic will dry faster than those that absorb moisture, such as wood. Placed side by side, a powder-coated wire grid seat will be back in service much faster than a flat wood bench. Seats that trap water or have their drain holes plugged by leaves or debris may be so slow to drain that the water evaporates rather than drains, with the result that the seat is left with mineral or dirt stains when it finally dries.

Suitability for Function

A seat's location and design should fit its purpose or function. (See Chapter 2.) The main seating functions that affect seat design are resting, watching, socializing, and eating.

For resting, a comfortable seat with a back as described earlier will work for most people. A seat with a deeper bucket and greater back tilt will provide comfort for more serious, longer-term relaxation.

For watching, a backless seat offers the advantage of allowing the sitter to face any direction, depending on where the action is at a given time.

4.13 A high-backed bench at Chicago's Millennium Park provides comfort for extended stays. Photo credit: Gustafson Guthrie Nichol Ltd.

4.14 Where there's a lot to look at, backless benches provide welcome flexibility and views in all directions. Photo credit: Bill Main

For socializing, movable seats, fixed seats around a table, and fixed configurations of seats facing each other or set at angles to each other within the social space of 4 to 12 feet are good options. Large flat benches or built-in steps or seat walls constructed at angles that allow people to face each other can also be effective.

For eating, things get a little more complicated. Most people, when eating, position themselves so that the mouth is just slightly over the edge of the table. Seats that are quite upright (i.e., have little or no bucket and an upright back) help position people up and forward—a good position for transporting food from plate to mouth but one that may feel a little formal or forced for casual conversation. Seats with a bucket and a tilted back require most people to lean forward, away from the back, in order to eat. (It is uncomfortable for most people to eat while leaning back, and this position increases the food-on-clothing risk.) However, this type of chair allows people to lean back after eating and assume a more relaxed, conversational posture.

The distance from the table is also important for eating. Movable chairs allow people to position themselves at a distance from the table that feels comfortable for them.

In the case of a table with fixed seats, the distance between the table and the seat must be a careful compromise between what is optimal for eating and what is optimal for ingress and egress. A fixed seat with a back should

4.15 Movable chairs make it easy to socialize. Photo credit: Bill Main

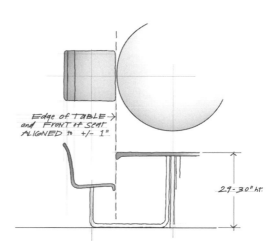

Edge of TABLE →
and FRONT of SEAT
ALIGNED to +/- 1"

29-30" ht.

4.16 Plan and profile of a table with attached seats. Credit: Robert G. Chipman, ASLA

be positioned so that the back is about 17 to 20 inches from the table edge. Fixed backless seats and picnic tables generally place the center of the seat about 12 inches from the table edge. Looking straight down from above, the bigger the gap between the front edge of the seat and the edge of the table top, the easier it will be to get in and out. A single seat will be easier to get in and out of than a long bench seat. Generally, a single fixed seat can extend up to the table edge, but a long bench seat should have a gap of several inches.

Types of Seating

The many different types of outdoor seating have characteristics and qualities that may make them more or less suitable for a particular application or for a particular user. Offering a variety of seating choices may be the best way to satisfy a diverse user population and multiple programming requirements. That said, regardless of the specific style or design, within types there are certain criteria that make a seating choice successful for the user and for the owner.

Benches

Benches are backed or backless. The typical North American bench is about 6 feet long. European and Asian benches are often a little smaller in scale and a little lower.

Backed Benches

Backed benches are more comfortable for longer periods of time. They provide more support, which may be crucial in some applications such as health care, or merely more pleasant in others. The demographics of an aging population suggest that the number of people who appreciate a comfortable seat is growing. Backed benches face in one direction, requiring careful consideration of how they are oriented and what views they offer. A 6-foot bench may accommodate several people, depending on how well they know each other and how large they are, but use by just one or two people is most common. Two individuals who do not know each other will seldom sit on the same 6-foot bench out of concern for violating personal

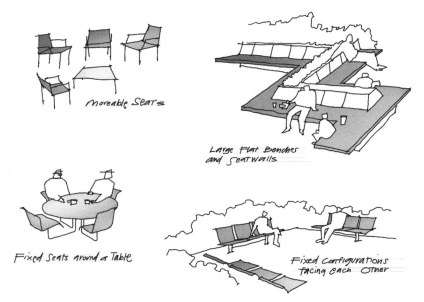

4.17 Some typical types of seating.
Credit: Robert G. Chipman, ASLA

4.18 Short steel benches are sometimes used as chairs in settings where furniture is meant to be movable . . . but not *too* movable. Photo credit: Bill Main

4.19 A bench placed perpendicular to the street provides a different view. Photo credit: Bill Main

space, except in heavily used areas where there is competition for good seats and in waiting areas at bus stops, airports, and so on.

Backed benches may be longer or shorter than the standard 6-foot length. When shortened to about 2 feet the bench becomes a very heavy and substantial chair for one. Sometimes these are used as movable chairs in settings where the design intent is that they not be *too* movable.

4.20 Long custom wood benches at Columbus Circle, New York City, complement the site design and allow people to find their comfort zones. Credit: OLIN

A 4- or 5-foot bench is a comfortable length for two people, although it doesn't leave much space for packages or a child. Four-foot benches in streetscapes are sometimes placed perpendicular to the street and at the end of a planted area, allowing users to look along the street rather than head-on at the street or surrounding buildings.

Eight-foot benches are a good choice when families and groups are expected—for example, at theme parks or outside family restaurants. Two strangers will sometimes sit at opposite ends of an 8-footer, just outside each other's personal space. Benches longer than 8 feet are usually custom-made or built in because they are difficult to ship. Really long or continuous benches are often chosen for aesthetic reasons, but they also make efficient use of space by allowing users to space themselves out appropriately for their comfort zones.

A well-designed and well-constructed bench will last for many years with minimal care. It is not uncommon for a bench to last ten to twenty years. While a bench may look worn after long use, it is usually replaced only when the space is being redeveloped or upgraded, rather than for structural failure, which is rare.

Armrests

Armrests on benches provide additional comfort and also aid people in getting up, especially if they are unsteady or in poor health. Depending on the bench, armrests may be integral to the design or an add-on option.

4.21 The message is mixed. Multiple armrests define individual space, but the sign warns visitors not to think of the space as home. Photo credit: Bill Main

Center armrests are frequently specified for seating in public spaces as a way of discouraging people from sleeping on the benches. This is usually effective but can compromise the spirit of the design. Armrests may also be used to discourage skateboarders from grinding on the front edges of benches. Armrests are sometimes used on backless benches for these purposes as well. Wider armrests without sharp edges will be more comfortable, although people seem to tolerate a wide variety of armrests, some of which are more aesthetic than functional. Armrests can be used to define personal territory along a bench (as is typical in airport seating). This approach can increase seating density, as people typically will sit closer together if their personal space is delimited by an armrest.

Tablets and Cup Holders

A few benches provide a tablet for food or drinks, a laptop, or a book. While a tablet can be an interesting and functional addition to a bench, the nature of public spaces requires that it be very strong and structural. Designers and owners should consider that someone, someday, is likely to sit on it, stand on it, or even jump from it.

Cup holders are another interesting option for benches. However, it is prudent to consider the strong possibility that in public spaces cups will be left behind in the holders, creating an unkempt look until someone comes along to clean up the mess.

4.22 A tablet arm provides a handy place for a laptop or lunch. Credit: Thomas Balsley Associates, photo by Michael Koontz

4.23 Back-to-back benches at Boston Harbor enable views in both directions: the harbor on one side and the promenade of people on the other. Photo credit: Bill Main

Back-to-Back Benches

Back-to-back benches provide the choice of facing in opposite directions. This may be appealing if the goal of the space is to provide a lot of seating capacity or if there is something interesting to look at in both directions. Back-to-back benches have a very large footprint, usually more than

4 feet across, which may make them too big for small or narrow spaces. And most people prefer more privacy than back-to-back seats provide. They are similar to airport seating, in that one's head is very close to that of the person seated behind, so unless the space is densely populated, people tend to space themselves out, even when seated on opposites sides. An alternative to the back-to-back bench is the simple placement of two benches in the back-to-back position. This configuration has the same advantages and disadvantages as a true back-to-back bench but offers considerably more design choice since there are relatively few true back-to-back benches available as standard products.

Reversible Benches or Two-Sided Benches

The reversible bench has a straight back that pivots at a hinge point near the ground, allowing the user to adjust it to face in either direction. The two-sided bench has a single back that is shared by seats on either side. Both types often sacrifice some comfort due to the geometric constraints of the concept.

Backless Benches

Backless benches are less expensive than benches with backs and are usually omnidirectional, which can be an advantage if there are things to see in all directions, as on a busy plaza. They are not as comfortable as their backed counterparts but may be fine for short perches. Backless benches may not be

4.24 This two-sided bench in a park is space-efficient, but seating comfort isn't a top priority. Credit: copyright 2006 Project for Public Spaces

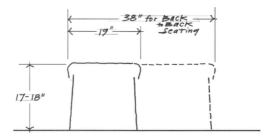

4.25 Typical backless seat profile
Credit: Robert G. Chipman, ASLA

suitable for the elderly, especially for extended stays, due to the lack of back support. Some backless benches have armrests, though they are usually there to prevent skateboarding or sleeping rather than for comfort.

The standard length for a backless bench is approximately 6 feet, although 5 feet works fine for two people and 8-footers are common. Widths range from a narrow ribbon, which may be used to save space or discourage sleeping, to a broad surface for back-to-back seating. The standard width is between 19 and 22 inches. A width of 30 inches is the minimum needed for sitting back-to-back on a flat bench, but 36 to 48 inches is better for this purpose. Strangers may sit fairly close together on the same backless bench, being careful to face in different directions to protect their personal space.

Modular Benches

Modular benches employ a seating module, typically about 2 feet wide, mounted to a beam to create a bench of indefinite length. In addition to dimensional flexibility, modularity has the effect of creating individual seats that offer people the sense of their own defined space. Seats may be backed, backless, or a mixture of the two. Modular benches typically have a metal structure with metal or wood seats. Table modules or backless seating modules may be placed between backed modules to create convenient, flat spaces on which food, beverages, or packages can be rested without tipping. More complex seating systems that enable angular configurations have been developed but to date have not been widely used.

Some modular bench systems employ a curved support beam to create a curvilinear structure. The combination of curves and indefinite length can create a strong, continuous visual effect, but in fact these systems usually consist of several independent support structures that are 6 to 10 feet long and placed end to end so that the seating modules are evenly spaced. Modular systems can be used to create a more customized, built-in look. However, quite often modular systems are used to create fairly conventional 6- or 8-foot benches using three or four modules. The goal in this case is usually to offer users the benefit of individual seat modules rather than indefinite length.

4.26 Modular seating example. Credit: Robert G. Chipman, ASLA

4.27 A long curved concrete seat wall with wood top on a Hudson River Park pier divides the paved pathway from the grassy area, encourages flexible use, and allows views in all directions. Photo credit: Bill Main

Seat Walls

Seat walls are low built-in walls that provide a top surface intended for seating. They are usually backless. Sometimes they also function as retaining walls, rims around planters, or edges around pools or fountains. (Whether their role as structural/design elements or seating came first is a chicken-or-egg question.) They are commonly used to integrate the site and architectural aesthetics.

Seat walls are usually constructed of the same materials used in the site's hardscape or buildings. Concrete, stone, and masonry are the most common seat wall materials. These may be slow to dry after rain, a condition especially prevalent with granite, which is often installed with no slope for architectural effect. Seat walls of stone often have crisp edges, which are hard on the back of the leg. Widths are similar to those for backless benches. Heights vary, especially if the site is sloped. The ideal height is about 17 inches. W. H. Whyte's research showed that "people will sit almost anywhere between a height of one foot and three" and will sit on places higher or lower under special conditions (for example, between 7 and 44 inches on the front ledge of the Seagram Building in New York).[1]

Seat walls are often used in addition to traditional seating as a mean of providing overflow or secondary seating in times of heavy use. Observations suggest that seat walls are more common and more heavily used in urban areas. This may be due to population density, building density, the lack of other seating, or some combination of the three. In less dense places there are fewer seat walls and people are more accustomed to finding a traditional seat.

Movable Chairs

Twenty or even ten years ago, movable chairs were uncommon in public outdoor spaces in North America. Thanks in part to the dramatic rise in coffee shops and their arrangement of tables and chairs outside on patios and sidewalks, the North American streetscape, in big cities and small, is starting to look a bit more European. Most café chairs and tables are privately owned and maintained by the café or restaurant that uses them. Proprietors keep a close eye on them and usually take them in or secure them in some way at night. Cafés add great variety and vitality to the streetscape because they provide lively, sophisticated settings as well as the food and beverage services that go with them. (Brew it and they will come.)

The publicity around the success of Bryant Park in New York City, which is often attributed to the use of movable chairs, has contributed to the growing interest in the use of chairs as general seating in outdoor public spaces. But some other spaces have been using this approach with great success for a number of years. (See the case study on the University of Wisconsin Memorial Union Plaza at the end of this chapter.)

Movable outdoor chairs come in a wide variety of shapes, sizes, materials, and designs. Seat height and back height are similar to benches, about 17 inches and 30+ inches, respectively. Seat widths vary considerably, from a very petite 15 or 16 inches to a very generous 21 or 22 inches. The typical width is about 19 inches.

Unlike most benches, weight can be an important issue in movable chairs. Chairs will be moved at least a token amount by virtually every user. There are a lot of trade-offs in chair design. Lighter-weight chairs are easier to move but are usually less robust and durable. Less weight also means less wear on chair glides and floors when chairs are dragged. Heavier chairs may be harder to move but are more durable and stabile. Anything under 10 pounds is considered very light and anything over 25 pounds heavy. The typical chair weighs in somewhere in between, at about 15 to 18 pounds. Armrests add a couple of pounds. Reducing the amount of material in a chair reduces weight and usually cost. In most cases it also reduces durability. Aluminum chairs are lighter than steel, and usually more expensive.

Armrests significantly affect the feel and function of a chair. The arm provides a handy handle for moving the chair. When used in conjunction with a table, the armrest will restrict the ease of sitting, requiring the seat to be pulled back completely from the table so that the sitter can enter the chair from the front. In very dense seating areas the extra space required for this maneuver may not be readily available, leading to awkwardness and collision of chairs. Armrests can also present problems for large people, who represent an increasingly significant portion of our population. Spacing of 19 inches between armrests is typical, but even that is a squeeze for big people.

The life expectancy of most chairs is shorter than that of benches, and may be as short as three to five years for a lightweight chair under heavy use. Even a tough chair that lasts ten years or more may benefit from refinishing after three to five years if it has been moved and banged around a lot.

At the point of contact with the ground surface better-quality chairs will usually have a "sacrificial" glide. Typically made of nylon or plastic, it will wear away as the chair is dragged along the ground. Glides are extremely vulnerable to wear and breakage, especially on the rough-textured paving often found outside. If the glide goes, the chair leg begins to grind on the ground. Depending on the material, this can lead to rusting, splintering, or the wearing down of the leg. Glides should be checked regularly and replaced as necessary before the leg starts to scrape the ground.

Sled bases, in which the material forming the legs is bent to form two continuous surfaces that rest on the ground, are useful for soft surfaces such as grass or gravel, where regular legs can poke in and cause the chair to tip.

Chairs may be stacking or nonstacking. Stacking chairs save a good deal of storage space, reduce shipping volume, and are simpler to secure and store when not in use. Designing chairs to stack does limit the design possibilities

4.28 Movable chairs are stacked and locked to tables for after-hours security in this San Francisco courtyard. Photo credit: Bill Main

somewhat, because the chairs must nest with each other. Stacking chairs usually have a recommended maximum number that can be stacked together; about six is typical. They usually have cushioning bumpers at strategic points to keep them from scratching or chipping each other when stacked, but the finish can still be damaged if they are stacked carelessly. There are special dollies available for some chairs that simplify moving a stack of chairs.

Folding chairs have the same storage and shipping advantages as stacking chairs and are typically racked side by side in the folded position. Folding chairs, such as the Bryant Park bistro chairs (see the Bryant Park case study in Chapter 9), are usually quite lightweight and light duty, and often relatively inexpensive. They are a good choice when storage space is very limited and there is enough management attention to ensure the quick removal of damaged chairs. They may also work well as additional chairs for peak periods.

Pedestals and Stools

Pedestals and stools are occasionally found in public outdoor spaces, most commonly in those that serve dense populations and/or in which space is at a real premium. They are sometimes built in, and they may be of the same material as the site hardscape. For example, a granite cube or cylinder about 17 inches high and 12 to 18 inches in diameter could serve as a seating pedestal. Pedestals may be useful for supplemental or overflow seating or near other seating to create social seating configurations. (See the Capitol Plaza case study in Chapter 2.) Care should be exercised in their placement, as they can be a tripping hazard if they are not clearly visible.

4.29 Granite stools and an ash urn create an elegant smoking area in a Tokyo garden. Photo credit: Bill Main

Leaning Rails

Leaning rails may be useful when space is limited, when short-duration "perching" is appropriate, and/or when loitering or reclining are to be discouraged. They are most often used at transit stops. A leaning rail can be freestanding or attached to a wall. Leaning rails are usually mounted about 6 to 8 inches away from the nearest wall and about 28 to 30 inches above the ground. They typically consist of a tube or bar, 2 to 4 inches across, in a form comfortable to the user's rear. They should not be flat on top, but should be shaped to shed water and debris.

Other Seating Forms

Though still unusual, interesting new seating possibilities are beginning to appear in some outdoor spaces. Chaise lounges are common around pools but have recently been appearing in a few adventurous public spaces. These chaises are usually modified versions that limit the amount of recline while allowing people to lean back and stretch out their legs. Chaise lounges in public spaces send a message that people are welcome and encouraged to get comfortable, relax, and have fun.

When a Chair Is Not a Chair

Landscape architect Ken Smith observes, "The great urban socialist William Whyte wrote often about the importance of providing places for urban sitting, but he rarely spoke of chairs. Sitting is an important urban activity and, as Whyte pointed out, some of the best urban sitting occurs on non-furniture—places like steps, ledges, parapet-like perches or other non-furniture objects. I have always taken to heart Whyte's startling conclusion

4.30 Chaise lounges in public spaces allow people to get *really* comfortable. Photo credit: Bill Main

4.31 Thanks, but I'd rather sit on the log. Photo credit: Bill Main

that "people tend to sit where there are places to sit" when thinking about urban space furnishings. For example, for a schoolyard in Queens, New York I installed recycled urban logs for seating in a circle so students would have a communal place to read outdoors." (See image in color photo "Playing"section.)

Organic forms and elements designed or arranged with the human body in mind can create wonderful opportunities for people to "sit" in new ways that are more liberating than the traditional bench or chair. These may be accents or novelties that supplement more traditional seating at a site.

Bariatric seating, specially designed to meet the needs of obese people, is now common in health care settings, where up to 25 percent of seating maybe be mandated to meet bariatric structural and dimensional standards. Bariatric seating is less common in outdoor spaces, but where it is called for, the general rule is that a 48-inch bench will seat one person and an individual chair should have a minimum seat width of 32 inches.

Amphitheater Seating

Amphitheater seating is used at outdoor venues for presentations, concerts, and other public events. The typical configuration is rows of seats arcing around and sloping down toward the stage. The priorities for amphitheaters are usually orderly ingress and egress of people, accommodation of a dense concentration of users, and good views of the show. Comfort may lose out to capacity. Depending on the situation, amphitheater seating may consist of anything from an arrangement of

4.32 Custom wood bleacher-style seating at New York City's Teardrop Park provides a pleasant vantage point for supervising kids on the slide. Photo credit: Bill Main

4.33 If it's Tuesday, this must be Venice: an ad hoc classroom on the steps outside a Las Vegas casino. Photo credit: Bill Main

rustic logs to flat bleachers, folding stadium seats, or full-size benches. The specific seating forms may be subject to local codes, especially if the venue is covered and is classified as a theater or stadium.

Steps

Steps in desirable locations may be used as seating. When this is anticipated, the steps can be curved or cornered to enhance the sitting opportunity.

CASE STUDY: THE REMARKABLE CAREER OF A MOVABLE CHAIR

Memorial Union Terrace, University of Wisconsin, Madison

In 1928 the University of Wisconsin broke ground for the Memorial Union Terrace, an outdoor space adjacent to the Memorial Union building, which had just opened as a gathering place for students, faculty, and staff. In the late 1930s a movable metal chair with a sunburst-patterned back was selected to replace the assortment of chairs then in use at the flagstone-paved setting overlooking Lake Mendota. Seventy-five years and several design iterations later, it remains the primary seating for this immensely popular outdoor space and enjoys special status as a university icon. In fact, the chairs are so popular they are offered for sale.

The choice of movable seating for the Memorial Union Terrace was a natural. The space was designed to be informal and to encourage interaction. Food and beverages were an important part of the program. (When it permitted beer service on the terrace in 1933, the University of

4.34 An overview of the terrace.
Credit: Univ. of Wisconsin

CASE STUDY: THE REMARKABLE CAREER OF A MOVABLE CHAIR

(Continued)

4.35 Movable chairs and tables provide flexibility and encourage sociability. Credit: University of Wisconsin, photo by Connie Reeves

Wisconsin became the first public university in the country to authorize the serving of beer.) Individual chairs and tables allowed campus regulars and visitors to arrange seating to accommodate one person reading a book or taking in the view, two or three students sharing lunch, or groups of various sizes out for a good time. And movable seating, with its smaller scale, nimbly accommodated changing densities within the space.

Four or five variations of the chair were tried and tested over the first twenty years. The current sunburst design with its tubular steel frame survived, primarily because its continuous rounded base provided stability and adjusted comfortably to the terrace's uneven paving. During this period the chair acquired its signature green, orange, and yellow colors. (The green color was known as John Deere green.) Over the next several decades, two companies successively manufactured the chair. When the second followed the first into bankruptcy, taking the manufacturing tools with it, a nonprofit organization affiliated with the Union, recognizing the chair's significance to UW culture, provided the necessary funds to commission the fabrication of the tools and dies needed to ensure production in perpetuity.

In 1987 the terrace was reconfigured and expanded out toward the lake. Ted Crabb, who served as Union director for thirty-three years until his retirement in 2001, headed up the project. "If there's one thing that drove us when we redesigned and expanded the terrace, it was William H. Whyte's book, *The Social Life of Small Urban Spaces*," he recalls. "Everything—the placement of furniture, places for people to see and be seen, and options to be in sun or shade—was right there. The stairs for the theater provide a place

4.36 The iconic Memorial Union Terrace sunburst chair. Photo credit: Jeff Miller, UW-Madison University Communications

4.37 The terrace offers a choice of other seating options: picnic tables, seat walls, and folding chairs for overflow crowds. Photo credit: Bill Main

for people to stand and see who's here and where their friends are. And the flagstone ledges are the right height for sitting, so they increase our seating capacity." Green spaces were planted at breaks in elevation to soften the hardscape. A wide center aisle was created to ease people through the space. More movable chairs and tables were added to the terrace, and picnic tables were installed in the lower area near the lake to accommodate visitors who bring their own food. There's entertainment on most weekdays and always on weekends, as well as Wi-Fi access. "But if we didn't have Wi-Fi, people would still be here," Crabb insists. "I don't think there's that much difference today than twenty-five years ago in terms of what people do. They come here to enjoy themselves, to relax. Whyte was right. People want to be where the action is."

The sunburst chairs see plenty of action. There are between 550 and 600 of them on-site at any given time. About two-thirds are armless and one-third have arms. The choice is based on cost ($110 vs. $130 apiece). But armless chairs are also easier to move around and better accommodate a population that is growing heavier and wider in the beam. The goal is to add forty chairs per year. Crabb estimates that the terrace could fill 800 to 900 chairs on a busy night, but "it's a question of money." (Folding chairs are kept in the wings to handle overflow crowds.)

The Memorial Union Terrace also replaces 100–125 chairs that disappear annually. (To help the local constabulary identify and return chairs gone

CASE STUDY: THE REMARKABLE CAREER OF A MOVABLE CHAIR

(Continued)

4.38 Several generations of tables on the terrace. Evaluation and improvement go on. Photo credit: Bill Main

AWOL, those purchased within 100 miles of Madison are offered only in red or white, to distinguish them from Union Terrace property.) "We made the conscious decision that we didn't want to start chaining the chairs together," Crabb explains. "We want Union Terrace to be a place where people can move the chairs around and be comfortable. So we bit the bullet and said, if we lose some, we lose some. It's worth it for what we gain." He is quick to add, "We've got a revenue unit that supports this, and revenue is dependent on the chairs and the tables and the atmosphere, so there's a real justification for spending money to do what we do."

The powder-coated steel chairs are sent out periodically for recoating at a cost of $55 each. "The ideal is a four-to five-year recoat cycle so they're always looking fresh," explains Paul Broadhead, assistant director, Wisconsin Union Facilities. The chairs wear well, the tables not so well. At present there are three or four different table designs on the terrace, some with bent legs and crooked tops. "If we were doing this over, we'd definitely increase the metal strength in the legs because of the amount of breakage we've had," Broadhead says. "People stand on top of them. We never anticipated they would have that kind of pressure on them." In past years chairs and tables were stacked and stored on the terrace for the winter. Last year they were packed up and moved to a university warehouse.

The Memorial Union Terrace and its furnishings have benefited from ongoing assessment and continuous improvement. New ideas were actively sought and put to the test. Some didn't work and were dropped. Others worked quite well and were gradually perfected. The chairs are pretty close to perfect now.

The terrace is a genuine community resource. In September 2008 *AARP the Magazine* ran an article on America's "ten healthiest hometowns," naming Madison, Wisconsin, number five. The photo used to illustrate the fine qualities of the place features the Memorial Union Terrace filled with people of all sizes and ages, every one of them sitting in a sea of bright color on a starburst chair. For three-quarters of a century this simple movable metal chair has provided utility, vivacity, and identity; it has worked hard and kept the customers happy; it has welcomed, supported, and sometimes gone home with the people who sat on it. And it still steals the show.

For more information on the history of the Memorial Union Terrace, visit http://digital.library.wisc.edu/1793/30750.

Endnote

1. William H. Whyte, *The Social Life of Small Urban Spaces* (New York: Project for Public Spaces, 1980), 31.

5.   Receptacles

Litter Receptacles

You can buy a plastic or galvanized trash can at Wal-Mart for about twenty bucks. A litter receptacle, on the other hand, is the trash can's sophisticated city cousin. It is typically purchased from a specialized supplier of commercial products at a cost ranging from $300 to over $1,000. Three primary factors account for the difference:

- Litter receptacles must be extremely durable to survive years of hard knocks on the street.
- Litter receptacles often have moving parts in the form of liners, lids, doors, locks, and other special features that complicate their construction.
- Litter receptacles are an important and highly visible element of street furnishings. Their design, or lack of it, reflects on the overall quality of a public space and projects an image that positions the space in the mind of the visitor.

Litter receptacles have multiple personalities to satisfy multiple constituencies. For such lowly objects, they lead fairly complicated lives. There is no perfect litter receptacle for every situation. The selection of the appropriate litter receptacle requires an understanding of how it functions, who uses it, who maintains it, and its role in the public space.

The receptacle is a mini transfer station. Its purpose is to provide a convenient, attractive, and safe way of collecting and storing trash and/or recyclables near their source until the start of the process that moves them on to the landfill and/or the recycling center. People put stuff into the receptacle in small, frequent deposits, and it comes out in periodic bulk removals by other people or machines.

The selection of the appropriate litter receptacle to meet the needs of a given setting requires an understanding of what's involved in the three processes of putting litter in, storing it, and taking it back out, as well the implications for the various stakeholders who use or have an interest in the receptacle and the space. But first it's important to understand something about the nature of litter itself.

5.1 Right: Where it all started: a 55-gallon barrel. Photo credit: Bill Main

5.2 Far right: Top-opening receptacle. Credit: Gramercy Trash Receptacle, copyright © Thomas Steele

5.3 Right: A wire basket in New York City's Wall Street district has a clear plastic bag inside. Some high-security areas require clear liners to reveal what's inside. Photo credit: Bill Main

5.4 Far right: The design of this litter receptacle complements the architecture of the bus stop and the building in the background. Photo credit: Bill Main

Litter Defined

Litter is paper or trash that is scattered about. According to Keep America Beautiful, Inc., "Litter is the result of too little attention to how waste is handled. . . . The careless and casual handling of waste creates litter." The organization's website goes on to state, "Research and experience prove that litter—intentional or unintentional pollution

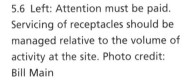

5.5 Far left: Pardon, your slip is showing. Photo credit: Bill Main

5.6 Left: Attention must be paid. Servicing of receptacles should be managed relative to the volume of activity at the site. Photo credit: Bill Main

5.7 Occasionally, critters are a problem. Photo credit: Bill Main

resulting from consumer waste products being carelessly handled or improperly disposed—attracts more litter."[1]

People who litter may be doing it out of laziness, the lack of a sense of civic ownership, a belief that they aren't really littering, or the conviction that it is some else's job to clean up. Litter may include waste that blew

5.8 An enclosure at a site in Port Douglas, Queensland, Australia, shields two very large-capacity wheeled bins. Photo credit: Bill Main

5.9 The Rolls-Royce of litter receptacles: a custom-made brushed stainless-steel receptacle at a Las Vegas site. Photo credit: Bill Main

out or fell out during handling or transport after it was dutifully placed in the receptacle. Some causes of litter and littering cannot be solved by receptacles alone. Nonetheless, a significant amount of litter and littering can be prevented by the proper design, location, and servicing of receptacles.

Putting Stuff In

Lunch is over, the cigarette is down to the filter, the straw is making that sucking sound at the bottom of the bottle. Now, where's the litter receptacle? Is there one in sight? If you are walking, is it on your route? If you are sitting, is it close enough to access quickly without giving up your seat or picking up all your belongings and taking them with you? Can you use it without touching it? It is overflowing? Can you put a cigarette in it? Is there a place to put a bottle, can, or newspaper for recycling? What are other people doing? These are some of the immediate questions that impact our use of receptacles. If the answers are the ones we're hoping for, there is a good chance that the litter will be deposited properly for the next step in its journey. It's also likely that we will feel good about doing the right thing.

On the other hand, doing the right thing might not happen if there is no receptacle in sight, or the nearest receptacle is overflowing, or other people are not using the receptacle, or the receptacle is confusing, awkward to use, or disgusting in its appearance and condition. *From the user's perspective, the receptacle should be simple, safe, clean, and close.*

The simplest receptacle to use has one or more large openings that can be readily seen. A large opening is one that is big enough to drop trash into without it getting hung up in the opening and requiring the user to force it through. Litter is often tossed into receptacles as people walk by, without breaking stride. An easy target helps avoid near misses. Utilitarian receptacles tend to have larger openings than high-design versions. Square or round openings of 7½ to 9 inches are adequate. Rectangular or oblong openings should be at least 5½ inches across in the small dimension so that empty lunch bags and drink cups will fit in. The opening may be on the top or on the side. Both work fine. Side-opening units are typically taller to allow adequate space for the openings without reducing capacity. Side-opening units may be better solutions in areas subject to heavy rain or snow because they keep precipitation from getting inside.

Most users prefer not to touch receptacles, for sanitary reasons. Receptacles with flaps or covers that must be opened by the user may negatively affect use. The flaps and covers on receptacles commonly used near food vendors to discourage insects and critters sometimes have the unintended consequence of also discouraging people. In using these receptacles, people often try to employ their trash as a tool to push the units open without touching them. As putting trash in and withdrawing the hand without making contact is almost impossible, the result is dropped litter and messy flappers. The need to touch the receptacle increases the likelihood that some people won't even try and will simply leave litter for others to dispose of. Disney uses receptacles with flappers at their theme parks, possibly because of all the insect-attracting sweets that end up in them, but their receptacles are kept spotless, and litter is picked up immediately by "cast members."

Storing Stuff

A critical requirement of the receptacle is that it effectively contains the trash or recyclables until it is emptied. It should prevent contents from leaking, falling out through holes, blowing out, and being dumped over. It is beneficial, for reasons of health and efficient grounds keeping, to prevent animals from getting in. It is also beneficial, though not essential, to keep rain and snow out.

The most commonly employed storage methods fall into three categories:

1. The simplest receptacle is a container into which trash or recyclables are dropped. The litter goes directly into the container and the container is lifted and dumped to empty it (see Figure 5.10).

2. Some units have a liner made of flexible polyethylene or galvanized steel. The liner fits inside the outer shell of the unit, the litter goes into the liner, and the liner is removed and dumped to empty it. Handling the liner is easier than dumping the whole unit, and using the liner helps keep the inside of the outer shell clean. Because the liner is used to both hold and dump the trash, the outer shell is subject to less damage, wear and tear. When a liner is used it is important that trash be directed into the liner and kept from falling between the shell and the liner. A lid or diverter can help. (See Figure 5.11)

5.10 A simple and very pretty wire basket in a park in Italy. Credit: copyright © 2003, Project for Public Spaces

5.11 An open-top wire basket with a poly liner is simple and has no moving parts, making it a basic solution for urban settings. Photo credit: Bill Main

5.12 Receptacle with metal liner and plastic bag. Credit: copyright © 2003, Project for Public Spaces

3. Many units employ a disposable plastic bag for containing the trash. To empty receptacle contents, the bag is simply tied and removed. Bags are most commonly used with liners, but are sometimes used on the unit itself. They help keep both the liner and the unit clean, provide a means of removing the trash that minimizes spilling and blowing, and tend to reduce wear and tear to the receptacle. On the other hand, as one more disposable plastic object, they present an environmental challenge. And they can present a visual challenge as well. When bags are used they sometimes are pulled out over the top of the exterior shell, creating a visual effect that can spoil the design of the unit (see Figure 5.5). This situation can be prevented by using the correct size bag and by instructing maintenance people on the correct method for securing the bag inside the unit (See Figure 5.12).

Keeping a Lid on It

A top or lid for the receptacle hides the contents, protects them from the elements and critters, and reduces the chance that they will blow out.

Hiding the contents has obvious aesthetic benefits. Without a top or lid, the contents will be on display to anyone taller than the unit. This may be acceptable in some rustic environments or at informal temporary events, such as street festivals, but is not the image most public spaces want to display.

In public places, receptacle tops and lids need to be secured to the base of the unit. Otherwise, they have a tendency to disappear. If the top needs to be opened in order to empty the unit, a hinge, pop-up, or cable attachment can be used. If cabled, the top will hang on the side of the unit while it is being serviced; if the top and base are both metal, there is a likelihood that the top will scratch or chip the base as it hangs from the cable. Plastic tops are often used to reduce this risk (See Figure 5.13).

In many areas, people search litter receptacles for bottles, cans or other valuables that can be sold or redeemed. If this is not planned for or managed, receptacle lids or doors may be left open and trash may be strewn about in the search process. One solution to this problem is to lock the door or lid of the receptacle and provide the maintenance people with the key. Another response is to manage the process by keeping an eye on the searchers, who are likely to be regulars, making sure they understand that they must leave the receptacles as they found them. A third response is to use receptacles that have a separate place for bottles and cans so that these items can be removed without going through the trash (See Figure 5.14).

Taking Stuff Out

Receptacles need to be emptied on a regular basis before they overflow and their contents begin to smell or attract critters. How a receptacle is emptied depends on how the litter is stored. Most receptacles are emptied by hand, though a few are emptied mechanically. People performing this task usually develop a regular routine, going through the same steps every time. Studying the process can reveal opportunities for improvements that will save time, prevent injuries, and reduce litter.

Emptying by hand generally involves one or more people coming to the unit (rarely is the unit moved to anther site for emptying) with a large cart or vehicle into which the material is placed. If the unit has a lid or door, it is opened (with a key, if it has been locked). Where the bag system is used, the bag is removed, tied at the top, and placed in the cart or vehicle. Oversized bags are often used so that there is enough material to make a knot. Sometimes wire or plastic ties are used, but simply knotting the bag eliminates the need to carry a supply of these around. A new bag is then installed.

If no disposable bag is used, the liner or the unit itself is lifted and dumped. A few hard thumps are usually necessary to get all of the trash out. Metal baskets or liners that are emptied this way quickly acquire dents. As noted

5.13 Metal litter receptacle with hinged metal top. Credit: copyright © 2003, Project for Public Spaces

above, the bag helps keep the liner and the unit clean. If no bag is used, the bottom of the container can quickly become coated with a sticky mess that will not come out easily, especially in the corners. This buildup will accumulate further over time and begin to smell. Pressure washing is usually needed to clean it out.

Receptacles with side doors are becoming more common because of concerns about employee injuries and worker's compensation costs associated with lifting. The door allows a liner to be pulled out of the side of the unit and emptied rather than lifted through the top. Although the trash will still need to be lifted, the side door reduces the lifting height and allows the person doing the work to exercise more control over the lifting position. Receptacles with doors are more expensive than the same receptacles without doors.

Mechanically emptied receptacles are usually made of rotationally molded plastic that can be gripped by the mechanical arm of a garbage truck, lifted, and dumped. They have a lid that flips open as the unit is dumped. To use this system the receptacles must be accessible by a large vehicle. These units tend to sacrifice design and aesthetic appeal in order to achieve mechanical processing.

Who's Responsible?

Some facilities within public outdoor spaces may own and maintain receptacles, either through their own initiative or by statutory requirement. For example, many municipalities and districts require food vendors to provide and maintain their own receptacles to avoid overburdening public receptacles in the area. Where this is the case, a requirement that the design and materials of the receptacles complement the other furniture elements in the streetscape or other public space may be wise.

Some owners/operators may not want a public litter receptacle in front of their business, especially if it blocks a window display or signage, is deemed unattractive, or is not serviced often enough. It may be necessary to develop written policies about receptacle placement, design, and standards of maintenance in order to resolve and manage multiple constituencies and their interests.

When Bad Receptacles Happen to Good Spaces

It is an unfortunately common phenomenon: a beautiful new office building or facility with a very unattractive receptacle placed prominently near the entrance. Ever wonder how this could happen? Typically it occurs with stand-alone office buildings and hotels when the people responsible for the design of the building do not include the selection of receptacles in the scope of their work. After the building opens, the need for receptacles becomes obvious to building management, and the task of selection is handed over to the maintenance staff. These folks are likely to select a product from what is offered by the maintenance supply companies they use. And while these units may function just fine, they often do not complement the site's architecture, design, materials, or quality standards. To avoid this, receptacle selection should always be included within the scope of the work of the design team.

Where and How Many

Where should receptacles be placed?

- Near settings and activities that generate trash, such as eating areas, food vendors, convenience stores, newsstands, and smoking areas.
- At transition zones where people seek to shed trash rather than taking it with them as they move to their next destination or activity. Transition zones include building entries, parking access points, and transportation entries and stations.
- At locations where people concentrate or are likely to pause. Such places include restrooms, plazas, special-event areas, vendor carts, kiosks, and major pedestrian nodes and intersections.
- Along urban streets and walkways (independent of the above triggers), at intervals such that people don't have to carry trash more than half a block or so. PPS recommends a litter receptacle at each corner of an intersection and one or two mid-block.

5.14 This San Francisco litter receptacle has a place in the top for bottles and cans to discourage folks from going through the trash to retrieve recyclables. Photo credit: Bill Main

The number of receptacles required in a space will vary depending on the population density and the activity level in the area as well as the frequency with which litters are emptied. Overflowing litter receptacles are a clear indication of the need for more receptacles or more frequent service. Litter dropped at a distance from receptacles may indicate a need for more receptacles or better placement.

Litter fills a receptacle loosely and not very efficiently. One fast-food lunch bag disposal with a large cup occupies about 2 gallons of volume. A small receptacle, 20 gallons, for example, will hold about ten lunch bags and cups. A larger receptacle, say 35 gallons, will fill somewhat more efficiently, compacting as it fills, and may hold as many as twenty lunches. Users won't compact trash in a public receptacle the way they will in their home receptacles, so the receptacles do not fill to capacity.

A receptacle plan showing activities that generate trash, as well as transition zones, concentration, and waiting points, should be included on the site plan to help drive receptacle quantity and placement decisions. Most facilities tend to place receptacles at appropriate locations and then add additional units later if the capacity is not adequate. They also bring out additional receptacles for special events and peak periods.

Size

Receptacle size is a significant issue. By convention, receptacle capacity is measured in gallons. The true capacity of a receptacle is the volume it can hold without overflowing the liner or rising above any of the openings on the outer shell. The actual capacity may be quite a bit less than it appears on units that have a big or tall outer shell with a smaller liner inside. Average capacity for streetscape receptacles is 25 to 35 gallons. Receptacles over 35 gallons are considered very large capacity and those under 25 gallons are generally considered small capacity. Using large-capacity units may reduce the number of units needed or the frequency of emptying. However, large units may look bulky and overpower the space, and they can be heavier to empty. On the flip side, using small units may increase the number needed or the frequency of emptying, but they are lighter, easier to handle, and may provide a better aesthetic fit. In Europe, small receptacles with small openings are often used to discourage people from depositing household trash.

Special Issues

Compacting

There are outdoor receptacles available that compact the trash deposited in them using solar energy to power the machinery. These may be desirable in

5.15 Poly liners in three sizes: small (15 gallons), medium (30 gallons), and large (40 gallons), with a 5-gallon bucket for scale. Photo credit: Bill Main

some outdoor spaces, but there are trade-offs. Their advantage is that they need to be emptied much less often. However, the units are big and bulky-looking because of the space required to house machinery inside where it is safely separated from the public. They have heavy flapper doors that users must operate to deposit trash (the design of the door prevents users from reaching in and risking injury), and people may avoid using them because they don't want to operate the flapper. The weight of the compacted material is considerably greater than that of loose trash. The initial cost is much higher than for conventional receptacles, although this may be recouped through less frequent emptying. (See Figure 5.16)

Fire Suppression

A few public places have special concerns about the threat of fire in receptacles. Receptacle fires may be intentionally lit or accidentally ignited with a cigarette. The fuel is almost always the trash in the unit, rather than the unit itself, although a wood receptacle may burn if ignited by the contents. Special airtight receptacles, designed with tight-closing flappers that starve a fire of oxygen, are available for these situations. These units may also employ a metal rather than plastic liner because of its ability to withstand heat.

Bees and Bears

Animals and insects are attracted to food left in receptacles. The most common culprits include flying insects such as flies, bees, and wasps, which

5.16 A solar compacting unit and smokeless ash receptacle have good intentions. The size and bulk of the unit pose designated placement issues. Photo credit: Bill Main

are drawn to sweets and sugary drinks. They usually appear in areas where food is being served or eaten. Placing the receptacle at least 12 feet away from where people sit or gather can reduce or eliminate the annoyance. If this is not possible and the problem persists, it may be necessary to install a receptacle with a flapper. In some locations, the scent of garbage may attract rodents such as rats or raccoons. Where this is a problem, receptacles should be emptied more often, moved to better-lighted or more-exposed locations, and checked to make sure there are no holes in the liner or bag. In towns located near bear populations, special heavy-duty lids specifically designed to be bear-proof may be necessary to prevent bears from becoming a nuisance.

Security

Increasing concern about acts of terrorism has led to new requirements at some public spaces, particularly transportation facilities. The concern is that explosives might be placed in receptacles. The new regulations call for either removing receptacles, installing blast proof receptacles, or installing clear receptacles. There is a level of secrecy about which requirements apply to which facilities, so it is necessary to check regulations for each specific facility.

Clear receptacles keep contents visible by using a clear liner, a clear bag, and an exterior shell that allows viewers to see into the liner and bag. Bomb-resistant receptacles are also available. Generally, these are designed with open tops and sides made of special materials that can deflect and direct the explosive force upward, where it is likely to do less harm. Bomb-resistant receptacles tend to be rather bulky-looking and are very expensive but may be required in some highly protected sites.

Built-ins

Receptacles are sometimes built into other elements of public space, such as transit shelters. Designers and owners should keep the following in mind before making a decision to do this. Receptacles may show wear and damage long before the rest of the facility. Whereas a separate receptacle can be replaced or relocated, a built-in receptacle cannot be as easily replaced or moved and may "age" the whole shelter before its time. And if receptacles are custom built-in units, replacement parts may not be available and replacement costs are uncertain.

Recycling Units

Recycling units may be separate elements or integrated with litter receptacles. Recycling units should also be simple, safe, clean, and close. A common problem encountered with recycling receptacles is that trash ends up being deposited in them. This can be minimized, though usually not eliminated

People watching *is an international pastime for which just about any seat with a view will do. Benches, chairs, stairs, ledges and walls all fill the bill. Multiple opportunities make it possible for people to choose their preferred perch.*

Gathering *is an instinctive human activity. There's no one right place or way to do it. The greater the variety of options offered, the greater the freedom allowed for self-selecting places and postures.*

Eating and drinking *in outdoor spaces is the most sociable of activities. Furniture frames these settings.*
Chairs, tables and umbrellas in variety and abundance expand the experience.

Playing *isn't just for kids but they certainly make the most of it. Who decrees what's a suitable seat? Who says seats are only for sitting? Why not offer opportunities that enable the unexpected?*

Water *is a magnet that creates the setting for the seating. It's a focal point that defines orientation while encouraging vari-ation. Benches around a fountain, a deck along a stream, stones in the water all suffice.*

Trees and plantings *act as anchors in outdoor settings. They provide a sense of comfort and a frame for an array of seating choices created to support a variety of activities in a diverse mix of spaces.*

Pathways *frame seating opportunities in a direct and linear way. They set the stage for stopping and resting in settings that range from stairs and ledges in plazas and streetscapes to solitary benches in quiet gardens.*

Refuge *is found in spaces that provide respite and protection. Seating in such settings may be set apart, arrayed against backdrops, nestled beneath structures. Sometimes it feels safe enough to fall asleep.*

5.17 A litter receptacle and two recycling units on a college campus. Openings and labels identify materials to be deposited. Redundancy in messaging is necessary to keep people from depositing trash in all three places. Photo credit: Bill Main

entirely, by providing very clear information/signage about what should be deposited in the unit. The information is typically doubly or triply redundant: the deposit hole is appropriately shaped for the material (a narrow slot for paper, a small circular opening for cans or bottles, etc.), and signage near the opening indicates the approved materials in words, images, or both. (See Figure 5.17)

Smoking Receptacles

The need for outdoor smoking receptacles began to grow exponentially when interior smoking bans first began sweeping the nation. It continues to grow today as more places are added to the no-smoking list, including bars and restaurants in many places. Smokers pushed outside plus the lack of good outdoor smoking receptacles led to numerous problems: piles of cigarette butts on the ground, ugly ash pans full of cigarette butts greeting people at the entrances to buildings, and "butt soup," the unfortunate result of rain on an ash pan that doesn't drain. Fortunately, there have been numerous improvements since then, but problems still remain. Most smokers flick their ashes on the ground and use the receptacle for extinguishing and disposing of the butt. Cigarette butts are today probably the most common form of litter. They are made of cellulose acetate, which does not break down readily, and once they are on the ground, their small size allows them to be carried by water and wind. They can find their way into the stormwater system and ultimately into streams and lakes. Perhaps because of their small size, or perhaps because they appear to be

5.18 An ash pan. Photo credit: Bill Main

more "natural" than they really are, many smokers drop cigarette butts without regarding them as litter. As with other forms of litter, there is an educational aspect to cigarette litter that cannot be completely addressed with ash receptacles. Nonetheless, good receptacles conveniently located can have a major positive impact.

There are three basic types of outdoor ash receptacles:

- *Ash pan:* an open-top pan or bowl with or without sand or fine gravel in it. The pan or bowl may be set on top of a small base unit or it may be installed in the top of a combination ash/trash receptacle. The sand or fine gravel helps hide the butts to some degree and extinguishes the burning cigarette when the butt is pushed in. Maintenance people remove butts with a slotted scoop (or sometimes a screen hidden under the sand) and will need to freshen up the sand or gravel as needed. The disadvantage of this type is that the cigarette butts may be highly visible and the unit can fill with rain or snow. Combination ash/trash units reduce the number of separate furniture pieces required, saving some space and money, but they do not serve either function ideally. This approach may be suitable for spots where people are expected to drop their butts but not linger and smoke at the receptacle (such as entries that do not serve as major smoking areas).

- *Covered ash receptacle:* a pan or bowl with a cover to protect it from rain and to screen the view of the cigarette butts. These are usually stand-alone units, but there are a few that attach to litter receptacles. They do not usually require sand or gravel and will instead have a place to snuff out the cigarette prior to disposal.

5.19 A covered ash urn. Photo credit: Bill Main

- *Smokeless receptacle:* a receptacle with a single hole just large enough to receive the cigarette butt. The butt disappears inside, and the lack of oxygen inside extinguishes the burning tobacco. These are often designed with the capacity to hold hundreds or even thousands of butts, hidden from view and protected from the elements. These are becoming very popular because of their simplicity and capacity.

Ash urns should be located wherever smokers are expected or directed to congregate. Many facilities have successfully pulled smokers away from entrances by creating better spaces nearby, with receptacles and perhaps some weather protection and seating.

Trash-and-Ash Combos

Some receptacles are designed to accept both litter and smoking ash and butts. This is typically accomplished with an ash pan that is mounted in the lid or hung off the side of the unit. While this feature eliminates the need for a stand-alone ash urn, there are some trade-offs. Depending on the design, an extra step or two may required to empty the trash, rain may collect in the ash pan, and visible burn marks may appear on the unit as a result of people snuffing out smokes on the finish.

Endnote

1. Keep America Beautiful, Inc., www.kab.org/site/PageServer?pagename=Focus_litter_prevention.

5.20 A smokeless receptacle. Photo credit: Bill Main

6. Other Site Furniture Elements and Accessories

Seating and litter receptacles are the staples of site furnishings, but a host of other elements add functionality, personality, and amenity to outdoor spaces. Tables (with and without attached seating), umbrellas, planters, wayfinding elements, bollards, borders, bike racks, news racks, tree grates and guards, railings, lighting, and transit shelters all contribute to the usefulness, attractiveness, and pleasure of public places. Here are their stories.

Tables

Tables can be hard to find in outdoor spaces, and that's a shame. Even a small table can make outdoor activities more convenient and enjoyable. A table is a natural place for eating and drinking, socializing, organizing, studying, and Web surfing. A round or square table positions people for eye contact and easy socializing and provides a comforting mass to lean on or relax behind. Bistro tables are often found at outdoor cafés and coffee shops, and family-style picnic tables are often provided at recreational parks, but the potential for tables in public spaces is much greater than that. Tables and chairs can be used at many of the same places benches are used to enhance the user's experience.

Standard table height is 28 to 30 inches, which is comfortable for eating and accommodates most dining chairs. Standing or bar-height tables, suitable for use while standing or sitting on a bar-height stool, are about 42 inches high. Low tables (coffee table height) are about 17 to 25 inches high and are fine for holding drinks or for very casual eating.

Some tables, usually those made of wood, have legs at their perimeter. But outdoor tables more commonly mix and match tabletops with table bases that support the table at the center, allowing easier access. This gives designers options to choose the right top for the situation and the best base to go with it.

Tabletops are available in round, square, rectangular, and occasionally other shapes. Square and round tables allow everyone to sit facing each other in a very sociable orientation. Round tabletops occupy an area roughly 20 percent smaller than square tables having the same cross dimension, while accommodating the same number of people. Round tables may be awkward

6.1 Sometimes a low table is nice.
Credit: copyright © 2003, Project for
Public Spaces

6.2 Fresh snow creates the opportunity
for a birthday cake table. Photo credit:
Bill Main.

for use with square cafeteria trays and are difficult to gang together for
larger groups and dense applications. Outdoor restaurants often use
small square and rectangular tables on movable bases, which can be easily
clustered together, to create long rectangular tables with side-by-side seating
to accommodate groups.

6.3 Bar height works at this temporary beach cabana in Berlin. Credit: copyright © 2007, Project for Public Spaces

Surfaces that are hard, smooth, and stain-resistant are very desirable for tabletops. Common examples include stainless steel, powder-coated metal, UV-resistant solid-surface acrylics, granite, and fiberglass. Galvanized finishes should not be used on tabletops due to the risk of contaminating food with the sacrificial zinc. Tabletops are subject to scratching from objects slid across them, such as trays; patterns or perforations in the top make scratches less noticeable.

When a table is intended to hold an umbrella, a tabletop and base specifically designed for this purpose must be selected. Generally, tables less than 36 inches across are not robust enough to provide adequate umbrella support. If there is a chance that a table will be used with an umbrella, it should be manufactured with an umbrella hole and a base that will secure the umbrella, or at least should allow space for an umbrella base to be added. Be aware that these features may be difficult or impossible to add later, as cutting the umbrella hole may compromise the table finish and the original base structure may not accept an umbrella.

Pedestal Base

A pedestal base is a column that attaches to the tabletop near its center and spreads more broadly where it contacts the ground. This type of base uses a combination of weight and geometry to hold the table steady. Heavy materials such as cast iron or concrete may be used because of their mass. However, a heavy base can make the table difficult to move without a cart.

6.4 Attractive tables and chairs enhance a pleasant outdoor eating venue. Photo credit: copyright © Jim Powell

6.5 Tabletops and stool tops are heavily perforated to dry quickly after rain and prevent heat buildup in the sun. Sydney, Australia. Photo credit: Bill Main

Lifting the table by the edge may damage the tabletop or the connections to the base, and rolling the base may damage the base itself or the paving material. That being said, a heavy base is especially beneficial for use with an umbrella.

Pedestal bases usually have glides to prevent the base from damaging the paving, and vice versa. Glides are typically made of nylon or plastic and are sacrificial in nature, wearing down or even breaking off, so they should be checked and replaced from time to time. Glides will wear especially quickly on heavy bases and on rough surfaces such as concrete.

Legs

Legs positioned around the edge of the table are more common on tables designed for indoor use, but they may also be found on some bistro tables and wood tables. Individual legs may be more vulnerable to bending or breaking than pedestal bases, especially when being moved, and like pedestals, they require glides. Legs limit the location of chairs around the table.

Fixed Supports

Permanently fixed supports usually consist of a simple metal column attached at the center of the table and fixed to the ground, either with anchor bolts or by means of a concrete embedment. In most cases, the tabletop can be removed and replaced if necessary without removing the base. This method is sometimes used to stabilize small standing-height tables (which tend to tip easily), to fix small tables at intervals along a bench, or to anchor tables, chairs, or stools in settings where furniture migration is an issue.

Tables with Attached Seats

In this design, seats and table share a common support structure. This furniture type will be covered in more detail later in this chapter.

General Issues with Tables

Beware that in some public settings tables may be sat upon, leaned against, or even stood on, placing impossible structural loads on the tables, especially at their edges, and creating safety hazards for ill-advised users and people nearby. The life of a light-duty table in these environments is likely to be much shorter than is typical of street furniture.

"Tippy" tables are a common frustration. Tipping is usually caused by an uneven surface under the table, a condition that is especially likely with stone or tile surfaces. For small tables, strategies to eliminate tipping include using three-legged table bases or using heavy bases, such as cast iron or steel plates that make broad contact with the ground surface. Adjustable glides

6.6 Lightweight tables take a beating and have a shorter life span than most site furniture. Photo credit: Bill Main

don't work well on small tables because they are moved around a lot. For larger, heavier tables that aren't moved very often, the simplest remedy is to rotate the table base until it no longer tips. If this doesn't work, adjustable leveling glides may. Or try using rubbery floor-protecting cups (sometimes called carpet protectors) under the glides.

Umbrellas

Umbrellas are more often used for shade protection than rain protection in urban spaces. People in cities want to be outside on nice days, and the sun may be bright or intense. On rainy days people in urban spaces generally do not stay outside for very long; they simply go inside or leave. If they use a canopy for temporary rain protection, it is usually just until they can make plans to get to a drier venue. Special events planned for outdoor spaces often include a tent or canopy brought in for insurance.

Umbrellas of many types may be suitable for use in public spaces, depending on the situation. Wind is a major consideration. Umbrellas catch a lot of wind, which can exert considerable force on the canopy, the pole, the tilting mechanism, and the supporting table and/or base. Most umbrella warranties do not cover wind damage. It is difficult to find dependable data on how much wind a given umbrella system can withstand. One of the reasons for this is the huge variety of combinations of canopy sizes, shapes, materials, mechanisms, poles, and bases, few of which have undergone any standardized wind testing. Most umbrellas simply are not designed to remain up in windy conditions; however, lowering umbrellas before it gets too windy requires having available and attentive staff nearby. Wind can damage an umbrella, usually by blowing it over, and this can be awkward and dangerous for people in the area.

How windy is too windy? It depends, but unless an umbrella system is designed to withstand strong winds, it is probably best to assume that a moderate breeze (13-19 mph), as defined by the Beaufort wind scale (13-19mph), will begin to move the umbrella canopy, and higher winds (fresh breeze, 20-24 mph, or strong breeze, 25-31 mph) can begin to cause damage. Umbrellas should be left in the down position when staff are not available to tend them.

Winds can sometimes lift the whole umbrella. Most bases provide for a clamp or bolt to lock the umbrella into the base. Use of umbrellas is not recommended on roof decks and roof gardens because strong winds and unpredictable updrafts can occur there. If they are used, extraordinary care should be taken to ensure that they cannot be blown off the roof, possibly taking their bases with them.

Umbrellas may be fixed or collapsible. Collapsible umbrellas can be raised and lowered, but fixed umbrellas are always in the up position. The latter typically have rigid canopies made of aluminum or fiberglass. Most can be disassembled for storage, but they are often left in place year round. Because they cannot be lowered and are out in all kinds of weather, fixed umbrellas should be designed to handle strong winds. To provide the necessary support for a fixed umbrella, the base needs to be securely anchored to the ground. This is often accomplished by installing the umbrella in a table engineered to hold a fixed umbrella and then securely anchoring the table to the paving surface. A major advantage of fixed umbrellas is that they don't require staff to put them up when needed and take them down when it gets windy or they are not required. Manufacturers of fixed umbrellas can usually provide wind test data.

Collapsible umbrellas are more common than fixed, and come in a wide variety of shapes, sizes, and configurations. Many of these have been designed for residential pool and patio applications and will not last long under regular use in a public space. For durability, every component of the umbrella must be robust: the fabric canopy, the pole, the struts, and the base.

Canopy

Cheap fabrics will deteriorate quickly with exposure to wind, rain, and sun. Ultraviolet waves will fade the fabric and break down its structure. A high-quality fabric woven from solution-dyed acrylic fibers will cost more but will perform much better and last longer. Some canopies have vented tops, which are designed to shed wind and reduce lift.

Pole

A sturdy one-piece pole with no tilts, cranks, or joints is usually best for public spaces because there is less to break and tamper with. Good poles can be made of stainless steel, heavy-gauge or double-tube aluminum, or hardwood.

Struts

Cheap umbrellas may have springy wire struts that deform in the wind or flimsy connections between the strut pieces. For greater durability, look for strong, rigid struts made of extruded aluminum, aluminum tube, or hardwood and well-thought-out and executed connections.

Base

A large (36 inches across or larger), sturdy table with a heavy or anchored base can provide excellent umbrella support. The base of the umbrella pole should be bolted, pinned, or clamped to the table base to prevent the umbrella from lifting out in the wind. The hole in the tabletop should have a protective ring that prevents the pole from moving and damaging the table edge around the opening.

When the plan calls for small tables that aren't substantial enough to hold an umbrella, special bases designed to support an umbrella without a table should be specified. These bases typically have a long vertical tube that holds and supports the umbrella pole up to about the same height as a table would. Several small tables may be clustered around a large umbrella supported in this manner.

Another umbrella alternative is the cantilever or side-support type, in which a fabric canopy is hung from a cranelike support located off to one side. The cantilever requires a base that is quite massive and may have a large footprint. Cantilever umbrellas employ a crank mechanism to open the canopy. Large square cantilever umbrellas are sometimes used at outdoor cafés to shade several small tables, and may be placed edge to edge to completely cover an area.

The perimeter of an umbrella should be at least 6 feet 6 inches high to enable people to easily walk under it. Tilting umbrellas, popular around pools and residential patios, are not normally used in public areas because tilting lowers one side of the canopy, blocking people from walking under it. Tilting umbrellas are also more subject to breakage than fixed-pole umbrellas.

Tables with Attached Seating

Attaching the seats to the table accomplishes a couple of closely related objectives. First, it keeps the seats from being stolen (unless, of course, the table is taken, too). Second, it prevents them from being moved away

6.7 Large umbrellas cover multiple small tables on this urban plaza. Photo credit: Bill Main

6.8 An interesting combination of movable seating with fixed tables and umbrellas outside the Environmental Design Building at UC Berkeley. Photo credit: Bill Main

from their planned location and keeps them neatly organized. Finally, this design may deliver some economy, as the seating and table share a common structure.

The theft of movable chairs in public spaces and the steps required to prevent it can present significant concern and expense. Public places such

6.9 Beijing: a serious policeman under a silly umbrella . . . and he's lovin' it. Photo credit: Bill Main

as Bryant Park in New York City that report a very low incidence of theft almost always have twenty-four-hour security or staff presence. Other spaces with no presence late at night, especially after the bars close, have experienced losses and other mischief. Stacking and locking chairs at night is a viable approach, but it takes time and involves some costs.

Migration of chairs from their intended location may also be seen as a problem, as it requires staff to periodically round them up and put them back where they belong. Some managers of spaces prefer the organized and geometric appearance of tables and chairs in a single unit, plus there's no straightening up and no chairs on the grass or in the fountain.

While most users and designers voice a preference for movable seating, there are clearly situations and spaces where attached tables and seats are called for. There are two basic configurations that meet these needs. The first is the common picnic table arrangement, in which seating is fixed along one or both sides of the table. The second is a round or square table with seating radiating around the table.

The picnic table configuration offers simplicity and economy. It has a very casual, family-style feeling. The seating is linear, and picnic tables can be placed end to end to accommodate large groups. Most have backless benches that can be awkward to get into, especially the middle seats. Some have individual seats, with or without backs. Individual picnic table seats with backs are easier to get in and out of if they swivel. The tabletop may be extended beyond the seats to provide wheelchair access to the table.

The radiant configuration offers a more social arrangement because the people sitting at the table can more easily face each other. This type usually seats four people, but some versions seat more. One or more seats can be omitted to allow wheelchair access.

6.10 Fixed umbrellas on tables with attached seating. Credit: Robert L. O'Boyle, FASLA, OCBA photo

6.11 In Paris these two big tables with attached seating and umbrellas are attracting a lot of users. Credit: copyright © 2008, Project for Public Spaces

Tables with attached seating may be freestanding, anchored to the ground, or embedded. Most are available in versions that will hold an umbrella.

Transit Shelters

Transit shelters are an important element of transit systems that would like to attract more riders who have a choice between using mass transit or not. Upgrading transit system amenities is one way to attract this group of riders. Transit shelters are a prime target for upgrade, both to increase ridership and to improve the streetscape environment. They are important and distinctive elements in the streetscape and the urban environment for several reasons:

- They are large structures compared with most other streetscape elements.
- They occupy prominent curbside locations.
- There are many of them throughout urban areas, often at important, busy locations.
- Many people use them on a regular basis and may spend considerable time in them while waiting for buses or trains.
- They often display wayfinding information and maps, which are useful even to people who don't use the transportation system.
- They may be lit at night, increasing their visibility.
- They are often designed to help establish or reflect local identity.

Transit shelters are intended to provide a clear, convenient, and safe place to wait for arriving transit vehicles and to get on and off those vehicles. Not all transit stops have a shelter. Transit systems typically provide different types and levels of amenity depending on the location and ridership at the particular stop. Amenities that may be provided include:

- Seating
- A roof for protection from sun and precipitation
- Side panels for protection from wind and weather
- Transit system maps and schedules
- Real-time information (RTI), such as the time of the next arrival
- Local area maps and information
- Lighting
- Litter receptacles

The available footprint for a transit shelter is often linear and limited, which results in the use of backless or shallow seating and leaning rails to save space. There is rarely more than a single row of seats.

Side panels, where present, are usually tempered glass, so people in and around the shelter are highly visible. Frosting or other markings on the glass signal its presence so people don't walk into it. Transit drivers should be able to easily see if anyone is waiting in the shelter, and the people waiting should be able to clearly see the approaching vehicle.

Advertising may be a significant source of funding for transit systems, especially larger urban systems, because of their prime locations and large captive audience. Advertising at transit shelters usually involves a large advertising panel located at the end of the shelter farthest from the arriving vehicle. It may also include one or more advertising panels on the rear of the shelter, although care must used to preserve good visibility in and out of the shelter. A number of large companies use a business model of providing and maintaining transit shelters and other urban structures, such as kiosks and newsstands, as part of an agreement to secure exclusive or special advertising rights in a particular geographic area.

Installing transit structures may be more complex than other site furniture because of the size and stresses involved. Some of the issues that may be encountered are:

- Grade changes and leveling
- Connecting to existing sidewalk or, if not sufficient, pouring a new slab
- Footings, if required by the structure

6.12 Ad revenues support the placement of these transit shelters in Chicago. Photo credit: Bill Main

6.13 San Francisco: A compact transit shelter designed for a small space. Photo credit: Bill Main

- Rainwater runoff
- Wind load and snow load
- Connecting to data and power
- Location relative to adjacent structures and activities

Planters

Planters generally serve one or more of the following purposes:

- To create a place for growing plants where it is not practical to plant in the ground
- To elevate plants above ground level for greater prominence
- To provide a pleasing aesthetic element in itself
- To define the space, as an edge or border
- To direct vehicle or pedestrian traffic
- To provide a security barrier

Planters come in a wide variety of sizes, shapes, and materials. Smaller planters are often called pots. Large planters may be 4 or 5 feet across and 3 feet high, and sometimes even larger. Raised planting beds, which don't have a bottom, have a soil mix that is contiguous with the soil of the site; these are not considered planters for the purposes of this discussion.

Many manufactured planters and pots are suitable for use indoors or out, with one crucial difference: indoor planters must contain water without leaking on floors and carpets, whereas outdoor planters must drain excess water so they don't fill with rain or irrigation water and drown the plants. (Water content in indoor planters also needs to be monitored to prevent overwatering and control planter weight.) Outdoor planters usually have several drain holes in the bottom and are raised or have channels in the bottom to let water flow from the holes.

When using planters on roofs and other structures where weight is a critical factor, it is important to recognize that a planter full of water may weigh many times what it does when dry. Water weighs 8.35 pounds per gallon and 62.4 pounds per cubic foot. Thus, a large planter saturated with water can weigh several thousand pounds. This water is not visible because it is under the surface, so in these locations it is especially important to be sure that water is properly draining out of the planter.

Managing water is an important aspect of growing any plant, but it is especially important in a container because extreme conditions of draught and saturation can be quickly reached. Water management is accomplished by controlling the materials in the planter and the water flow through the planter.

There are usually three or four different layers of material in a planter. The bottom layer is intended to allow excess water to flow easily to the drain holes. This is often accomplished by using a few inches of an inert, highly permeable aggregate covered by a soil-separating fabric. This fabric keeps the finer growing media from moving down and clogging the aggregate layer. Some planters are made with an integrated soil-separating barrier, which eliminates the need for the fabric and the aggregate. Above this is the soil mix or growing medium, in which the plants will root out and grow. It accounts for the largest volume of material. The soil mix should be appropriate for the selected plants and of a texture that will hold the right amount of moisture. Sometimes a top layer of bark or mulch is added to help retain moisture.

In some cases planters are filled almost entirely with lightweight foam filler, such as packing peanuts. Small pots of flowers are then pushed in and a cover of bark or mulch is added to conceal the foam and pots. This creates a lightweight system that can be easily moved and quickly changed.

Watering to supplement natural rainfall may be accomplished by means of an irrigation system or hand watering. Because planters are often spread out along streetscapes or around plazas, it may be impractical to reach them with an irrigation system or even with hoses from fixed water supplies. These locations may need to be serviced by vehicles with water tanks and portable hoses. Alternatively, there are watering systems designed to be built in or added to planters. These have a reservoir or bladder of water that is released into the soil mix over time, reducing the watering attention required.

Planters are probably used most often to introduce splashes of color with flowers and other interesting and colorful seasonal accents. For these short-term plantings a relatively shallow planter is fine. Planters are also used for more permanent greenery such as grasses, shrubs, or trees. The size of the planter should be adequate for the mature size of the plants. The environment of a planter may, over time, become challenging to permanent plantings due to heat, cold, freezing, limited root space, and deteriorating soil conditions. It may be necessary to remove and replace permanent plants and the other contents of the planters if the plants become stressed.

Planters need to be structurally strong enough to hold the weight and withhold the stresses to which they may be subjected. This is especially true for large planters with straight sides. The weight and pressure of soil and water and expansion from freezing will bow out the sidewalls. Some planters use an inside liner to isolate the outside planter walls from this pressure. A thick layer (2 inches or so) of foam lining on the inside and a light soil mix can be used to provide some protection from frozen soil expansion.

Planters set on sloping surfaces should be leveled for best appearance. When doing this, especially on large planters, care should be taken to support the planter weight evenly and to avoid blocking the drainage holes.

6.14 Concrete planters. Credit: Kornegay Design, LLC

6.15 Decorative planter.
Credit: Haddonstone (USA),
www.Haddonstone.com

6.16 Very large planters cross a retail
center in Roppongi Hills, Tokyo. Photo
credit: Bill Main

Wayfinding and Signage

Wayfinding is the process of learning to navigate in and around an area or
a space. People are more likely to visit a given area and stay longer if they
enjoy it, are comfortable in it, and are not frustrated or intimidated by it.
Knowing where you are and how to get to where you want to be is part
of feeling comfortable in a space, and a good wayfinding system can help.

Wayfinding systems can be designed for a range of project types and sizes: a single facility, a large site, a district, a campus, a community, a transit system, and so on.

People use a variety of aids and techniques to help orient themselves and find their way. These may be outdoor elements designed for that purpose, personal or interpersonal communications, or existing features and qualities of the area.

Wayfinding aids include:

- Signage and graphics
- Landmarks, monuments, and distinctive features
- Maps and guides, either posted or personal
- A clear layout of streets, spaces, and routes
- Prominent businesses and activities
- Verbal directions

People will use the wayfinding methods that they are most comfortable with. A good wayfinding system recognizes this and integrates existing wayfinding aids with new ones as needed. For example, significant landmarks may be shown on all maps, guides, and signs and called out with the same graphic image in all visual resources as they are made available.

Signage is one of the most important aids to wayfinding. There are many types of signs:[1]

- Identification
- Directional
- Warning
- Regulatory and prohibitory
- Operational (open hours, available services, etc.)
- Honorific
- Interpretive

A signage system is a unified and comprehensive approach to creating signs for a particular client or location. The system must be flexible enough to address many physical features in an area and the needs of many different users. A signage system consists of three subsystems:

- *An information system.* This is the message content and the distribution (locations) of that content.
- *A graphic system.* This includes the fonts, images, symbols, arrows, colors, and graphic design standards used to organize these elements on signs.

- *A hardware system.* This is the physical object(s) to which the graphics are applied. It includes all necessary materials, finishes, mountings, connections, power, and lighting.

A good signage system has the following characteristics:

- It is clear, simple, and intuitive. (Note that people may need to interpret signs while driving or moving.)
- It covers the range of sign types needed.
- It is capable of conveying comprehensive, custom messages, rather than just stacking multiple messages on top of each other.
- It expresses identity and distinctiveness, contributing to the branding of the place or client.

Today, an increasing number of signs are electronic and may be interactive or offer real-time information. These signs have screens and electrical and data connections that must be protected from vandalism as well as from weather.

The signage hardware system may include signs, maps, kiosks, and other freestanding objects that become part of the furnishings of the exterior site. Like other furnishings, they must be durable and resistant to weather, UV exposure, and vandalism. Perhaps more than most other furnishings, signage is subject to change. As areas evolve and things come and go, signs may need to be altered, added, or removed. Thought should be given to this process and responsibility assigned to ensure that the signage is kept up to date and is not corrupted by ad hoc elements that don't fit within the system.

Steel, aluminum, and other common materials are used in sign structures, but the range of materials used in sign displays, panels, and graphics is vast and constantly evolving. Whatever materials are used, they must be robust enough to withstand use outdoors in sun, rain, snow, ice, humidity, and wind.

Sign clutter is a common problem in public areas. Urban environments are full of signs and images from many different sources. There are street signs, storefront signs, advertising signs, warning signs, and on and on. While most of these signs are helpful and well intentioned, their cumulative effect is often visual clutter and visitor confusion. It can be a challenge to garner the authority to establish and control a coherent wayfinding and signage system while respecting the needs, rights, and demands of merchants, advertisers, public safety authorities, and property owners. Many districts and communities have sign ordinances. Good sign ordinances can help create the environment for an effective signage and wayfaring system.

6.17 Bollards separate the plaza from the street. Photo credit: copyright Jim Powell

Bollards

The name *bollard* is borrowed from the posts found on wharfs and used for mooring ships. In concept, bollards are among the simplest of urban elements. In reality, they are a bit more complex. A bollard is a short post around 3 feet tall, usually intended to provide traffic control. Placed parallel with the road, they prevent vehicles from being parked on curbs and accidentally entering the pedestrian right of way. This is accomplished by spacing the bollards close enough together to prevent vehicles from passing between them, but far enough apart to allow people to walk or propel a wheelchair between them. (If neither vehicles nor people are to be allowed entry, a fence or guardrail might be used). Typical bollard spacing is about 3 feet, which is sufficient to accommodate luggage and wheelchairs. In other applications, a series of bollards may be used to define an area, or one or two bollards may be used to block a specific entry.

Bollards are sacrificial. They are not expected to suffer vehicle impact without damage. Rather, they are expected to help protect something more valuable. It is likely that a bollard hit by a vehicle will need to be either repaired or replaced. The exceptions are some bollards mounted on a spring or made of flexible materials that discourage vehicles, but bend out of the way when actually struck. These are used where the consequences of vehicle penetration are not judged to be severe.

Bollards range from simple and utilitarian to highly designed and detailed. At the most basic end of the continuum are timber or painted steel posts vertically embedded in the ground. The most utilitarian bollards are more often found around parking lots and alleyways than at public entries to important spaces and places. At the other end of the continuum are a variety of more detailed forms and refined materials that are intended to complement surrounding architecture and urban elements and support local identity. These latter types are generally considered to be part of the public area furniture and amenity package.

While the general purpose of bollards is to prevent vehicles from entering pedestrian areas, there are other specific tasks that bollards are expected to perform, and these require specific design and engineering characteristics. Adding more features adds cost and complexity to the bollard and to its installation, so determining just what is needed at each location is important.

Design

Bollards can be anything in form, from sleek and contemporary to ornate and traditional, to complement architectural styles. Materials and finishes can be chosen to fit with other exterior elements in the area.

Security Level

Bollards provide both a visual barrier and a structural deterrent to vehicles. However, most bollards have not been designed to meet an established standard for stopping vehicles, so the structural deterrent aspect may be relatively insignificant. A car sliding slowly on ice or accidentally backing into a bollard may be stopped, but a car that is fully out of control or a truck driven by a terrorist may destroy the bollard and keep going.

Some sites, particularly federal buildings, now have stringent security standards for the building perimeter that require being able to stop a speeding truck on impact. Although these applications are limited, bollards designed, tested, and rated to meet these standards are available. They are broader and built of heavier materials than typical bollards and require large and complex footings that support tremendous impact resistance. (See the U.S. Department of State Bureau of Diplomatic Security website for standards: www.state.gov/m/ds.)

In the immediate aftermath of the September 11 attacks, the increased demand for security led to the "hardening" of many existing sites with rows of bollards and barriers. Since that time, security design has evolved to include measures such as grade changes that meet security requirements without the need for excessive hardening by redundant rows of bollards and barriers. But bollards remain an important security tool because they can be engineered to provide a predictable level of security in a small footprint.

6.18 Bollards protect a pedestrian crossway at a median. Photo credit: Bill Main

6.19 Bollards with solar LED lighting perform multiple functions. Photo credit: copyright Jim Powell

Fixed or Removable

A fixed or stationary bollard is one that is permanently fixed in one position. A removable or retractable bollard is one that can be selectively moved or removed to allow access by selected vehicles. Removable bollards vary in sophistication. Some simply slide down into a vertical sleeve in the ground and are removed by manual lifting. Some have a pin mechanism that allows them to be attached and released at ground level. Either of these first two types may have a keyed lock, with keys held by service personnel, public safety departments, and other parties with legitimate needs for access. A retractable bollard has a mechanism, usually hydraulic, that allows it to be raised and lowered from a remote location, such as a guardhouse.

Lighting

Some bollards also provide lighting. This may be either marker lighting or area lighting. Area lighting is significant lighting of the ground plane around the bollard. Marker lighting provides a glow that highlights the location of the bollard. The photometrics of the unit (i.e., brightness and illumination coverage) will vary, depending on the particular lighting system in the bollard. Some marker bollards are solar-powered, eliminating the need to connect to the electrical grid, but at this time there are no solar-powered area lighting bollards. Where a light mounted on a low post is needed but the strength of a bollard is not required, a path light might be a better choice.

Garden Borders

Garden borders are very low decorative fences that enclose planting areas. They are typically found in urban areas between the sidewalk and the curb, where they serve to discourage people from walking across planted areas and from allowing their pets to relieve themselves there. Keeping people and pets out protects plants from damage and soil from compaction.

Borders are usually about a foot tall, making entry merely awkward, not impossible. They are commonly made up of short sections of ornamental cast metal or of metal rods formed into upside-down U shapes and placed in an overlapping pattern dense enough to keep all but the smallest critters out. Some borders are held in place by stakes that are simply pressed into the ground. Others are fixed to the edge of the surrounding paving. Adjacent sections should be connected for alignment.

Urban garden borders seem to be like snowflakes—from a distance they look similar, but when you look closely there's a lot of variety. This is typically the result of borders being provided piecemeal by adjacent

6.20, 6.21, 6.22. A trio of garden
borders. Photo credit: Bill Main

property owners rather than being selected and installed as part of a larger streetscape project.

For a more elegant appearance and to create a raised planting bed, a concrete or stone curb can be formed around the planting area with the metal border rising above it.

Bike Racks and Bike Lockers

Bike racks are intended to provide a convenient place for bike owners to securely lock their bicycles. To make this possible, a bike rack must provide a lock attachment loop that is proximate to a good locking location on the bike's frame. This varies from bicycle to bicycle. In practice, many riders prefer to lock both the front wheel and the bike frame to the rack. The location for this on the bike is typically about 2 feet above the ground, give or take a few inches.

There are many different bike rack designs that allow this locking method. One that doesn't is the old schoolyard bike rack that holds just the front wheel. Owners of expensive bikes do not like holding the bike from that point because it puts stress on the wheel rim. This type of rack may be fine for kids' rugged bikes but not for the better bicycles of more serious riders. The Association of Pedestrian and Bicycle Professionals recommends that the bike be supported by its frame. Racks must be securely anchored to the ground in such a way that potential bike thieves cannot free the bike by freeing or breaking the rack.

In locating bike racks, the planner needs to allow for possible placement of the bike(s) as well as the rack. The bikes should not protrude into walkways or present hazards for blind pedestrians.

The consequence of not providing bike racks, or not providing enough of them, is that people will lock their bikes to whatever is available. This might be a railing, a tree, a bench, or any other stable object that offers security. They will not leave their bikes unlocked. The consequence of locking bikes to these objects include scraped bark, chipped and scratched finishes (locks and chains can be very tough on furniture finishes), and bikes in places they weren't expected to be.

It is worth noting that colleges tend to have huge bike riding populations and have huge needs for bike racks. In recent years a common solution for colleges has been installing rows of inverted-U racks in slabs of fresh concrete throughout the campus.

Bike lockers are becoming increasingly common as more people seek long-term bike storage or commute on very expensive bicycles and want a more protected place to secure them. Bike lockers are enclosures within which riders can lock their bikes. As bicycle commuting continues to increase, bike lockers will become more prevalent. In the absence of good lockers, good bikes may be brought inside.

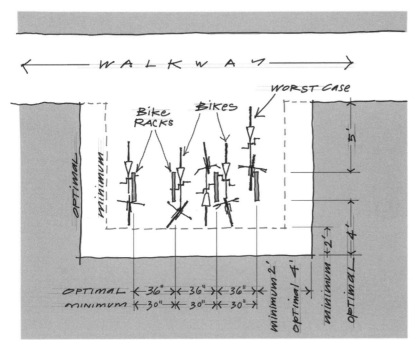

6.23 Layout for inverted "U" Credit: Robert G. Chipman, ASLA

6.24 Inverted-U bike racks on a university campus wait for spring. Photo credit: Bill Main

6.25 A sculpture (bike rack?) made from recycled guns in front of San Francisco City Hall. Photo credit: Bill Main

6.26 A surface-mounted bike rack. Credit: Copyright © Madrax

Newspaper Racks

Today these elements are still often called news racks, despite the fact that they are actually large metal or plastic boxes that enclose and dispense newspapers and handbills. The news rack is where street furniture meets the first amendment.

News racks come in several sizes depending on whether they are dispensing broadsheets (the standard newspaper), tabloids (a large vertical format with the fold on the left), or handbills (a smaller-size format). They have a spring-loaded hinged door on the front for accessing the papers. They may be coin- or card-operated or free, depending on the paper. A typical broadsheet or tabloid news rack is about 20 inches wide, 16 inches deep, and 36 to 48 inches tall. A handbill rack is smaller. Multiple units are larger, of course, but more about that later. Some news racks are plain cubes that rest on the ground, while others, such as the ubiquitous *USA Today* racks, are mounted on a pedestal.

Traditionally, news racks were placed at busy public locations by papers as part of their effort to sell their product. The box was usually boldly branded with the paper's name and colored for identification and to attract attention. The cost of putting these out and operating them was borne fully by the paper. Naturally, papers wanted to place their racks at prominent, busy locations for better sales. And naturally, competing papers wanted to be at the same spot. The result was long rows of boxes in different sizes and shapes, with many colors and logos, in prominent locations throughout cities. They would appear along streets, in plazas, at airports, and near major buildings. Some might be chained to trees, receptacles, signs, or poles for security. The result was visual clutter, damage (from chains and locks) to other streetscape elements, and sometimes awkward or unsafe obstructions of sidewalks, trash receptacles, bus stops, and entries.

As a consequence, cities began to regulate the placement of news racks and to require all papers to use a standard rack. The papers fought back, claiming interference with their First Amendment rights to free speech. A series of court decisions rendered since the mid-1980s have provided some guidance regarding the rights of each party. Basically, the courts said that news racks can be regulated, limited, and even prohibited in some cases for the purposes of public safety, property protection, and beautification. The regulations need to be carefully crafted, cannot exercise control over content, and must be applied uniformly to all news rack users.

The result is that in some places rows of individual news racks have been replaced by a smaller number of large racks that dispense multiple papers. These racks are provided by the city or other administrative entity, which can also control design and placement. The newspapers fill their own racks, collect their own money, and usually provide and service their own collection devices on the rack. The city may charge a rental fee, though if the fee is set high in order to discourage the newspapers, it may find itself in court.

Tree Grates and Guards

Trees are vitally important to the urban experience and environment. Among their many benefits, they provide shade and cool spaces, buffer wind and noise, replenish oxygen, define space, and lift spirits. But hard-surface

6.27 Multiple newspaper racks in assorted colors, shapes, and types create visual chaos. Photo credit: Bill Main

6.28 A standardized, uniform news rack consolidates multiple units and imposes visual order. Photo credit: Bill Main

urban spaces can be very tough on trees, and to grow healthy trees in these settings attention must be given to creating the right environment for the trees, caring for them, and protecting them. Urban horticulture is a big subject, and there are entire books devoted to it. For our purposes we will focus on tree grates and tree guards, which are used in paved pedestrian areas to help protect trees and their environment, and to keep the area around the tree trunks safe and usable.

Trees in paved areas are planted, and replaced when necessary, through an opening in the paving that is usually about 5 feet across but can be larger or smaller. A new tree typically has a root ball that is about 12 inches in diameter for each inch of trunk diameter, and it weighs several hundred pounds. The root ball requires an excavation that is large enough to accept it and an appropriate soil mix placed around it.

The large opening in the paving around the tree needs to be finished in some way. How it is done is a matter of design and practical considerations. It could simply be covered with shredded bark mulch or other ground cover. However, in areas where it is likely that people will purposely or accidentally walk on it, as might be expected along a busy urban sidewalk, a tree grate should be used for the protection of the tree and the safety of pedestrians.

A tree grate surrounds the base of a tree with a hard, walkable, water-permeable surface that is installed smooth and flush with the sidewalk. The tree grate covers the entire opening in the paving and allows people to safely walk and stand on it without grade change or stepping in the soil. Grates are usually made of metal, often cast iron, and have many small openings that allow water to flow into the pit and the soil to breathe. A gap of a few inches between the grate and the soil surface allows the roots to grow and the soil to expand and contract without raising the grate. It also protects the tree roots from soil compaction that would be caused by foot traffic over time.

Tree grates come in many patterns to complement the identity and design of the surrounding space, and they can be very handsome and interesting features. They are offered in numerous standard sizes and are usually square, round, or rectangular. Grates come in two or more pieces so they can be installed around the tree. There is an opening in the center for the trunk. Some have expandable openings to allow for tree growth, and some have openings for uplights. Tree grates are usually set into a metal frame that is installed in the pavement opening. The frame must be installed flat and true for the grate to sit properly.

Objects such as canes, high heels, and wheelchair wheels can get caught in tree grate openings. To prevent or minimize this problem, grates with small openings are available. Americans with Disabilities Act (ADA) compliance requires that surface openings be no greater than ½ inch wide and that the long direction of elongated openings run perpendicular to the primary direction of pedestrian traffic.[2]

Cast iron is the material most commonly used for tree grates, but cast aluminum, cast bronze, plastic, and fabricated steel are sometimes used.

6.29 This tree grate provides a flush,
safe walkable surface on the sidewalk.
(The same cannot be said
of the abandoned bike in the
background.) Photo credit: Bill Main

6.30 Now what? Trees sometimes
outgrow their grates. Photo credit:
Bill Main

6.31 It's hard being a tree in the big
city: what happens when enough bike
racks aren't provided. Photo credit:
Bill Main

Slippery surfaces and finishes should be avoided. Applied finishes can be problematic due to the wear and tear of foot traffic, snow shoveling, and other activity. Cast gray iron is usually left unfinished and weathers naturally to a dark rusty patina.

A tree guard is a vertical cage structure that surrounds and protects the tree trunk from impacts, scrapes, bike chains, initial carving, and other injuries. Tree guards are not as commonly used as tree grates, but when they are the two are usually used together, with the guard bolted to the grate. Tree guards are another level of protection for trees, which they need most when they are young and small. A tree guard can be removed if the tree outgrows the guard. Tree guards can also provide ornamental qualities.

A typical tree guard is about 5 feet high, is fabricated from steel, and is painted or powder-coated. While the tree guard protects the tree, what protects the tree guard? Guards are often used as makeshift bike racks and are subject to the impacts and scrapes that otherwise would have damaged the tree. A tough finish and occasional touch-ups may be in order.

Railings

Railings are used primarily for safety—as barriers to keep people from falling over edges and as handrails for navigating steps and slopes. In outdoor spaces with many edges or ground level changes, railings can become visually important by virtue of their quantity and prominence. Local building codes establish regulations regarding the location and design of railings.

One challenge presented by outdoor railings arises from the fact that they are often fabricated and finished locally, due to the variety of pieces required and the need to fit them to as-built site conditions. If sophisticated finishing capabilities are not locally available, it may be difficult to control colors and finishes and match them exactly with furniture and site elements obtained from other sources.

Lighting

Exterior lighting is a complex subject that goes well beyond the scope of this book. However, a discussion of outdoor furniture and elements would be incomplete without at least touching on the aspects of lighting that relate to furniture and furniture selection.

Lights are important both functionally and visually in the landscape.

- Lighting makes spaces usable at night, allows people to move about safely, and helps people feel more secure.

- Lighting is an aspect of security and can play a role in reducing crime and vandalism.
- Lighting can and should play an important aesthetic role, both in the quality of illumination and in the design and placement of poles, fixtures, and related support structures.

We will focus here on aesthetic issues, more specifically on the physical light fixtures and poles rather than on illumination.

Definitions:

- *Lamp:* the actual source of the light
- *Fixture:* the housing that holds the lamp and other parts necessary to produce the proper light and protect the lamp
- *Pole:* the support structure that holds the fixture, positioning it properly in space so that the desired area is illuminated and providing an electrical conduit from the fixture to a connection to a power source

Fixtures and poles can be categorized as either decorative or functional. Decorative elements have been designed with aesthetics in mind and are intended to be seen and enjoyed. Functional fixtures and poles are often built-in, hidden, or used in areas where aesthetics are not emphasized, such as a parking lot.

Decorative fixtures and poles can be significant visual features in the landscape:

- They are found wherever light is needed in public spaces.
- Light poles are tall, visually prominent elements.
- There are many of them, spaced regularly along streets and throughout spaces.
- People tend to be near them because that is where the light is at night.
- Poles may also serve to hold signage, banners, planters, or seasonal decorations.

Local building codes establish numerous regulations covering outdoor lighting, and these should be consulted before undertaking any lighting project.

Path lights and lighted bollards are roughly 3 feet tall and help to define spaces and/or illuminate walkways and building entries and exits. Path lights are located at regular distances along the path. The spacing depends on the level of lighting required on the path and the characteristics of the lamp and fixture.

Pedestrian lights along sidewalks and in open spaces start at about 12 feet high and go higher, depending on the illumination required and the characteristics of the lamp and fixture. A taller pole will spread the light over a greater area. Seeking economy in initial project costs and ongoing maintenance costs may lead to using taller, brighter lights because fewer will be needed. On the other hand, using more lights may increase the ability to deliver more specific, controlled effects and environments. Poles for pedestrian lights are often bolted to a concrete footing, which supports the load and allows leveling of the pole. The footing may be below grade and hidden by paving that abuts the pole. Alternatively, the footing may be above ground with the anchor bolts concealed by a shroud at the base of the pole.

Light pollution is a growing concern. Light pollution is defined as light that escapes into areas in which it is not desired, whether into a residence's window or up to the sky. Light pollution wastes energy and annoys people and communities subject to it. The design of the fixture, its positioning on the pole, and the use of highly directional light sources (e.g., LEDs) can help control light pollution.

Light poles may be multifunctional. They can hold banners, planters, signage, and seasonal decorations. Brackets, which typically clamp around the pole rather than penetrating it, can be attached for this purpose. Check with the manufacturer regarding attachments, as these may affect the structural strength of the pole and the load requirements (including wind load) that it must meet.

People are aware of light because it provides such an essential function. They don't use poles and fixtures in the same way, but these elements are also very important. Poles and fixtures should be designed to please the eye, deliver the light, resist the elements and vandalism, and be easy to service. The design of the pole and fixture should complement the space. Consideration should be given to both the overall view of the pole and fixture and to the base of the pole, with which pedestrians may get much closer. The color and finish of poles may be coordinated or matched with the furniture used in the area.

6.32 Ornamental bases for street light poles come in many styles. This one has acquired a distressed patina. Photo credit: Bill Main

Endnotes

1. Chris Calori, Signage and Wayfinding (Hoboken, NJ: John Wiley & Sons, 2007), 71–75.
2. Susan Goltsman and T. Gilbert, "Access to the Outdoor Setting," in *Landscape Architectural Graphic Standards*, ed. Leonard Hopper (Hoboken, NJ: John Wiley & Sons, 2007), 278–79.

7.   Selecting Site Furniture

Six Categories That Drive Selection

Good site furniture design meets requirements in six categories:

- Durability
- Safety
- Form and character
- Function
- Sustainability
- Value

The weight given each will depend on the situation and the client. Site furniture design is the process of creating outdoor furniture solutions to meet this set of six needs in such a way that the resulting products are compelling and suitable for use at a particular site or at a range of different sites. Custom furniture is usually intended to be site-specific, while standard catalog furniture is intended to be more broadly applicable.

High levels of durability and safety are to be expected from virtually all site furniture (exceptions are described below). The importance placed on the other four factors may vary considerably, depending on the project. Each type of furniture (bench, chair, receptacle, etc.) presents a different set of design challenges driven by functional demands. Understanding how these six design issues are to be addressed is critical to achieving great outdoor space solutions.

Durability

Durability is often cited as the first requirement of site furniture. Most owners want to "set it and forget it." They expect many years of public use with minimal need for repairs, touch-ups, or replacement.

How long should site furniture last? While life span varies, a reasonable goal for most locations is for the furniture to last until the space undergoes its next renovation. This may be ten, fifteen, or twenty years. When selecting furniture keep this timeline in mind.

Chairs and umbrellas are the exceptions to the rule. Some lightweight chairs and fabric umbrellas have life spans as short as three to five years. They are often made of thin materials to save weight and money, and consequently may fail sooner under heavy use. The sun will quickly fade cheap umbrella fabrics.

Good durability is the outcome of thoughtful design, an ample quantity of quality materials, good engineering, careful fabrication, and appropriate installation. Site furniture should not require much maintenance, but if it does, timely attention may add years to its life (See Chapter 11).

In the United States there are almost no required tests or standards for durability or structural integrity of site furniture. A few clients have established their own standards for bollards, but these are for crash resistance, not true durability. Some manufacturers do their own testing, and it is a good idea to ask manufacturers if and how their products are tested for durability.

Useful structural and mechanical tests include:

- Static load tests
- Drop tests
- Repetitive load tests
- Tip tests
- Repetitive operation tests

Finish tests include UV and salt exposure tests. Wind and snow load tests may be appropriate for umbrellas and overhead structures.

Site furniture failures can occur in numerous ways. The most common failures occur to finishes, structure, moving parts, and connections.

Finish failures may be the result of manufacturing defect, impact, vandalism, UV exposure, or simply the wearing away of the finish through use. These failures degrade the appearance of the furniture, but they may not affect its structure or function if they are repaired before the underlying structural materials are compromised (see Chapter 10). Skateboards often cause damage to finishes, for example, but much less often cause structural damage.

Structural failures may occur because of manufacturing or materials defects, impact damage, connection failures, or structural designs that are just not adequate for the public environment. For example, jumping on a bench may break wood slats if they are thin or contain a flaw.

Most site furniture pieces don't have moving parts, but those that do, such as receptacles and umbrellas, may suffer failures of hinges, locks, and mechanisms. Very robust mechanisms are essential to stand up to the rough service and repeated slamming common in public spaces. Finishes will usually wear off moving parts quickly, so these should be made of stainless steel, aluminum, brass, or other materials that don't rely on their finish to prevent corrosion.

Connection failures can happen when bolts loosen, screws pull out, rivets pop, glues fail, seams tear, or welds are defective. These usually occur gradually, through repetitive use of the furniture. Connection failures can lead to progressive structural failure. For example, loose bolts or screws on a bench may lead to racking and twisting, which further stress the connection, leading to a complete collapse of the bench when weighted. Complete failure can often be prevented by periodically checking connections and tightening any that have loosened.

Durability is the result of the absence of any failures or the timely repair of minor ones.

Understand what is covered in the product warranty and for what length of time. It is fairly common for finishes to be covered differently than structures, often for a shorter period.

7.1 Heavy weights are used in static load, drop and repetitive cycle testing to verify the strength and durability of benches. Photo credit: Bill Main

Safety

By its nature (robust materials, few moving parts) site furniture is relatively safe, but there are things to look out for. Safety requires good-quality furniture to begin with, appropriate installation, and periodic inspection and maintenance over time. Manufacturers should provide detailed installation and maintenance requirements.

Stability is the key to seating and table safety. Seating should be securely anchored (see Chapter 11) or, if freestanding, should not tip, even if users sit on the edge. Folding umbrellas should be lowered when the wind comes up to keep them from blowing over and taking the tables with them. Fixed umbrellas must always be anchored to the ground. Chairs with bent legs should be discarded rather than straightened, which can cause metal fatigue. All furniture should be free of sharp edges, splinters, finger traps, protruding screw tips, and similar hazards.

Some clients prefer side-opening or tilting litter receptacles, rather than those that require lifting trash out of the top, due to concerns about back strain and workers' compensation claims stemming from lifting injuries.

Form and Character

Site furniture selection often starts with the design theme of the space. Whether it's contemporary, transitional, traditional, or something else, the site furniture should fit with and support the overall design of the space.

7.2 This long granite backless bench is a great visual fit with the rectilinear architecture and planters at the site. Photo credit: Bill Main

Because site furniture is often used in settings with a range of architectural styles, the right appearance may be one that fits in rather than stands out. In this way the furniture can help unify the overall appearance of a site rather than introduce yet another look. Other situations may call for a signature or statement piece that adds interest, a focal point, or identity.

Given the long life of site furniture, the design selected should be one that will stand the test of time, and not appear outdated or tired in just a few years.

Function

Every piece of site furniture should perform its intended function well—and for a long time. Functions will, of course, vary a great deal depending on the type of furniture. The functions of furniture should be intuitive (easy to understand without instructions) and simple for people to use. Functions for service within furniture elements may be concealed to limit tampering. For example, litter receptacles are sometimes equipped with concealed latches or locks to discourage people from opening them and going through the trash. For more about function in specific types of site furniture, see Chapters 4, 5, and 6.

Sustainability

Sustainability is becoming an increasingly important factor in all product selection, site furniture included. Site furniture in general has many sustainable attributes. (See Chapter 12 for details.)

Sustainability factors to consider when selecting outdoor furniture include:

- Expected life span
- Use of sustainable materials
- Embodied energy
- Energy consumption (for example, lighting)
- Contribution to sustainable activities or practices (for example, bike racks, recycling receptacles, planters, and mass transit shelters)
- Recyclability at the end of the item's useful life

Additionally, a strong case can be made that good site furniture contributes to positive outdoor experiences and the attendant health and healing benefits.

Value

The value of the site furniture is the perceived monetary worth. Price alone does not create good value. An item is a good value if the total experience it provides—its collective features and benefits—is worth more than the dollars asked for purchase and installation.

The purchase and installation of site furniture is a one-time capital expense, whereas the benefits are realized over time. Therefore, the value equation should consider long-term and even intangible benefits such as warranty coverage, future availability of replacement parts, coordination of furniture with project management, and timely and accurate information. Some furniture may be shipped unassembled, requiring on-site assembly labor and oversight.

It has been said that the initial happiness of a low price is long forgotten if it is followed by frustration and disappointment in a product that hasn't measured up to its expectations. Good value is the total package.

Context Is Key

Some of the most celebrated furniture designs for interiors are renowned precisely because they make iconoclastic statements about form, function, materials, or the zeitgeist. Furniture for outdoor spaces, in contrast, is typically designed to address context: the architectural surroundings and the natural environments in which the furniture is placed.

The relative impact of furniture design may be tempered by the context. The design of benches placed at intervals along a wilderness path to provide occasional rest for bird watchers may be less critical than the design of seating in an urban plaza where it may play a role in defining the character of the place and attracting people to enter and stay.

Criteria for Design Selections Depend on the Selector

Design professionals typically have three constituencies to take into account: themselves, the owner, and potential end users.

Designers

Form is critical to professional designers. Our discussions reveal that architects and landscape architects are most often attracted to furniture elements on the basis of their visual qualities, view the design of the furniture as integral to the design of the space, and consider furniture decisions essential to maintaining visual control of the site. For this group, the aesthetics and appropriateness of the furniture design to the particular place are critical. Designers may see their role as helping the owner stretch beyond their initial comfort zone to understand and support an investment in design.

Owners

The design preferences of owners often tend toward furniture that makes statements about themselves or their organizations, and frequently have a lot to do with the bottom line. (That includes a consideration of real cost and perceived cost. In an interesting twist, some public agency clients have expressed the caveat that furniture in their public spaces should not look "expensive," regardless of actual cost.) Clients may want to match furniture they already own. Or they may have an image they want to project or an identity they want to incorporate. Owners are very concerned with maintenance, management, and functional issues because they will live with the furniture. They may opt for designs that promise durability, convenience, and minimal care.

End Users

End users most often have a say in the selection of furniture design in public projects where community input is required. Users of neighborhood spaces may have a sense of ownership and notions about what "looks right." They may insist on basic utility and on what makes them feel comfortable, both physically and emotionally. The issue of comfort is particularly important in furniture that will be used by the elderly. Benches with backs, armrests, and contoured seats are particularly important for these users.

Sourcing Furniture That's Right for the Site

There are three major avenues for sourcing outdoor furniture: standard products, special products, and custom products.

Standard Furniture Products

Most standard manufactured outdoor furniture products are designed to blend into the landscape and complement prevailing architectural styles. This is usually accomplished with simple forms, common materials, neutral colors, and structural characteristics (e.g., slats or perforations) that allow some transparency. The goal is to provide furniture elements that contribute positively to the general impression of a site without making a strong individual statement. The standard furniture available in the market achieves these objectives with varied degrees of sophistication and success. Most manufacturers of site furniture typically try to include a variety of styles and materials in their collections to address a range of architectural and site conditions. Whether the site aspires to look sophisticated or rustic, formal or fun, contemporary or traditional, or perhaps express a theme (nautical, for example), a design that will satisfy the need can almost always be found.

Standard products are almost always the less expensive options. There is good, better, and best site furniture out there. In general, as the level of

7.3 Standard product: a four-seat steel bench. Photo credit: copyright © Jim Powell

design refinement, engineering elegance, material quality, and workmanship increases, so does the cost.

Custom Furniture

On the other end of the spectrum there is custom furniture—elements designed specifically as part of the design professional's overall vision for a space. Landscape architect Tom Oslund explains, "We see the furniture on our projects as sculptural pieces that resonate the ideas of the design for the entire space." Custom design and manufacturing services are offered by some major commercial manufacturers and by dedicated custom shops. Some designers report success using local craftsmen for simple custom projects. Custom designing and building is a luxury not supported by most project budgets. Oslund's fallback position is the one followed by most design practices: "For the projects that need more cost efficiency in construction, we find the most beautiful standard furnishings that will work."

Specials

In between standard and custom are specials. These are standard furniture products modified by the manufacturer to meet specific needs on specific projects. Specials may involve modifications to function (a higher

7.4 Custom product: a bench at Surfer's Paradise, Australia, clearly designed to express the identity of the place. Photo credit: Bill Main

back on a bench), materials (aluminum slats instead of steel), finishes (signature colors), or identity (a laser-cut logo). They almost always involve an upcharge from standard product costs but are typically less expensive than custom-designed furniture. (See Table 7.1.)

Setting Standards

Designers have a vested interest in creating and maintaining a common design language, reflected in consistency of forms and colors, throughout the spectrum of furniture and related elements in a space. Establishing an overview with standards is important to the initial design of the project and to the preservation of project character over time. Furniture elements may consist of a family of related products from a single manufacturer, a collection of furniture elements with complementary characteristics assembled from several manufacturers, or a combination of standard and custom-designed elements.

For construction projects, designers will prepare a detailed set of plans and specifications that clearly describe the selected site furniture and acceptable alternatives.

For municipalities, urban districts, or campuses developing longer-term amenity, identity, or wayfinding systems, the design firms involved may publish guidelines that include selected and approved products in all the

7.5 Special product: a logo laser-cut into a standard product exemplifies a common special request. Photo credit: Bill Main

Table 7.1: Advantages and Disadvantages of Standard, Custom, and Special Products

	ADVANTAGES	DISADVANTAGES
Standard product	Lower cost	May not find what you're looking for
	The bugs have been worked out	No special identity
	Quick delivery	
	Simple to order and specify	
	Outcome more assured	
	Warranty	
Special products	Meets specific needs	More costly
	Can be tailored to the site conditions	More planning and fabrication time
	Outcome fairly assured	May be harder to get replacement parts
	Standard product, modified	
	Warranty	
Custom products	Unique identity and design	Expensive
	Do something never done before	Requires extensive design and engineering attention
		Outcome less assured
		Limited warranty
		May be difficult and expensive to get replacement parts

7.6 A completed project in Austin, Texas, includes a package of designs: a custom stone bench, standard steel benches, and bike racks, all acquired from a variety of sources and coordinated to achieve visual coherence and integrity. Photo credit: Bill Main

7.7 Las Vegas: love it or hate it, there's no mistaking this district's identity. Photo credit: Bill Main

major categories: seating, litter receptacles, lighting, bollards, bike racks, planters, and so on, along with plans and descriptions for how they are to be located, oriented, and installed. This practice is a good means of controlling design direction and site integrity in both the short and long term in cases where implementation will take place over an extended period and perhaps be carried out by municipal employees.

8.   Accessible Design

It has been about a half century since "accessible design" entered the lexicon to describe the elements and process that enable people with disabilities to more fully engage in the built environment. We've come a long way since that time, from the first national standards for accessible design, published by the American National Standards Institute (ANSI) in 1961, to the Architectural Barriers Act of 1968, which was the first federal legislation to mandate accessible design in federal facilities, and the landmark Americans with Disabilities Act (ADA) of 1990, which provided new civil rights protections for people with disabilities and ADA accessibility guidelines (ADAAG).[1]

The codes and guidelines set forth in these acts were developed to address the needs of people in wheelchairs and the blind. Fortunately, thinking about accessible design continues to evolve. In 1997 the Center for Universal Design at North Carolina State University published version 2.0 of the Principles of Universal Design, which moves beyond a focus on removing barriers and mitigating obstacles for specific classes of people to defining more general and universally applicable criteria of usability for products and spaces. The Center defines "universal design" as "the design of products and environments to be usable by all people, to the greatest extent possible, without the need for adaptation or specialized design."[2]

The seven principles of universal design are the starting point for the design of accessible furniture and spaces.

The Seven Principles of Universal Design

Principle 1: Equitable use

 The design is useful and marketable to people with diverse disabilities.

Principle 2: Flexibility in use

 The design accommodates a wide range of individual preferences and abilities.

Principle 3: Simple and intuitive use

 Use of the design is easy to understand regardless of the user's experience, knowledge, language skills, or level of concentration.

Principle 4: Perceptible information

   The design communicates necessary information effectively regardless of ambient conditions or the user's sensory abilities.

Principle 5: Tolerance for error

   The design minimizes hazards and the adverse consequences of accidental or unintended actions.

Principal 6: Low physical effort

   The design can be used efficiently and comfortable and with a minimum of fatigue.

Principle 7: Size and space for approach and use

   Appropriate size and space are provided for approach, reach, manipulation, and use regardless of the user's body size, posture, or mobility.

Universal design, also referred to as "inclusive design," takes into account the needs of a broad range of people, including those with physical disabilities, learning disabilities, and the frailties of age. In addressing not just physical features and conditions but human factors such as experience, knowledge, language skills, and preferences, these principles broaden the scope and substance of what genuine accessibility entails.

Susan Goltsman, a landscape architect and principal of MIG, Inc., is a respected advocate for the disabled and designer of accessible spaces. She explains, "Universal design is seamless design that is friendly and inclusive. It doesn't mean that everyone who uses the space uses it in the same way. It means that there's some way to design the space so that it both accommodates the widest range of abilities and is also flexible enough for anyone to use it."

This inclusive approach to spaces applies to the furniture in those spaces as well. We propose that furniture elements and their placement in outdoor settings follow three principles of universal design to achieve accessibility:

1. It accommodates everyone who wants to enjoy outdoor spaces: young children, teenagers, and seniors; parents with strollers; individuals, families, and groups; people with disabilities, including the blind, people in wheelchairs, and those using walkers and canes.

2. It segregates no one, intentionally or unintentionally. The goal is to make spaces and experiences available without physical obstacle or social marginalization.

3. It provides choice and quality of experience for as many users as possible.

Comprehensive guidelines for achieving accessibility in site planning and design are provided in "Access to the Outdoor Setting," by Susan Goltsman, FASLA, and Timothy Gilbert, ASLA, in *Landscape Architectural Graphic Standards*.[3] We highly recommend this source, which draws on the authors' deep commitment to inclusive design and extensive experience in the design of accessible spaces. Some of the standards included in that reference document are based on ADA regulations. But "Access to the Outdoor Setting" goes beyond ADA mandates, reflecting Goltsman's conviction, echoed by many advocates of universal design, that "you can meet the letter of the ADA law and still not have true universal design."

That being said, some projects require designers and clients to meet ADA guidelines. When it comes to furniture in outdoor public spaces, this can occasion some confusion. The only outdoor furniture for which ADA regulations have been specifically written is tables with attached seats (picnic tables). Regulations for other outdoor furniture elements are derived from those written for interior furniture.

In an effort to clarify applicable ADA requirements for furniture in outdoor spaces and help designers achieve ADA compliance on projects for which it is mandated, we offer the following information.

About ADA

The Americans with Disabilities Act of 1990 was signed into law on July 26, 1990, and later amended with changes effective January 1, 2009. The ADA is a wide-ranging civil rights law that prohibits, under certain circumstances, discrimination based on disability. Disability is defined as "a physical or mental impairment that substantially limits a major life activity."

Under Title III of the act, "Public Accommodations and Commercial Facilities," no individual may be discriminated against on the basis of disability with regard to the full and equal enjoyment of the goods, services, facilities, or accommodations of any place of public accommodation by any person who owns, leases (or leases to), or operates that place. Public accommodations include most places of lodging (such as inns and hotels), recreation, transportation, education, and dining, along with stores, care providers, and places of public displays, among other things. Title III specifies that all new construction (that is, construction, modification, or alterations) after the effective date of the ADA must be fully compliant with ADAAG.[4] Title III also applies to already existing facilities.

Whether or not a given project is required to comply with ADA guidelines depends on the type and location of the project. States, counties, and/or municipalities assess and approve projects and may set additional accessibility requirements. For example, many state and/or municipal codes now require fast-food venues to provide wheelchair access. Enforcement agencies employ oversight committees, often staffed by disabled persons, to review drawings and provide comment. Design practitioners should review ADA guidelines and check with local and state agencies to confirm applicable mandates and reporting requirements for individual projects.

ADA Guidelines

ADA guidelines applicable to (but not necessarily written for) site furnishings address how benches, tables, tables with attached seating (picnic tables), and trash receptacles must accommodate people in wheelchairs. They also address the safe placement of site furnishing elements in relation to walkways and ramps to ensure that they do not endanger the safety or hinder the mobility of people in wheelchairs and the blind.

Bench standards are designed to enable people in wheelchairs to pull up next to stationary benches and, if desired, transfer safely to a bench. (Transfer implies arms installed at appropriate locations along the bench, although arms on benches are not specified in current ADA guidelines. Transfer, however, is more likely to be needed in a changing area such as a locker room than outside.) There are no ADA requirements for chairs. (People seated in wheelchairs typically do not transfer to standard chairs. In most cases they want to be able to pull up to tables in their wheelchairs and comfortably join the party.) Table standards are designed to enable occupants of wheelchairs sufficient surface space and proximity to attain comfortable reach and enough undertable space volume to provide access and maneuverability.

Seat walls are not addressed in ADA guidelines. To support universal accessibility in practice, one could follow the requirements for benches and design seat walls within a setting in such a way that a wheelchair can be positioned with wheels parallel to the end of the wall at a suitable height. Note that minimum dimensions for walkways must be maintained. (See "Circulation," page 193.)

Benches

- Benches must be installed in place (attached).
- Benches must be affixed to a wall or provide back support.
- Clear ground space for wheelchairs (minimum dimension 30 by 48 inches) must be provided beside installed benches.

Dimensions

- Minimum seat length: 42 inches
- Minimum seat back length: 42 inches
- Seat depth: 20 inches minimum, 24 inches maximum
- Minimum back height (measured vertically): 18 inches

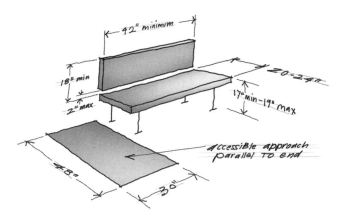

8.1 Clear ground space for a wheelchair next to an installed bench. Credit: Robert G. Chipman, ASLA

- Seat height (above the ground or floor): 17 inches minimum, 19 inches maximum
- Maximum space between the top of the seat and the bottom of the back: 2 inches (no gap is required)

Structural Strength

- Allowable stresses shall not be exceeded for materials used when a vertical or horizontal force of 250 pounds is applied at any point on the seat, fastener, mounting device, or supporting structure.

Wet Locations

- The surface under benches installed in wet locations shall be slip-resistant and shall not accumulate water.

Clear Ground Space

- Clear floor or ground space for wheelchairs shall be positioned at the end of the bench and parallel to the short axis of the bench. (See Figure 8.1.)

(Note: all drawings in this chapter are based on graphics in *Landscape Architectural Graphic Standards*.)

Practical Recommendations

Current ADA guidelines for benches do not specify arms. However, the next version will specify arms, which provide necessary support as sitters lower themselves into and lift out of the seated position. This is especially

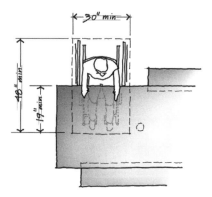

8.2 Clear floor or ground space for a wheelchair. Credit: Robert G. Chipman, ASLA

critical for the weak and elderly and for people with a variety of disabilities including arthritis and poor motor control. *Landscape Architectural Graphic Standards* states: "Accessible fixed benches must have at least one armrest that can withstand 250 pounds of force in any direction" (p. 281).

Although not addressed in the ADA guidelines, experts recommend providing flat negative space in front of benches to allow sitters to push their feet back behind the front edge of the seat to aid them in getting up.

Clear Floor or Ground Space for Wheelchairs

Size and Approach

The minimum clear floor or ground space required to accommodate a single, stationary wheelchair and occupant is 30 by 48 inches. Clear floor or ground space for wheelchairs may be part of the knee space required under some objects.

Relationship of Maneuvering Clearance to Wheelchair Spaces

One full, unobstructed side of the clear floor or ground space for a wheelchair shall adjoin or overlap an accessible route or adjoin another wheelchair clear floor space. If a clear ground or floor space is located in an alcove or otherwise confined on all or part of three sides, additional maneuvering clearances shall be provided.

8.3 An example of a bench that conforms to ADA dimensional requirements. It has clear space for a wheelchair next to it. Photo credit: Bill Main

8.4 Most typical litter receptacles will meet ADA guidelines as long as there is clear access to them. Photo credit: Bill Main

Surfaces for Wheelchair Spaces

Ground and floor spaces shall be stable, firm, and slip-resistant. Changes in level are not permitted with the exception of slopes not steeper than 1:50.

Practical Recommendation

Although not specified in ADA guidelines, it is recommended that ground space for wheelchairs extend at least one foot behind the back of an adjacent fixed bench to enable shoulder-to-shoulder positioning of sitters. The goal is to provide the disabled with the most readily usable integrated settings possible.

Fixed or Built-in Seating and Tables

- Clear ground or floor space shall be provided. (See "Clear Floor or Ground Space for Wheelchairs," above.)
- Such clear ground or floor space shall not overlap knee space by more than 19 inches. (See Figure 8.2.)
- Tables and benches must have no sharp edges or protruding hardware that may be hazardous.
- The distance from the tabletop to the ground must be between 28 and 34 inches and the distance from the table bottom to the ground must be 27 to 29 inches. (See Figure 8.5.)

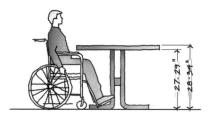

8.5 Wheelchair clearance under a table. Credit: Robert G. Chipman, ASLA

- A clear 36-inch space, measured from the back of the seat, must be provided around the table for wheelchair access.
- A minimum of 5 percent (or 1 of 20) of the individual dining table spaces of buildings and facilities must be accessible. (some experts recommend that 50 percent of all tables and benches on a site be accessible, and dispersed throughout the site. Actual requirements for any given site may depend on decisions by local authorities.)

Knee and Toe Clearances

Toe clearance is the space under the table between the ground and 9 inches above the ground. Knee clearance is the space between 9 inches above the ground and 27 inches above the ground.

Where seating for people in wheelchairs is provided at tables or counters, a space at least 27 inches high, 30 inches wide, and 19 inches deep shall be provided. (See Figures 8.2 and 8.5.)

The volume of space under the table is key. These dimensions were established to ensure adequate space for wheelchair maneuverability and comfortable reach. Clearances are measured in relation to the usable clear floor space. When determining clearance under a table for required turning or maneuvering space, care should be taken to ensure that the space is clear of any obstructions such as support structures.

Tables

Dimensions

- Minimum width: 30 inches
- Depth (under table): 19 inches
- Height (above the floor or ground): 28 inches minimum, 34 inches maximum
- A clear 36-inch space, measured from the seat, must be provided around the table for wheelchair access. (See Figures 8.2 and 8.5.)

Trash and/or Recycling Receptacles

- The receptacle must be located on stable, firm ground with a clear space minimum of 30 inches by 48 inches and a slope of 2 percent (3 percent allowed if necessary for drainage).
- The receptacle and/or operating mechanism must be between 15 and 48 inches above the ground for front approach and between 9 and 54 inches for side approach.
- Receptacle openings must be operable with a single hand manipulation and require less than 5 pounds of pressure to operate. This requirement

does not apply to hinged lids and controls designed to exclude large animals.

Practical Recommendation

Place dog waste bag dispensers and disposal container openings at the low range of receptacle openings as described above.

Circulation

ADA guidelines address site circulation in detail. For the most part, these regulations are properly the subject of general site planning. We are concerned here with regulations on the location and dimensions of walkways and ramps in relation to the placement of furniture.

- Walkways and ramps must have a minimum width of 36 inches. When a 24-inch deep bench is placed along the walkway, the walkway must be 60 inches wide.
- Where benches are used in outdoor spaces in which the slope is greater than 1:20, they must be placed on landings.

There is no ADA-mandated dimension for the distance between the front edge of a bench and a walkway; 30 inches is optimal to avoid sitters tripping those walking by.

Practical Recommendation

Circulation areas around furniture should be firm, stable, and continuous. Avoid uneven brick pavers, cobblestones, and wide gaps between pavers, which can cause pain in people with spinal disabilities, as well gravel and soft trail materials, which can get spongy and sink after rain.

Protruding Objects in Circulation Paths

An ADA advisory provides the following description of how blind people navigate through space. It is helpful for understanding the regulations governing protruding objects, which in the context of site furniture apply to elements such as wall-mounted benches and litter receptacles mounted to posts.

The two principal cane techniques are the touch technique, where the cane is arced from side to side and touches points outside both shoulders, and the diagonal technique, where the cane is held in a stationary position diagonally across the body with the tip just above the ground at a point outside one shoulder and the handle extended to a point outside the other shoulder. When one of these techniques is used and the element is in the detectable range, it gives a person sufficient time to detect the element with the cane before there is body contact.

- Objects projecting from walls with their leading edges between 27 and 80 inches above the ground or finished floor shall protrude no more than 4 inches into walks, halls, corridors, etc.
- Objects mounted with their leading edges at or below 27 inches above the ground or finished floor may protrude any amount.
- Objects mounted on posts or pylons at heights between 27 and 80 inches above the ground or finished floor may overhang a maximum of 12 inches.
- Protruding objects shall not reduce the clear width of an accessible route or maneuvering space.

ADA-Compliant Furniture Products

There are few standard exterior benches or tables with attached seating available that precisely meet ADA standards. We believe this is the case primarily because of limited demand and because the ADA bench guidelines were originally conceived for use in locker rooms, saunas, and steamrooms. These guidelines are sometimes, but not often, applied to outdoor spaces. Manufacturers of outdoor furniture often address wheelchair accessibility in ways that do not strictly meet ADAAG or by making modifications to existing products. These may involve significant changes in size or structure, or they may entail the simple reconfiguration of parts.

For example, on picnic tables with attached seating, one seat may be omitted to permit a wheelchair to approach the table. On rectangular tables a bench may be made shorter to allow a wheelchair to draw up at the end and still fit within the space defined by the tabletop. These solutions require adequate table height and a table structure that provides sufficient undertable clearance.

8.6 An accessible table with attached seats near the concession area of a city park and beach. Photo credit: Bill Main

In addition, custom-designed products are sometimes created to address ADA concerns.

How Designers See It

ADA guidelines provide useful minimal standards that help enable a vast group of people with physical disabilities to access and enjoy outdoor public space. But they only point in the general direction. "What's needed in our profession is a more nuanced understanding of how disabled people function," says Kevin Jensen, AIA, ADA disability access coordinator for the City of San Francisco Department of Public Works. "We have to be mindful that we are designing who can and who can't use a space." Many landscape architects and other design professionals have embraced the opportunity.

The results are evident in well-designed accessible outdoor spaces throughout the country. Kent Sundberg, ASLA, a landscape architect at WRT in Philadelphia, has worked on many ADA-compliant projects. He says, "We do it because it's right to give everyone the same opportunities. If we're conscientious about social equity, we will design for ADA. The idea is to maximize the number of people who can participate in outdoor spaces without obstacle, embarrassment, or pain."

Jerry Smith, a landscape architect with MSI, Inc., and chair of the ASLA Healing Gardens Practice Network, sums up how ADA mandates relate to his work: "ADA is an understood regimen," he says. "But accessible design is so much more than that."

Landscape architects have used ADA guidelines to configure nonlinear outdoor settings that facilitate social interaction for people in wheelchairs. Design practitioners have creatively adapted guidelines to emerging conditions to ensure accessibility in outdoor spaces, for example, by specifying that bollards and planters (common as security barriers) used in lieu of or at curbs be placed at least 30 inches apart to ensure wheelchair clearance. WRT has used ADA guidelines for tables as a starting point to create custom-designed planters for healing gardens.

Endnotes

1. On ADAAG, see www.access-board.gov/adaag/html/adaag.htm.
2. Center for Universal Design's website, www.design.nscu.edu/cud/about_ud/udprinciples.htm.
3. Leonard J. Hopper, ed., *Landscape Architectural Graphic Standards* (Hoboken, NJ: John Wiley & Sons, 2007), 278–93.
4. See www.access-board.gov/adaag/html/adaag.htm.

9. Management

Management can play a critical role in maximizing the short- and long-term success of exterior spaces. But the importance of management is often under-recognized. Many projects invest heavily in initial capital spending to achieve a desired physical space but make a limited commitment to funding the management of ongoing operations and activities at the site. The result can be underutilization of the asset and loss of control over the destiny of the space.

Good, proactive management is essential to help a space achieve its goals and keep its constituents happy. Managers must understand the needs of users, owners, and the employees who take care of the space. Managers and employees who are regularly present on-site have a unique opportunity to make the space successful, however that is defined. Planners and designers of new spaces should work closely with the people who will manage those spaces so that design and operations support each other.

Good management requires:

- Leadership to establish goals and plans, and to direct the effort to get them done
- A workforce to perform necessary tasks
- An operating budget sufficient to the challenge
- Good relationships with key constituencies of the space

The scope and scale of management will depend on the size, type, location, and goals set for a space. Every space will benefit from looking well cared for. The "broken window" theory suggests that taking care of the small things, whether it's a missing windowpane or overflowing trash, will help prevent bigger problems by sending the message that people are paying attention to the space. Managers of successful spaces often find it necessary to supplement basic municipal services to accomplish this goal.

A relatively passive space might simply require:

- Regular maintenance such as trash removal, lawn and plant care, snow removal, and cleaning
- Ongoing inspection, repair, and replacement of elements in the space

In addition to those basic efforts, a more active space may also require an expanded set of management tasks:

- Developing sources of revenue
- Programming activities and special events
- Managing food and service vendors (including kiosks and cafés)
- Managing specialized venues such as ice rinks, running tracks, and dog walks
- Overseeing the daily and seasonal logistics of movable furniture such as chairs, tables, and umbrellas
- Establishing and enforcing smoking policies
- Organizing seasonal activities such as holiday decorations and flower plantings
- Generating publicity, advertising, and promotion
- Dealing with negative behavior and complaints
- Providing site security and safety
- Conducting postoccupancy evaluations (POEs)
- Promoting continual improvement

Some of these tasks involve site furniture in a major or minor way.

Regular Furniture Maintenance

- Litter removal

  Don't let litter receptacles overflow. This can be achieved through a combination of an adequate quantity of receptacles and frequent emptying. Anticipate peak use times such as lunch periods and special events, and bring in extra service staff and/or additional temporary receptacles. Pick up litter around the site.

- Lawn care

  Make sure mowing equipment does not strike the legs of furniture.

- Snow removal

  Make sure plows and shovels don't strike the furniture.

- Plant care

  Plant seasonal flowers in pots and planters. Water the plants and remove dead and dying ones.

- Cleaning

  Wipe off noticeable dust from chairs, tables, and benches. Remove bird droppings. Periodically pressure-wash litter receptacles and liners.

- Furniture inspection

  Staff members should keep an eye on the furniture in the course of their other duties and be on the lookout for any loose connections or broken parts. A thorough inspection and repair should be done at least once a year, with special attention to tightening connections, including all nuts, screws, and set screws. See Chapter 11 for more information.

Expanded Furniture Management Tasks

- Developing revenue sources

  Finding sources of revenue beyond the allocated budget is becoming a key management function. Major sources being developed today include parking, concession contracts, and income from sales, user fees, and donations. Some donation programs, such as the popular "donate a bench" program, involve putting the donor's name on the furniture.

- Programming activities and special events for the space

  Regular activities and special events can bring great crowds and vitality to public spaces. Kathy Madden of PPS says, "We propose a goal of ten activities you can do within a space. This supports triangulation, which means building one activity off another so that you can stay there for a while. So it's not just a ten-minute space. It could be a two-hour space." Activity settings such as children's play areas, refreshment stands, and outdoor reading rooms often include furniture. Special events, such as festivals, celebrations, rallies, concerts, sidewalk sales, and markets, may require rearranging furniture to clear space, adding temporary chairs and receptacles, and increasing the frequency of emptying the trash.

- Managing food and service vendors (including kiosks and cafés)

  Where there is food there is likely to be a need for tables, chairs, umbrellas, and litter receptacles. These may be owned and maintained by the vendor or by the owner of the space. Whoever owns them will be responsible for taking care of them; this usually includes arranging tables and chairs in the morning, stacking and locking them at night, putting umbrellas up and down as needed, and emptying the trash.

- Managing specialized venues such as ice rinks, running tracks, and dog walks

  These may present special furniture issues such as skate blade damage to benches caused by people using them for support while they tie their skates. The answer may be to use benches with sacrificial slats that can be replaced easily and economically.

- Overseeing daily logistics related to movable furniture such as chairs, tables, and umbrellas

  Many people favor movable furniture over fixed, but it comes with management issues attached. Simply put, the issue is that it does indeed move. Or more correctly, people move it. They move it around its home space, they move it to other spaces, and sometimes they remove it altogether.

  Movable chairs and tables may require regular collection and rearrangement to keep them in their home area. And, contrary to some wishful commentary, in the absence of security movable chairs do disappear. So if movable furniture is chosen (and there are many compelling reasons to choose it), plans should be made to manage it. This typically involves oversight, and locking when oversight isn't available. Chairs are usually secured by cabling. Sometimes this is done in place, using a long cable to lock the chairs to the table. Alternatively, the chairs can be stacked and cabled together. Another option is to forgo security and accept a level of "shrinkage."

- Establishing and enforcing smoking policies

Because smoking is prohibited or discouraged in so many interior spaces, a great amount of smoking now occurs outdoors. As a result, a significant number of venues are beginning to ban or limit outdoor smoking as well. This puts management of outdoor public spaces in the position of establishing and, if necessary, enforcing smoking policies. Alternatives include an outright ban, limiting the places in which smoking is permitted, or permitting smoking throughout the space. Smoking can be a very personal and emotional issue for both smokers and nonsmokers. Getting input from those affected may be helpful in establishing a workable policy, or at least in understanding the range of responses likely to be encountered.

When smokers were first forced out of buildings they congregated just outside entries or huddled under overhangs in the rain. This created a gauntlet of sorts for visitors and other employees and resulted in an accumulation of cigarette butts at entrances—not a welcome sight. In response, many facilities moved smoking areas further from entries, sometimes creating attractive break areas with seating and overhead protection to lure smokers. Today, some policies and local regulations restrict smoking in certain outdoor spaces such as eating areas, spaces near buildings, lines, stadiums, and, more generally, places where people congregate and secondhand smoke becomes an issue. In addition to establishing and enforcing policy, management must provide and service an adequate number of smoking receptacles in the appropriate places. The consequence of not doing so will be a rapidly accumulating abundance of cigarette butt litter.

- Overseeing seasonal activities such as storage, holiday decorations, and flower planting

Most good-quality site furniture does not need to be stored in the off-season unless it is in the way of other activities. You can bring the fabric umbrellas in and let the others remain outside. They may weather a bit more if left out, but the hassle and cost of moving and storing them probably outweigh any negative consequences. Holiday banners, lights, and decorations may need to be put up on light poles. These are usually clamped around poles rather than installed by drilling through them. Seasonal flowers should be planted in pots and planters and faded ones removed.

- Dealing with "undesirables"

The matter of dealing with homeless people and others deemed "undesirable" who may wish to use a space and its furniture falls to management. The consequence of not dealing with this issue is that the presence in numbers of people who behave in unusual or generally unacceptable ways may deter or frighten others who would otherwise use the space. There are several approaches to this dilemma:

- Safety in numbers

  The objective of this approach is to attract so many people to the space that a relatively few undesirable users don't seem scary. This works well in areas with high population density and a large user base.

- Accept and manage

  A corollary approach is to accept the presence of all visitors to the space as long as their behavior remains within the bounds of acceptability and they abide by the rules. In these cases staff typically keep an eye on the regulars and get to know them. Anyone who creates problems or violates the rules is spoken to, and progressive levels of enforcement are exercised. These first two approaches work well together.

- Go on the defensive

  A very different approach is to limit amenities and make the furniture itself defensive. In effect, this makes the furniture, or lack of it, do some of the enforcing. Examples of defensive furniture strategies include adding center arms on benches, tilting benches to prevent sleeping on them, and using sociofugal seating arrangements to reduce personal interaction. Unfortunately, defensive methods affect the comfort and experience of the space for everyone, not just those whose behavior management wants to discourage.

- Solving for skateboarding

Skateboarders may be fine and fun-loving young people, but they have become the bane of many public spaces. The common skateboard maneuver of sliding or "grinding" boards along the edges of urban features, such as seat walls, picnic tables, and benches, scrapes off the finish of the furnishings and grinds down the edges. The damage and disfiguring effects can be dramatic. And while some folks find skateboarders entertaining to watch, others find the sharp clacking sound of the boards hitting hard surfaces over and over intensely annoying. There are four approaches to dealing with the problem:

- Maintain vigilant oversight and prevent any skateboarding.

  The vigilance must be constant, as it only takes a few minutes to do a significant amount of damage.

- Provide a dedicated skateboard park.

  This may be a fine idea on several counts, but unfortunately it does not ensure that skateboarders will use only the designated skateboard park. (More is more.)

- Make the furniture defensive.

9.1 Skateboarding deterrence: Raised stainless steel pieces set into the joints of a stone seat wall provide a fairly discreet solution. Photo credit: Bill Main

9.2 Skateboarding deterrence: Multiple arms have been added to a wood seat wall to prevent sleeping as well as skateboarding. Sometimes the cure is worse than the disease. Photo credit: Bill Main

The usual method is to make any smooth, grindable edge unappealing by installing breaks or interruptions every 2 or 3 feet. These can be raised bumps, deep cuts, or objects such as armrests. The goal is simply not to provide any edge that's long enough to grind.

• Design for damage control.

The two most common furniture design strategies to limit damage by occasional skateboarding are fabricating vulnerable edges out of

9.3 Skateboarding deterrence: Stainless steel elements added to a stone seat wall are small, simple, and discreet. Photo credit: Bill Main

rugged materials that don't require a finish, such as stainless steel, and using rounded edges that are less likely to be ground down. A variation is to use a sacrificial material that can be economically replaced. A drawback of this approach is that, in the absence of vigilance, it may actually encourage skateboarding activity.

- Doing a postoccupancy evaluation (POE)

The POE is a tool for collecting and analyzing data about the use of a space. Often thought of as a follow-up tool for use by space designers to discover what's working and what's not, a POE is also a great tool for ongoing management of the space. A POE can point out areas where the design and management functions intersect. "Design cannot be divorced from management," write Clare Cooper Marcus and Carolyn Francis.[1] "Some problems can be resolved by management entirely. For instance, a dark corner of the park could have its lights kept on until late in the evening to increase use and safety. On the other hand, some design changes have to be accompanied by suitable management practices to be effective. New lights may be put in a dark corner of the park but if they aren't kept on long enough or maintained well nothing is resolved."

Postoccupancy evaluations are done by observing and documenting the use of a space during key periods. Data are collected, mapped, and charted for factors including the number of people in the space, what they are doing, where in the space they are, who they are (man, woman, child, etc.), and other relevant data, such as weather, for defined time intervals (morning, lunchtime, afternoon, evening, weekend, etc.). An evaluation of a space as designed can reveal what is effective and what needs improvement and can be done again after changes are made to evaluate their effect. Unfortunately, designers are rarely paid to do POEs, so this useful feedback loop is often missed. When done by the managers of a space or by third parties, a copy of the POE should be provided to the original designers to help them improve their design process.

For detailed instructions on how to structure and conduct a POE, see Marcus and Francis's *People Places*.[2]

- Promoting continual improvement

Continual improvement is a conscientious, proactive process of becoming better. Continual improvement processes generally involve many smaller ongoing and achievable projects rather than one grand project. Examples might include developing a trash collection schedule that eliminates overflowing receptacles without increasing labor expense, reducing cigarette butt litter through better placement of ash urns, or increasing visitor use of seating by trying out different locations and configurations. Measurable data should validate the improvement and build accountability into the process. Small experiments can be used to test ideas before committing to the expense of a more permanent solution. Continual improvement should be part of the culture of the organization that manages the space (see Management and PDCA cycle in Chapter 2).

- Providing safety and security

Management should include regular inspections (see "Regular Furniture Maintenance," p. 190) in its process to ensure that all furniture is in safe working order. It should also take steps to prevent the unsafe use of furniture or moving furniture to unsafe areas. (Examples of unsafe practices are standing on tables and positioning seating to permit climbing over protective railings.) Management should also promote employee safety by making sure workers use good lifting practices when moving furniture; this might entail offering training in proper lifting methods and requiring that workers get assistance or use equipment to move heavy pieces. Some spaces, such as transit terminals and courthouses, have security requirements that affect site furniture use. For example, removable bollards and transparent trash receptacles are now required at some transportation facilities.

There are numerous instances in which good management has helped make a great place. There are a few in which inspired management has raised the bar and established a model for successful public space that is admired worldwide. Bryant Park is such a place. The following case study describes the scope and depth of management, from generating grand ideas to finessing the daily details, that makes this place an icon and sets an example for best practices in the field.

CASE STUDY: MANAGEMENT

Bryant Park, New York City

History

In 1974 Bryant Park was designated a historic site by the New York City Landmarks Preservation Commission, which called it "a prime example of a park designed in the French Classical tradition." Five years later the long-neglected park had been virtually abandoned to addicts, drug dealers, and other bad actors. In 1980 the Rockefeller Brothers Fund created the Bryant Park Restoration Corporation (BPRC) under the founding leadership of Daniel A. Biederman, a Harvard Business School graduate and systems consultant, and Andrew Heiskell, then chairman of Time, Inc., and the New York Public Library, and charged them to develop a master plan to turn the park around. Biederman took the lead and set a vision and operating plan for a park that, under his continued leadership, has become a model for parks and public spaces worldwide. Bryant Park reopened in 1991 with some basic physical improvements: new entrances that increased visibility from the street, enhanced garden design, and upgrades and repairs to paths and lighting. In 2008 the park teemed with more than six thousand people during peak summer lunchtime hours and attracted audiences of up to ten thousand for its morning concert series.

What Happened?

New entrances were designed to open up the park so people would feel more comfortable entering, but Bryant Park's elegant bones remained essentially the same. The way the park was operated and managed made the difference. The plan for Bryant Park established a dynamic concept for a densely occupied space and a management strategy to make it work.

Bryant Park wasn't just wasted space in the middle of a busy commercial district. It was a liability to businesses and real estate development and a threat to civic life in the area. The reenvisioned space was designed to address the interests of business and property owners, office workers, library users, residents, and visitors to the city. The park, which with the library occupies an entire New York City block and includes a great lawn that is 300 feet long and 215 feet wide, was to become a vibrant civic common with the comfort and welcome of a great urban living room.

CASE STUDY: MANAGEMENT

(Continued)

9.4 Bryant Park: an informal grouping of chairs, exactly as the last visitors left them. Credit: Bryant Park Corporation

9.5 A Bryant Park hospitality employee maintains the site and mixes with the crowd. Credit: Bryant Park Corporation

Jerome Barth, director of operations for the Bryant Park Corporation, explains, "The park has a great mix of spaces in their character and their climates, sun and shade." The furniture, most of it movable, is key to how those spaces are used. It allows people to choose their spaces and create their own settings. "Movable furniture really works because you

9.6 Emptying litter receptacles is an ongoing process. Well-trained park employees make the task a seamless part of life in the park. Credit: Bryant Park Corporation

9.7 Multiple activities provide something for everyone. Credit: Bryant Park Corporation

can determine where you want it. You can't do what we're doing if you don't have it," he says. Aesthetics really matter. "A lot of what we do is about beauty, in a classic sense," he explains. The casual ambience and intentional informality of the park belie an obsession with quality design that begins with furniture, lighting, signage, and plantings, extends into the well-appointed restrooms (considered by many the best public facilities in

CASE STUDY: MANAGEMENT

(Continued)

9.8 Movie night at Bryant Park. Credit: Bryant Park Corporation, photo: Jose Luis Cortes

the city), and is reflected in day-to-day operations that offer an exceptional experience for park users. "We didn't pioneer the concept," Barth says. "I think Paris probably did that. But we are pioneers in the sense that we are systematic about it. We've made it into a science. Into a business."

Management Strategy

Bryant Park Corporation (BPC) is a not-for-profit business improvement district (BID) that operates Bryant Park. The BPC staff also runs the 34th Street Partnership BID. Together, these constitute the largest effort in the nation to apply private management backed by private funding to a public park. Revenues come primarily from four sources: vendor rents, advertising, contributions from real estate owners through the BID, and usage fees for programming and events. The genius of Bryant Park has been the fluid relationship between capital investment, operational funding, and the creative evolution of programming and activities.

The process by which the park became the place it is today was incremental by intention. It reopened with a simple platform: it was attractive, clean, and safe. It offered basic amenities—gardens and planters, benches and movable chairs, food kiosks and restrooms—and supported them with security and maintenance. Programming was introduced gradually. "It was a careful accumulation of one element after another, aggregating each into the operation, observing and learning and in that way gradually expanding the body of experience," Jerome Barth explains. "After a historic conversation between Dan and the chairman of HBO, an outdoor film series was begun, and that, I think, more than anything, started the love affair between the people and the park." Regular summer season programming in addition to free movie screenings now includes fifteen Good Morning America concerts, yoga, piano recitals, and a reading room. There's an ice-skating rink in the winter and numerous special events throughout the year. With a body of successful programming in place, the park began hosting commercial events for third parties, further expanding its revenue base.

"You don't need that much in the beginning," Barth says. "We had local stakeholders, the BID, who invested money on a regular basis, so we had a budget. We worked with that, creating new sources of income. And because we had a steady income stream we could finance projects. That allowed us to build things such as the restaurant. It's been a virtuous cycle for us. Credit goes to the public sector, which delegated sufficient powers to us that we could do all this."

Bryant Park management chose its investments carefully. "Most projects focus on big dollars and massive investment in hardscape," Barth says. "We focus on softscape, the small things that make a difference." They spent money on upgrading and maintaining bathrooms because that sends a strong message that somebody's in charge. They set up a protocol and budget for changing the flowers in planters four times a year. "Our flowers are not sophisticated botanicals because of the scale and the realities of operating a space where you have so many people, so much traffic, and less than ideal conditions. But they are beautiful. We do the very best we can with the environment we have," Barth reports. And they invested in furniture. "Furniture is crucial to the functioning of the park," he says. "You can't have thousands of people in the space if you don't have thousands of seats. And it's crucial because it's cheap. Compared to $6 million in renovations, a $60,000 furniture budget is minimal and it gives you results."

Furniture Elements

Bryant Park reopened in 1991 with 1,000 movable chairs. Today there are about 4,200 of them, along with 800 tables, 65 umbrellas, and 200 stools. There are 40 high chairs and 12 high tables on the upper terrace. Some 220 trash receptacles, augmented with basic barrels during periods of heavy use, are strategically placed throughout the site. (A custom litter receptacle now being developed by the 34th Street Partnership will soon be introduced throughout the business district.)

"Every year we kept adding, seeing how it feels and what it needs," explains Barth. "Managing all that furniture can be daunting. We train our crews and our programming partners to handle it, and add more as we can. If you started from scratch with that much, it would be overwhelming." Furniture volume is highest at the beginning of the season and diminishes through the year as breakage and loss take their toll. (About 95 percent of replacement

CASE STUDY: MANAGEMENT

(Continued)

is necessitated by breakage. Tables and chairs last an average of three years.) The park used to reorder tables and chairs, all of which are imported, once a year. Now it's done on a continuous cycle.

Logistics

Bryant Park provides security twenty-four hours a day with a staff of twelve to eighteen. Thirty-five people work the twenty-four-hour sanitation detail. Attendants staff the two restrooms from seven o'clock in the morning to eleven o'clock at night. The furniture crew has five regulars plus outsourced labor for very large events. The horticulture staff of four is augmented by outside contractors during planting seasons.

Nothing is left to chance. Barth posts weekly schedules covering every program and activity in the park, on every day, with a detailed enumeration of operations required for each, in intervals of time sometimes broken down to less than a quarter hour. For example:

Tuesday, 11:05 a.m.: *Yoga*

Return tables, chairs, and umbrellas to upper terrace.

Remove mats from upper terrace, transport w/horticulture cart to Library storage.

Chairs

Bryant Park hosts numerous events requiring the moving of chairs. Prior to an event, chairs are set up in rows, and after the event, they are returned to their former disarray. "We set the chairs back up in a way that they look random, as though somebody just walked away," Barth explains. "We have an aversion to what we call military rows. It all comes back to the natural appearance of the park. It is randomly set up—but it is not random. It's something we train the staff to do."

For big events all exit paths have to be cleared for security purposes. Chairs are folded and stacked in designated areas in groups of about two hundred. As soon as the event is over the crew comes back and unfolds everything. "We may have a major pop concert at eight-thirty in the morning, but at noon it looks like nothing happened," says Barth. "The cost is borne by the promoter. Our partners work with us. They understand how the park works."

Tables and Umbrellas

Tables are bused and spray-cleaned three or four times a day. Freestanding umbrellas are used because they provide more shade for more people throughout the day than do table-mounted types. The staff do their best to discourage park users from moving umbrellas themselves because they are heavy. "But people feel like this is home, so it still happens," Barth says. "We worked with manufacturers to invent bases with wheels that would withstand frequent moving. Now every manufacturer makes bases like ours, but I'd like to think we had something to do with it."

Litter Receptacles

Every year management reviews the site map and places receptacles where people can readily reach them and where they fit the usage patterns of the park. "Not one of them is randomly placed," says Barth. "We try to make sure that they're not in major sightlines. We put them slightly off to the side and at least three feet from seating, so when you are entering the space, all you perceive are the chairs and tables, the other people, and the gravel and grass." On regular days the park uses its 120 standard receptacles. When there are very large crowds, the crew sets out barrels in spots where they know they will be needed. "It doesn't make sense to overwhelm the park with all these little receptacles at all times," Barth explains. "We opt for a more flexible approach, putting them out at eleven-thirty and taking them back in at two-thirty. During those hours they will be drowned in a sea of people and you won't see them. But they're necessary because we never want to have overflowing trash cans." During a busy lunch period maintenance staff may handle up to three hundred 45-gallon bags (about 7,000 cubic feet in volume). It's a continuous cycle. One crew picks up the bags, and a separate crew comes around and takes them to designated collection spots. Bags are often moved by hand because of the difficulty of maneuvering carts through the dense crowds.

Restrooms

Bryant Park restrooms feature quality tile, sconces, full-length mirrors, good lighting, fragrant oils, and classical music. Attendants are on duty during all open hours, and bathrooms are cleaned throughout the day. Seven hundred thousand people use these facilities every year; management knows this because it does regular spot tallies, counting visitors every hour of the day once in every month, to ensure that staff and services keep up with demand.

Slow Days/Down Time

There are few slow days at Bryant Park. The number of days on which visitors numbered three thousand or more increased by 40 percent in 2008. Management credits the growth to more programming, increased real estate density in the area, a younger demographic that tends to spend more time outdoors, and technology such as cell phones and BlackBerry devices that extend the time people can be away from their desk. The park also offers Wi-Fi so that people can use their laptops. "Our problem is not

CASE STUDY: MANAGEMENT

(Continued)

too few people but the perception that the park is too full at certain hours," Barth explains. "That's important for me. Do we make physical changes, like taking out some ivy and putting in gravel, or do we just increase some of the sightlines so that people realize that they can, in fact, find a chair without too much difficulty?"

There is also almost no off-season in the park. Soon after the summer and fall seasons end, the ice rink opens for the winter. A majority of the furniture is removed from the park and stored. But some is kept in place. Litter receptacles are needed, people still come and sit when there's snow on the ground, and a few umbrellas are left out around the ice rink. Capital work is scheduled during March. Then spring planting begins.

User Feedback

The number one metric of success for Bryant Park management is attendance. The park uses clickers to count visitors. (It judges current electronic counting technology impractical for outdoor spaces.) Management values the gender count because it believes that a high number of females are an indication of the safety of the place. The ratio at Bryant Park is roughly 52 percent male and 48 percent female, a figure it considers "exceptional," as most outdoor spaces are skewed much more toward males. In addition to positive feedback expressed in steadily growing attendance, management gets e-mail and letters from visitors. And staff regularly interact with people in the park, keeping a pulse on how people are feeling about the place. Complainers are treated very seriously. Barth answers every complaint by hand. "It's exhausting to run this place," he admits. "The messages we receive from visitors and the way people care about the park are what really gets the staff up and keeps them going. "

Bad Behavior

Vandalism, skateboarding, and graffiti are kept under control by tens of thousands of "eyes on the street" during the day and security at night. Undesirable behaviors are treated as a management issue. "We enforce the same rules for everybody," Barth explains. "We don't allow people who are homeless or deranged or drug-addicted to impose their rules on others. If the rules say you can't place things on the ground, or can't be inebriated, or can't be aggressive to others, we apply them to everyone." That, he says, takes care of most problems. The danger that people who may be viewed as undesirable will steer others away from the park is mitigated by creating an environment that is so full of people and activity that the eye doesn't pick out anything amiss in an initial glance at the space. (Barth's test is whether a family from Kansas who looks in would feel it's safe.) And finally, the park staff gets to know problem constituents, who tend to be few in number and regular customers. "We know their names, histories, families, and habits," he explains. "We form a relationship with them, which is the opposite of what many agencies do. We do not have an anonymous approach. We have a very individual approach." People are rarely removed from the park. Instead, a staff member is right there keeping an eye out to reassure others that things are under control and to remind the person who is out of line that he can't just do whatever he wants. "It's very subtle and soft. Sometimes we call his family on the phone and tell them things are bad and they should step in. In most cases this is all that is needed. Occasionally bad things happen but we really try."

Culture and Commitment

Bryant Park management nurtures a culture of service and excellence that permeates all levels of the organization. Its success is reflected in the high regard in which the park is held and in the longevity of management and staff. "It's a credo," Jerome Barth says. "I try to inspire the staff to believe that we can create something that's exceptional, to bring public spaces to the next level. I want Bryant Park to be remembered as something that mattered for this civilization at a moment in its history. We are trying to build a wealth of knowledge about public spaces and spread it, so that if this place goes away, what we have learned and accomplished will live on."

Bryant Park is one of the most intensively managed parks in America, and perhaps the world. It is a stunning example of what is possible when committed management is exercised with caring and knowledgeable attention. Is the model replicable in other spaces? "Yes," the director of operations says. "We do it in four other spaces and it works just as well. In fact, we are discussing with the city taking over a park in one of the poorest neighborhoods in New York, and we can't wait to do it because we want to prove that you can do this in the wealthiest neighborhood in Manhattan and you can do it in the poorest and it will work. From an ideological standpoint, it could mean so much to us. The staff is really chomping at the bit to take that on."

For information about Bryant Park, including webcams, visit www.bryantpark.org.

Endnotes

1. C. Cooper Marcus and C. Francis, eds., *People Places: Design Guidelines for Urban Open Space*, 2nd ed. (New York: John Wiley & Sons, 1998), 354.
2. Ibid., 345–56.

10. Materials and Finishes

Several key factors drive choices of materials for site furniture:

- Exterior environmental factors—including how well a material withstands humidity, rain, snow, sun, temperature, freezing, salt, acid rain, sand, dust, and wind
- Public environmental factors—including how well a material stands up to rough service, unintended uses, lack of attention and maintenance, vandalism, graffiti, and skateboarding
- Functionality for the desired use—including comfort, form, strength, and weight
- Aesthetics—including how the material fits with the overall design and other materials in the space, and how it helps achieve the designer's intent
- Sustainability—does the material support the sustainability goals of constituents? (See Chapter 12 for a detailed discussion of sustainability of materials used in site furniture.)
- Value—is it a compelling investment, especially over the long term?

Many materials and finishes (including connections, fasteners, and glues) that are perfectly fine for interiors are unsuitable for outdoor use. Furthermore, many that are suitable for some exterior uses are not suited to the special rigors of site furniture. The primary exterior environmental threats to site furniture are:

- Water, including extremes of rain, snow, ice, and humidity
- Sun, including ultraviolet rays
- Salt, on the ground from deicing, or airborne near the ocean and other salt water
- Temperature, including extreme heat and cold and the effects of temperature changes
- Wind, especially in regard to umbrellas, shelters, structures, lightweight chairs and accessories, poles, signs, and banners

The first three factors are especially damaging over time to vulnerable materials, gradually breaking them down cosmetically, structurally, or both. And all factors can sometimes conspire—for example, near a warm ocean beach, where water, sun, salt, temperature, and wind all work together to create a corrosive atmosphere for some metals.

Exterior materials need either to be naturally resistant to these threats or to have some protective treatment or finish added to help them resist. For this reason we address the material and the treatment or finish together in this chapter. Product design can aid or hamper a material's resistance to environmental elements. Consider design characteristics such as how connections are made and whether a product sheds or traps water.

In addition to exterior environmental threats, public site furniture faces significant challenges from abuse by people who may lack feelings of ownership or concern for the furniture. In some cases rough treatment by users or maintenance staff may be unintentional. In other cases, as with vandalism and graffiti, it may be intentionally destructive and even against the law.

Beyond environmental threats and abuse, site furniture must also endure the wear and tear of normal use, which over a ten-to-twenty-year life span can be significant. All of these challenges must be addressed through the proper choice of materials for the given set of circumstances. Together, the challenges posed dramatically limit the number of materials and finishes suitable for use in site furniture.

What makes a material suitable for use in exterior site furniture? Desirable characteristics include:

- Resistance to fading or degrading due to ultraviolet radiation from the sun
- Resistance to the effects of extreme humidity and precipitation, which can include rotting, rusting, delaminating, discoloring, and supporting mold or mildew
- Resistance to the effects of temperature extremes, including freezing (heat can soften some materials and cold can make them brittle)
- Resistance to impacts, nicks, and scratches
- Resistance to insects
- Surfaces that are pleasant to the touch, without splinters or sharp edges
- Colors that maintain their integrity and do not leach and stain surrounding surfaces

Materials and finishes used together in one product must be physically, chemically, and thermally compatible with each other. Examples of common compatibility problems include:

- Erroneously specified screws that pull out of soft woods and plastics
- Sharp-edged umbrella struts that wear holes in the canopy fabric
- Reactive metals that corrode (galvanic corrosion) when used in direct contact with each other
- Bowing and twisting in benches, due to differences in thermal expansion between parts
- Cracking or peeling of hard coatings and finishes when used over expanding and contracting woods

Relatively few materials have demonstrated the ability to satisfy the demands of site furniture, and the ones that have are the most commonly used. They include coated metals (steel, aluminum, and iron), stainless steel, exterior hardwoods, a few plastics, cast aggregates, and cut stone. These and a few others with more limited application for site furniture will be covered in the following pages.

Simply put, decisions about site furniture materials usually boil down to whether to use metal, wood, or stone. Metal is used primarily because of its perceived strength, durability, and low maintenance. Wood is used for its warmth and naturalness. Stone is used for its earthiness and to match architectural materials.

Metal and Metal Finishes

In the 1970s and 1980s, powder-coated metal site furniture began to receive wide acceptance because it offered exciting new forms and colors that couldn't be done in wood. It didn't weather and fade like wood, either. Site furniture, which had been primarily wood-surfaced, gradually transitioned to be predominantly metal. Metal finishing, on which most metal site furniture depends, also improved over those years, so today the reality of durability is much closer to the hype.

Metals can be hot or cold to sit on, depending on the sun and temperature. Obviously, lighter colors absorb less solar heat than do darker colors. One misconception about metal furniture is that it necessarily becomes extremely hot in warmer climates. In fact, because steel is so strong it usually requires less mass, and the use of perforations or narrow straps on seating surfaces creates airflow and radiates heat away.

Thicker metals are tougher but also heavier, more expensive, and more difficult to fabricate. The required thickness of a part can be reduced by forming the metal into inherently strong shapes such as cylinders and angles, or by adding reinforcing gussets or braces.

Metal parts are usually bolted or welded together in site furniture. Welding is forever, never loosens, and requires no on-site labor for assembly. Nuts and bolts need occasional checking and tightening but may save on freight by enabling unassembled delivery.

Steel

Steel is one of the most commonly used materials in site furniture due to its high strength, durability, wide availability, ease of fabrication, and economy. It is available as sheets, plates, tubes, beams, and angles, and steel fabricating capabilities are widely available. Steel rusts easily unless completely protected by a finish material. Steel site furniture must be designed with finishing in mind so that coverage will be complete, including in hard-to-reach areas. Once rust starts it will creep under finishes that are not bonded to the metal. The finish must be robust enough to hold up to wear and tear and occasional impacts.

Advantages

- High strength, economy, durability, availability; many standard shapes, forms, and sizes; ease of fabrication.

Disadvantages

- Rusts readily unless finished. Can be hot or cold to sit on.

What to Look For

- A tough finish with complete coverage is essential.
- Smooth welds matter (poor welds are ugly and hard to finish).
- Thin sheets with little support can dent or "oilcan."
- Consider perforating broad surfaces such as tabletops to lessen graffiti problems.
- Wire grid panels can give steel furniture lightness and transparency and provide good drainage.

Recycled Content

- Steel is highly recyclable. More than half of the available steel supply is made from recycled steel. [1]

Finishes

- Powder coat

  Polyester powder coat, properly applied, is an excellent finish for steel site furniture. (Epoxy powder coats are intended for interior use.) It offers good color selection (though not as wide as liquid paint) and excellent durability and wear resistance. It is a uniformly smooth finish that is available in a variety of gloss options. Powder coat must be applied in a highly controlled factory environment. The plastic powder is applied over the part and subjected to heat, which liquefies the powder and causes it to flow evenly over the part. Powder coat does not bond well directly over oxide layers, so good cleaning is essential, and a primer, which bonds to both the steel and the powder coat, must first be applied. Powder alone will not cover tight corners and will not fill caverns or recesses, where a phenomenon called "Faraday's cage" causes the charged powder particles to repel each other. Thus, the furniture needs to be designed with finishing in mind to avoid creating places that can't be coated. Custom powder-coat colors are available, but be aware that using them may greatly raise the cost of future replacement parts.

- Galvanizing

  Hot-dip galvanizing is a sacrificial zinc coating that provides excellent corrosion resistance and durability, typically measured in decades. It has very good impact resistance. Its silver color may have a crystalline spangled appearance. The texture is rougher than most cosmetic finishes, especially on the underside, where the liquid runs off after dipping. It is not possible to galvanize tubular products without drain holes. Galvanizing is not suitable for food service surfaces such as tabletops. Galvanizing is sometimes used as a primer when corrosion resistance is paramount, but getting additional finish coatings to bond with it is very difficult due to the oxide layer that forms.

- Plastisol

  Plastisol is a flexible PVC dip that creates a thick coating. It is available in a limited color selection due to the economics of maintaining tanks of each color. Plastisol shows drip marks where it runs off after dipping. The "drip side" usually becomes the back or underside. Plastisol is often used on play structures and utilitarian site furniture. Plastisol does not bond to the metal and instead relies on a tight, elastic fit. It resists cuts and scrapes well, but because it is not bonded to the steel, once rust begins to form it may creep under and raise the finish.

Stainless Steel

Stainless steel is steel with chromium and nickel additives that make it more resistant to corrosion. Different grades of stainless steel offer different levels of resistance. Grade 304 offers good corrosion resistance, and the more expensive grade 316 is better for highly corrosive environments (such as near seashores or chlorinated pools). Stainless steel is very expensive and requires special welding and fabricating. It is an excellent surface for food service, such as tabletops. In sunny areas the glare from stainless steel can be unpleasant. Cast stainless steel is available but is very expensive.

Advantages
- Corrosion resistance, durability, and authentic metal aesthetic.

Disadvantages
- High cost, glare. Can be hot or cold to sit on.

What to Look For
- Grade 304 or higher. Passivation, a special chemical cleaning process, is required if contaminants have been introduced during fabrication.

Recycled Content

- Has a high average recycled content and is highly recyclable.

Finishes

- Requires no coating and offers a choice of several mechanically applied surface finishes (electropolishing, hand polishing, scratch brushing, bead blasting) Smoother finishes better resist staining.
- Like steel, can be powder-coated if desired to achieve both color and corrosion resistance, though this is an expensive approach.

Aluminum

Aluminum combines light weight, corrosion resistance, and versatility of fabrication. It has many site furniture applications and is often used because cast and extruded forms and shapes can be more economically achieved than with steel.

Advantages

- Does not rust to a red color, and is less expensive than stainless steel.
- Lightweight, readily available in many standard sizes and shapes, and can be cast or extruded in designed shapes and forms.

Disadvantages

- More expensive and weaker than steel.
- Welding requires more skill.

What to Look For

- Available in many alloys; the one used must match the structural requirement.

Recycled Content

- Has a high average recycled content and is highly recyclable.

Finishes

- Due to a very inconsistent oxide layer, aluminum will "white rust" if not finished. Two favored finishes are anodizing and powder coating.
- Anodizing is a thin conversion coat that allows the aluminum to keep its surface texture and metallic look. Dyes can also be used to tint the color of the finish.
- Powder coating also works well. Cast aluminum can be challenging to powder-coat because when heated it releases gases that can cause finish imperfections.

Ductile Cast Iron

Ductile cast iron is a cast iron that is heated for an extended period to improve its strength.

Advantages
- Useful for creating designed shapes and forms.

Disadvantages
- Heavy; must be coated to prevent rust.

What to Look For
- Often used for bench end frames and ornamental receptacle parts.

Recycled Content
- Iron has a high average recycled content and is highly recyclable.

Finishes
- Generally the same as steel.

Gray Cast Iron

Gray cast iron is a basic cast iron that is somewhat brittle, with little ability to bend under loads or impact. To gain strength it is typically cast with more thickness.

Advantages
- Economical way to create castings with high mass, such as tree grates and manhole covers.

Disadvantages
- Brittleness.

What to Look For
- Make sure it is well supported and not subject to heavy loads or sharp impacts that might cause it to break.

Recycled Content
- Iron has high average recycled content and is highly recyclable.

Finishes
- When used as a ground surface (such as a tree grate), gray cast iron is often left unfinished. It will rust, but the mass of the casting limits this from becoming a structural problem.
- Typical steel finishes may also be used.

Wood and Wood Finishes

Wood is often chosen for its naturalness and warmth. Wood is an insulator, so it does not conduct cold to the body to the same degree as metal; however, it does hold heat and can get quite warm depending on the mass and airflow of the product design. Wood is well suited to seating surfaces.

Exterior woods must resist rotting, decay, and insects, as well as excessive twisting, cracking, and warping when left outside. Woods that are naturally suited to being outside, such as teak, ipe, or jarrah, are best for site furniture. Other woods can be protected with a finish, but wood finishes don't last long in public spaces and refinishing can become an annual event.

The hardness of wood used on site furniture is also an important consideration. Soft woods are easily damaged by knives, pens, skateboards, and even mischievous fingers; thus unfinished exterior hardwoods are preferred for site furniture. Exposure to the sun will weather the wood to a silver or gray patina. Some clients don't like or understand the fading and seek to preserve or restore the original color. Doing so requires regular treatment or refinishing, most likely on an annual basis. Wood has a largely undeserved reputation for being high maintenance. An exterior hardwood that is left unfinished and allowed to weather should not require any maintenance. The irony is that by finishing the wood the owner creates the need for a high level of ongoing maintenance.

Wood site furniture is assembled with mechanical connections such as screws, bolts, or pinned mortise-and-tenon joints. Glues are generally used to secure mechanical connections rather than as the primary connection.

Exterior Hardwoods

Ipe is a widely used tropical hardwood. Jarrah is temperate-forest hardwood. Teak is a tropical hardwood; teak furnishings are typically fabricated in Asia using mortise-and-tenon joinery, then assembled at or near their destination. Black locust, a domestic temperate hardwood, is gaining popularity, but the supply is very limited. Purpleheart is a less commonly used tropical hardwood whose distinctive color weathers to gray quickly in the sun. There are many other exterior hardwood varieties, mostly tropical, but their availability will fluctuate.

Advantages
- Warm, natural, and durable.

Disadvantages
- Wood weathers and changes over time. Like it or not, wood fades, small cracks open and close with humidity changes, and it can be slow

to dry after a rain. Hardwoods can dull saw blades and woodworking equipment quickly.

What to Look For

- Every tree variety has somewhat different lumber qualities and characteristics, and some are not suitable for furniture. Stick with varieties that have demonstrated their appropriateness for exterior furniture.
- While wood density is usually a good indicator of strength, it is not the only factor. Moisture content and natural resistance to microorganisms are equally important.

Renewability

- Most commercially available exterior hardwoods are tropical. Check the source and/or rely on third-party certification of forestry practices, such as the certifications conferred by the Forest Stewardship Council (FSC).

Finishes

- Finishing is not recommended. If you must finish wood or use a color restorer, plan on redoing it annually.

Exterior Softwoods

Redwood, cedar, and mahogany are examples of soft exterior woods. They can be fine for use in more protected or private spaces. Good-quality woods are dimensionally stable and don't warp or twist.

Most pressure-treated woods are lower quality soft woods that are not good candidates for furniture because of their tendency to twist, warp, and crack.

The use of exterior softwoods in site furniture has been declining as the harvesting of the best old-growth timber has fallen into disfavor.

Advantages

- Softwoods are less prone to checking and cracking than hardwoods because they can absorb and release moisture easily.
- They are easier on woodworking equipment.

Disadvantages

- Softer woods can be easily damaged by impacts.
- Screws may not hold well under stress.

What to Look For

- Avoid flat-grained pieces that can snag clothes.

Renewability

- A number of softwoods come from domestic sources. Check the source and/or rely on third-party (such as FSC) certification of forestry practices.

Finishes

- Finishing is not recommended.
- If you must finish wood or use a color restorer, plan on redoing it annually.
- Avoid hard-shell finishes over softwoods.

Plastics

Plastics are not as commonly used in site furniture as metal or wood, but there are some great applications for it. Different plastics have dramatically different characteristics. In most plastics the color is integral, so nicks and scratches have limited visual effect. Most plastics are not affected by water, but they have varying responses to temperature, sun, and impact.

Polyethylene

Polyethylene is a relatively soft, opaque plastic that needs thickness and mass for strength. It is used both as virgin material and in its recycled form. The recycled form is sometimes thought of as "recycled milk bottles," though it can include many other items. It is durable and comfortable to the touch, and the color is integral (not an applied finish). Virgin polyethylene is well suited for rotomolding into large objects such as litter receptacle bodies and planters. Recycled polyethylene (HDPE) is extruded into slats or molded into more complex shapes. Polyethylene's bending or flexural strength weakens in warm temperatures. Recycled polyethylene cannot span as much distance as wood of the same cross-section even though it looks similar. Sometimes glass fiber is added for strength or wood fiber is added as filler to recycled polyethylene, both of which may reduce its end-of-life recyclability.

Advantages

- Offers a comfortable seating surface.
- Very durable in all sorts of weather.
- The color is integral, penetrating the material.
- Very resistant to stains.

Disadvantages

- Sags when warm.
- Achieving strength through mass can lead to clunky-looking furniture.
- Colors are limited.

What to Look For

- Spans should be less than for wood of similar cross-section or it will sag.
- Polyethylene boards can be crosscut, but because of the material's "skin," they may deform (like a split hot dog) if rip-cut.
- Screws can pull out or cause material breakage. Follow the manufacturer's recommendations closely for cutting and attaching.
- Pigments tend to fade with sun exposure. Color stabilizers are often mixed into the material to reduce fading.

Recycled Content

- Pure polyethylene is highly recyclable.
- Use of fillers and additives may limit recyclability.

Finishes

- None—the color is in the material.

Polycarbonate

Polycarbonate is a high-performance engineered plastic. It is the extremely hard plastic commonly used as headlamp covers on automobiles. It can be injection-molded, and it is widely available as extruded sheets, which can be thermoformed to create clear or translucent panels for use as seat panels or other infill. Polycarbonate is also useful in landscape lighting because of its toughness and clarity. Polycarbonate is not naturally resistant to ultraviolet radiation, so it needs a UV-resistant coating or layer to prolong its life.

Advantages

- Extremely hard and tough.
- Used for its clarity or translucency.
- Can be tinted.

Disadvantages

- Expensive and requires specialized fabricating techniques.

What to Look For

- Should have a coating added for UV resistance.

Recycled Content
- Can be recycled.

Finishes
- May have a smooth or frosted surface, or be engineered for special purposes.

Acrylic Resin

Acrylic resin is naturally resistant to UV radiation, but it does not have the impact resistance of polycarbonate, so thin sections are not ideal. Acrylic is commonly opaque or translucent; it is available in sheets or can be compression-molded under pressure. Acrylic, also known as solid surface, works well for tabletops because it is easy to clean and maintain and can be molded into various sizes and shapes with an integral edge form.

Advantages
- Smooth, hard, cleanable surface with integral color that is very desirable for tabletops.

Disadvantages
- Expensive.

What to Look For
- Available in a variety of colors and patterns.
- For exterior use, pigments should be protected by a UV stabilizer in the material.

Recycled Content
- Can be recycled under limited conditions.

Finishes
- Color and patterns are integral, so no finish is necessary.
- Polishing determines the gloss.

Fiberglass

Fiberglass is molded and laminated to create products that are lightweight, opaque, and of virtually any color. The use of fiberglass is declining as rotomolded polyethylene becomes more popular. Fiberglass is an economical material for producing low volumes of large molded objects such as planters and tabletops. Gel coats and paints can be applied after molding to add unique looks such as faux or distressed finishes. Fiberglass is vulnerable to chipping and scratching because, unlike other plastics, the color is a surface coat.

Advantages

- Can be economically fabricated into large forms. (They make boats out of it.)

Disadvantages

- Scratches and chips rather easily.

What to Look For

- Fiberglass is a labor-intensive, handmade product, so quality depends on the skill and attentiveness of the individual fabricator.

Recycled Content

- Cannot be recycled.

Finishes

- Fiberglass is laminated, and the topcoat is the color and wearing surface. Some fiberglass is postfinished, meaning the finish coat is applied after the product comes out of the mold.
- Postfinishing offers great choices in color and pattern, but the finish coat may be too thin for rough service areas.

Cast Concrete and Aggregate

Cast concrete is a natural, earthy-looking material that employs mass to achieve strength. It is used for a variety of site furnishings, including planters, receptacles, bollards, poles, and benches. Various additives can be used to manipulate color, texture, strength, and weight. It can be molded into a vast array of forms and shapes. Steel reinforcing rods help prevent cracking. Fiber additives and new technical concretes can be used to reduce thickness and weight.

Cast concrete is durable and sturdy. It may be used to make standard products or be custom-formed at the job site. It is often used for steps, ledges, and walls that can also serve as seating. New additives and processes are beginning to increase the design choices available in this ancient material.

Advantages

- Heavy weight keeps cast concrete furniture in place with limited or no anchoring (depending on the piece).
- Not attractive to vandals or thieves.

Disadvantages

- Heavy weight can make shipping expensive.

- Often has a rough texture, which is not an appealing seating surface; may be slow to dry.

What to Look For

- Check the reinforcement methods used. Steel bars require a thicker concrete form; fiber additives may reduce weight and thickness.
- Check the manufacturer's method of eliminating air pockets during casting.

Recycled Content

- Can be recycled on-site.

Finishes

- Can be smooth, lightly sandblasted, or rough exposed aggregate.
- Pigments can be added to the concrete to achieve various integral colors and tones.

Stone

Natural stone comes in many forms. Granite, marble, slate, sandstone, and limestone are among those most commonly used in site furniture. Each takes on its own "personality," depending on color and pattern. Used in site furniture, stone is often an extension of the surrounding architectural materials as, for example, when stone used for a building is extended into the site to create seating and planters. Stone is often cut into rectilinear slab forms but can be machined into softer forms as well.

Few standard products are made of stone. Stone site furniture is almost always done as a custom project. Stone is often used for steps and ledges that can also serve as secondary seating.

Advantages

- Can match or complement nearby architectural materials.
- Long-term durability.
- A natural material with potential for unique patterns and colors.

Disadvantages

- Heavy and consequently costly to ship.
- Expensive to custom-fabricate.
- Commonly used slab forms with sharp edges may be uncomfortable for seating.
- Porous stone, such as marble, may stain.

What to Look For

- Mechanical connections may require machining or drilling into the stone.
- Grouts must be carefully selected to complement the stone.

Reuse

- May have residual value for reuse.

Finishes

- Can be left rough or polished to a gloss.

Fabrics

In public spaces the primary use of fabrics is in umbrellas. Dyed acrylic fiber is the standard for creating a fabric that is tough and fade-resistant. Good fabric will raise the cost of the umbrella, so be skeptical of the fabric on cheap umbrellas. It may fade or deteriorate quickly.

Advantages

- Fabric adds color, texture, and sometimes movement to a space.
- Light and thin, providing contrast to more structural site materials.

Disadvantages

- Bright colors may get dirty from air pollution and require cleaning.
- The umbrella frame may outlast the fabric.

What to Look For

- If exact color is important, get a fabric sample rather than rely on printed color sheets.

Recycled Content

- Fabrics may contain recycled materials.

Finishes

- The color is in the fiber, so no finishes are used.

Table 10.1: Comparison of Common Site Furniture Materials

MATERIAL	ADVANTAGES	DISADVANTAGES
Steel	High strength Modest cost Readily available Recyclable Many standard shapes and sizes Easily and commonly fabricated	Rusts unless coated
Stainless steel	Corrosion resistant Minimal maintenance required	Expensive Mostly available in sheet or tube Lower grades will corrode Should be fabricated on dedicated equipment
Ductile cast iron	Heavy Modest cost Custom shapes Stronger than gray iron	Fewer domestic foundries Rusts easily
Aluminum	Light weight Recyclable Extrudable, castable Custom and standard shapes	Higher cost Production consumes lots of electricity
Wood (depending on species)	Readily available Renewable Readily and commonly fabricated Structurally strong Low maintenance (proper woods should not require finishing)	Must select an outdoor wood Will weather to gray or silver Some species stain the concrete initially Checks and cracks with the humidity Soft woods subject to carving and impact
Recycled plastic (HDPE)	Color throughout Extrudable, castable	Structurally very weak High thermal expansion Limited colors Can't cut "skin" without deforming it
Polyethylene	Can be rotomolded into big shapes Economical Can be recycled Color throughout	Not readily machinable High thermal expansion
Acrylic	UV Stable Formable (cast) or sheets Machinable	Sharp edge when it breaks Special fastening required Thin sheets are weak

Fiberglass	Economical Custom shapes Weather resistant Strong and light	Fabricating is a smelly, sticky task Not recyclable Fabrication uses VOCs Oxidizes (needs annual freshening) Can have sharp edges
Precast concrete and stone	Heavy (not easily moved) Modest cost Can be colored throughout Various surface effects possible Custom forms and shapes	Chips and stains can mar surface Expensive to ship Bulky (unless reinforced or strengthened with additives)
Natural stone (granite, marble)	Weather resistant Can be polished Can match architecture materials Heavy (not easily moved) Each piece is unique	Expensive Limited shapes and fabrication Special fastening required

Table 10.2: Comparison of Common Table Top Materials

	ADVANTAGES	DISADVANTAGES
Steel, powder coated or plastisol	High strength Modest cost Readily available Recyclable Easily and commonly fabricated	Finish may scratch (perforated metal won't show scratches as much) Can rust if not coated properly
Stainless steel	Corrosion resistant Easy to clean and care for Recyclable	Expensive Lower grades will corrode Should be fabricated on dedicated equipment Shininess may not be appropriate
Woods	Readily available Natural and renewable Readily and commonly fabricated Structurally strong	Must select an outdoor wood Will weather to gray or silver Spills may leave stains Checks and cracks with the humidity
Acrylic	UV Stable Formable (cast) or sheets Machinable Easy to clean and care for	Expensive Requires special fasteners

(Continued)

Table 10.2: (*Continued*)

	ADVANTAGES	DISADVANTAGES
Fiberglass	Economical Custom shapes Weather resistant Strong and light Easy to clean and care for	Fabricating is a nasty job Not a green product Oxidizes (needs annual freshening) Finish may scratch
Stone (granite, marble)	Weather resistant Can be polished Can match architecture materials Heavy (not easily moved) Natural product Each piece is unique	Expensive Limited shapes and fabrication Special fastening required
Polyethylene	Can be rotomolded into big shapes Economical Can be recycled	Not readily machinable Finish may scratch

Endnote

1. Meg Calkins, *Materials for Sustainable Sites* (Hoboken, NJ: John Wiley & Sons, 2006), 363.

11. Installation and Maintenance

Installation

The installation process is a brief but vulnerable phase in the life of site furniture. It is important to use skilled and attentive installers and contractors. Shipping, unpacking, assembly, and installing all expose furniture to threats very different from those it will be exposed to during its years of use. Proper care at each stage of the process is essential. Installation quality will influence the life and performance of the furniture. Be sure to follow the manufacturer's recommendations, carefully assess the site conditions, and use the correct hardware.

Shipping

Most site furniture is shipped by truck, due to its size and weight. Trucking firms seeking to maximize their load will stack containers on top of each other in the trailer. Most common carriers use a hub system much like airlines, unloading and reloading containers at regional terminals until they reach their final destination. One container may be handled several times. During the road trip the trailer bumps and vibrates and the load can shift if not properly secured. At the final destination, often a construction site, a proper loading dock and/or a forklift may not be available.

If the furniture has been packaged and handled properly, it should arrive in perfect condition. However, if the finish has rubbed against corrugated packaging paper during the trip, the container was dropped or crushed, the container was lost, or very long pieces were bent, the installation process will have to stop until matters are corrected. It is very important to document damaged packages at the time of delivery. Trucking firms will not accept responsibility for damage if the shipment has been accepted and signed for without a written explanation of damages. And most manufacturers will not accept responsibility for freight damage. If damaged packages are accepted at the destination, the owner may end up footing the bill.

It is the manufacturer's responsibility to package products properly for the journey. It is the buyer's responsibility to unload and store products carefully and to inform the shipper of any damage to the packaging or the products.

Unpacking

There are two rules for unpacking. The first is to unpack systematically and inspect carefully to make sure all parts and documents are present and in good condition. The second is to set all unpacked parts in a safe place. A surprising number of small pieces, especially hardware, get lost or thrown out with the packaging during unpacking. Loose parts should be set on a protective sheet, such as a piece of carpet or a blanket, not on the ground or on concrete, which is abrasive. It is usually best to open hardware containers just as the products are being assembled and installed in order to minimize lost or damaged parts. Packaging materials should be recycled if possible.

Assembly

Site furniture may be shipped assembled, partially assembled, or knocked down (KD), which means it requires complete assembly. Furniture shipped assembled requires no assembly labor at the job site and will almost certainly be assembled correctly. KD furniture may cost less to ship due to smaller package volume but will require assembly labor at the job site and incurs a greater risk that it won't be assembled properly. Manufacturers should include assembly instructions in the package, but often these are consulted only after something has gone wrong. Assembly should be done on a protective surface such as carpet or a blanket to prevent scraping or marring the finish. It's a good idea to come back and retighten all connections within thirty days of assembly. In some cases, installation and assembly are an integrated process—for example, when final assembly is done after the furniture support is anchored.

Placement

Installation may be as simple as setting freestanding furniture in its final location, but more commonly it involves permanent anchoring or embedding. Fixing problems is more complicated once the concrete has set, so it is a good idea to double-check the product prior to installation. Permanent installations require special considerations for exact location and leveling.

For more information about furniture placement, see Chapters 2–6. In general:

Place benches at least 9 inches in front of walls and other hard objects to prevent head bumping.

If possible, recess benches about 30 inches from walkways to keep sitters' legs clear of pedestrian traffic.

When placing benches end to end, leave 2 inches between them to avoid finger traps.

Avoid placing furniture where it could be used to climb over protective railings or fences.

When locating litter receptacles, be sure to consider the orientation of the trash opening and the space required to open the unit and remove liners for emptying.

In placing bike racks, consider all possible variations in bike parking and locking.

Anchoring furniture on sloping surfaces calls for a decision on whether to install horizontally or follow the grade. With most furniture, horizontal placement will look and function better. Benches on the horizontal plane will better relate visually to architectural features in the background, and doors and hinges on litter receptacles will operate more smoothly.

Surface-mounted benches will follow the grade, while embedded benches can be installed horizontally. Benches on a slope are usually installed with the correct height (typically 17 inches) at the center. Consequently, one end is higher above the ground than the other, which is acceptable and even interesting. If desired, a small level concrete pad can be poured for surface-mounting furniture on a sloping site.

More detailed information about anchoring follows. Also see Tables 11.1 and 11.2.

Freestanding Furniture

Freestanding furniture is a good choice when:

- Moving the furniture is encouraged.
- Security and theft are not a problem.
- The furniture must be moved for programming and activities in the space.
- Anchoring is impractical due to the ground surface material.

Exterior surfaces such as concrete and brick are very abrasive, and thus some provision needs to be made to prevent furniture from being damaged when it is moved. (Surface paving material can also be marred or damaged by dragging furniture across it.) Ideally, furniture should be carefully lifted and carried, but more typically it is lifted on one side and dragged to its new location, scraping the finish off the bottom or legs in the process. This can mar the appearance of the furniture, cause structural damage, and expose the base material to corrosion. There are three ways to prevent this:

1. *Use a sacrificial material, such as a nylon glide, to isolate the contact points from the main body of the furniture.* Glides will wear away and sometimes fall out, so they should be inspected frequently and replaced before they are worn down completely. If that is not done, both the furniture and the paving may be damaged. Chairs in very active spaces,

such as food courts and cafés, may require glide replacement every year or two. The manufacturer should be able to provide replacement guides for a nominal charge.

2. *Make the furniture too heavy to move.* This is commonly done with planters. Once filled with soil, they are too heavy for most people to move. Tables with heavy ballasted bases also discourage moving. But be aware that when these heavy objects do need to be moved, special care must be taken to ensure that they are lifted from underneath, not dragged or lifted by their tops, or else damage may result. Dollies or temporary furniture glides can help.

3. *Put wheels on the furniture so it can be moved easily.* This is often done with chaise lounges but is impractical for most exterior furniture.

Freestanding furniture may slide around on very smooth surfaces such as tile or terrazzo. Special nonslip glides and boots, usually made of rubber, may help. Adjustable glides are available for use on uneven surfaces. These typically employ a threaded bolt that is turned to adjust the height. They work best on furniture that is not intended to be moved around because they require adjustment with every move.

Fixed Furniture

Site furniture is anchored for one or more of the following reasons:

- To keep it from being stolen
- To keep it in a favored location or configuration
- To reduce management time and effort needed to reorganize it
- To provide necessary structure, support, or function
- To keep it in a safe or permitted location

The first three reasons address economic, aesthetic, and operational concerns. The fourth addresses site furniture elements that must be anchored in order to function properly. These include bollards, lighting, fixed umbrellas, most bike racks, and some bench and receptacle designs that are cantilevered or otherwise unstable on their own. Examples of locations where furniture needs to be fixed for safety reasons include rail transit stops and major streetscapes.

Anchoring Methods

Site furniture is occasionally wall mounted, but more commonly it is anchored to the ground plane. There are several methods for anchoring, and most furniture must be ordered for the specific anchoring method because the bases are designed differently for each method. Manufacturers should be able to provide CAD drawings and specifications useful in planning the installation.

Surface Plate Anchoring

In this method the furniture has one or more base plates or tabs that are predrilled. Anchor bolts going through the predrilled holes are tightened to secure the piece. Numerous styles and brands of anchor bolts are available. Some are screwed down into a socket from above, and others have a bolt coming up through the hole and employ a washer and nut. The former will usually look better when the anchoring is exposed. The strength of this method is dependent on the surface material as well as the plate and hardware used. Tamper-resistant hardware is often used if it will be left

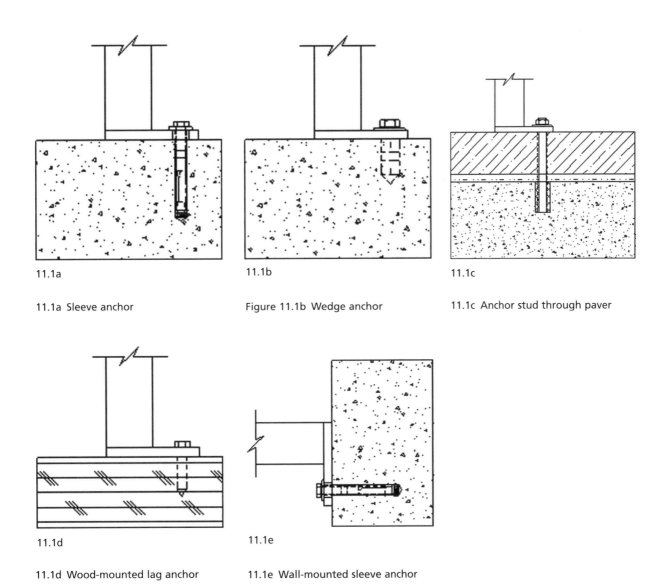

11.1a

11.1a Sleeve anchor

11.1b

Figure 11.1b Wedge anchor

11.1c

11.1c Anchor stud through paver

11.1d

11.1d Wood-mounted lag anchor

11.1e

11.1e Wall-mounted sleeve anchor

Five surface plate anchoring methods. Credit: Landscape Forms exposed. It usually requires a special tool to turn the screw or bolt. If the furniture is temporarily removed, perhaps for a special event, the hole in the ground should be temporarily plugged for safety and to allow the anchor bolt to be reinstalled.

Concealed Anchoring

The anchoring hardware in this method is hidden within the structure of the furniture. There are different ways to do this. One is to embed rods in the ground that extend upward into holes in the legs of the furniture. Setscrews in the legs are then tightened to secure the piece. Another is to place threaded rods extending downward in the bottom of furniture legs and fix these rods in the surface using a special epoxy. The strength of this method is dependent on the surface material as well as the hardware and epoxy used.

Embedding

In this method the support legs of the furniture extend into the ground and concrete or mortar is poured around them. This method has the advantages of being very secure, having no visible hardware, and working well on uneven surfaces. The paving surface is usually installed first and then holes

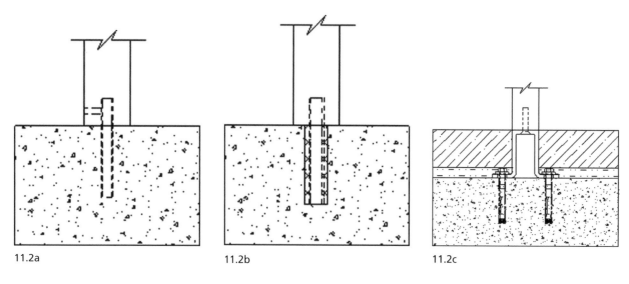

11.2a

11.2b

11.2c

11.2a Concealed anchor with setscrew

11.2b Concealed anchor in epoxy

11.2c Concealed surface-mounted paver adapter

Three concealed anchoring methods. Credit: Landscape Forms

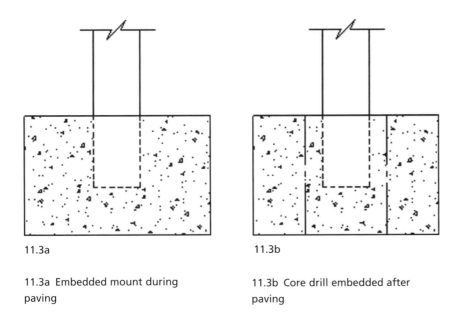

11.3a

11.3b

11.3a Embedded mount during paving

11.3b Core drill embedded after paving

Two embedding methods. Credit: Landscape Forms

are drilled or excavated for the embedded legs. The furniture needs to be held in place while the concrete or mortar sets.

Footing

This method requires making an excavation and pouring a concrete footing with anchor bolts extending upward in a pattern that exactly fits the base plate of the furniture. The size and depth of the footing will depend on the requirements of the furniture element and local soil conditions. This method is typically used for lighting and for some transit structures. Electrical conduit can be brought up through the footing if necessary. The anchor bolts allow leveling and truing of the piece using nuts and washers above and below the base plate. Footings must be built to close tolerances to ensure that the base plates fit over the anchor bolts. Manufacturers should provide CAD data or templates for this purpose.

Maintenance

Maintenance requirements depend on the type and materials of the furniture, as well as local conditions and patterns of use. Site furniture is intended to get along without much help, but a small investment in timely maintenance can add value by improving functionality and extending useful life. Loose connections, scratched finishes, and torn fabrics will typically worsen over time, and if not addressed can ruin the piece aesthetically or functionally. Check with the manufacturer for maintenance recommendations.

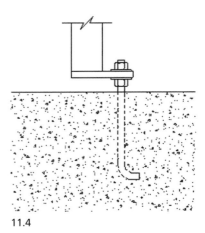

11.4

11.4 Footing method: embedded J-bolt with leveling nut. Credit: Landscape Forms

Table 11.1: Installation Types: Advantages and Disadvantages

TYPE	ADVANTAGES	DISADVANTAGES
Freestanding	Can be moved around the space Simple to install Easy to service	May rock on uneven surface Needs glides to protect surface Can be tipped over and damaged Can be stolen or moved
Surface mount	Can't be stolen easily Less work than embedded Can be removed for service or functions	Must "damage" the surface Requires an installer Requires secure surface Can be installed badly Anchor hardware is usually visible
Embedded	More integrated in to the landscape Can mitigate uneven surfaces Clean appearance Very solid anchor, no loose bolts	Impossible to remove for service Must be protected during embedding process Requires forethought and planning Requires more substantial tools and materials (core drill)
Wall mount	Can clean underneath Anchoring hardware usually hidden Saves space Can go against or on top of wall	Not very common Requires highly structural wall Requires coordination with architect/contractor Curves are difficult to align
Built-in	Very permanent Integrated look (use architectural materials) Saves space	Difficult to change Requires more planning and coordination Difficult to service

Most site furniture never gets cleaned except by the rain, but there are cases in which cleaning is recommended. Tabletops collect and show dirt, and cleaning them makes them much more pleasant to use. Wiping with a damp cloth will usually do the trick. Litter receptacles get gunky from spilled food and drinks, and pressure washing is a good way to take care of this. Pressure washers vary, so test a small spot to be sure it won't damage the surface or finish. Don't pressure-wash soft woods or painted surfaces.

The following is a schedule of suggested regular maintenance tasks:

Daily:

• Manage umbrellas: lower them when it is windy or they are not attended.

Every 1–7 days, depending on intensity of use:

• Wipe off tabletops.

Table 11.2: Compatibility of Surface Materials with Installation Methods

MATERIAL	FREESTANDING	SURFACE MOUNT	EMBEDDED
Concrete slab	Glides must endure rough surface	Easy	Core drill and add deep concrete—doesn't require structural slab
		Concrete must be thick and secure enough to hold anchor	Or, drill and epoxy method - which requires a structural slab
		Concrete should be fully cured	Concrete should be fully cured, if new (28 days)
MATERIAL	FREESTANDING	SURFACE MOUNT	EMBEDDED
Brick pavers	Easy	Attaching to pavers not recommended	Must have concrete slab or caisson beneath pavers
		May use an adapter or extension to slab below pavers	Cut pavers to trim around furniture
Asphalt	Easy—but watch for legs poking through in hot weather	Not recommended	Requires concrete caisson
Grass or gravel	Can be unstable, can sink in	Requires small concrete slab	Requires concrete caisson
	Sled base may help	String trimmers and mowers may damage	String trimmers and mowers may damage
	Glides may not protect legs Must be moved for mowing		
Wood deck	Easy, but watch bench/ chair legs and decking gaps	Lag bolt into deck or thru-bolt to backer plate, depending on structural needs	Not recommended
Roof deck	Wind conditions may prevent freestanding	Can't penetrate the roof membrane, usually requires a sub frame on top of the membrane to attach to	Not recommended
	Consider the weight	Consider the weight	

Table 11.3: Maintenance and Repair by Material Type

	CLEANING	STAINS	LIGHT SCRATCHES*	DEEP GOUGES*	GRAFFITI*	BURN MARKS* (SMALL)	SKATEBOARD DAMAGE*
Powder coat	Water and soft cloth	Mild detergent and soft cloth	Wax and buff	Touch-up paint	Graffiti cleaner	Touch-up paint	Touch-up paint
Plastisol	Water and soft cloth	Mild detergent and soft cloth	Ignore	Vinyl touch-up	Graffiti cleaner or mild abrasive	Touch-up paint	Vinyl touch-up
Stainless steel	Water and soft cloth	Stainless steel cleaner	Ignore	Ignore or replace	Stainless steel cleaner	Stainless steel cleaner	Stainless steel cleaner
Wood	Water and soft cloth	Ignore or sand	Fine sanding	Sand	Sand	Sand	Sand
Painted surfaces	Water and soft cloth	Mild detergent and soft cloth	Sand and repaint	Sand and repaint	Repaint	Touch-up paint	Sand and touch-up paint
Hard plastics	Water and soft cloth	Mild detergent and soft cloth	Wax and buff	Ignore or replace	Mild detergent and soft cloth	Ignore or mild abrasive cleaner	NA
Soft plastics	Water and soft cloth	Mild detergent and soft cloth	Wax and buff	Ignore or replace	Mild detergent and soft cloth	Ignore or mild abrasive cleaner	NA
Glass	Glass cleaner	NA	Ignore or replace	NA	Scrape with razor and soapy water	Glass cleaner	NA
Stone	Water and stiff natural bristle brush	Mild detergent and natural bristle brush	Ignore	Ignore or replace	Graffiti cleaner or pressure wash	Cleaner or mild abrasive	Wire brush (stainless steel bristles)
Concrete	Water and stiff natural bristle brush	Concrete cleaner and natural bristle brush	Ignore	Ignore or replace	Graffiti cleaner or pressure wash	Wire brush (stainless steel bristles)	Wire brush (stainless steel bristles)
Umbrella fabric	Water and stiff natural bristle brush	Mild detergent and natural bristle brush	NA	NA	NA	NA	NA

*Some cases may require use of abrasives (such as sandpaper, Scotch-Brite, and scouring liquids or powders) or pressure washing. Before proceeding, test the effect on the finish in an inconspicuous location.

- Check trash and smoking urns, empty as necessary.
- Repair any observed graffiti or damage (or remove from service).

Every 1–12 months, depending on intensity of use:

- Pressure-wash receptacles and liners; inspect doors, lids, and hinges.
- Inspect all connections and tighten as necessary.
- Inspect chair glides and bumpers; replace as necessary.
- Rinse off fabric umbrellas (if they haven't been adequately rinsed by rain).
- Touch up chips and scratches.
- Remove abandoned bikes from racks.

Every 6–12 months, depending on climate:

- Restore oxidized fiberglass surfaces.
- Inspect umbrella fabric for wear and tear; repair or replace as necessary.

See Table 11.3 for material-specific recommendations.

Storage

If furniture is to be stored, clean and dry it prior to storage.

Skateboard Damage

Skateboarding on site furniture causes impact damage and finish damage. The long edges of some benches are vulnerable. Examples of impact damage include ground-down horizontal edges and loosened anchor bolts. Finish damage can range from minor rubs to deep gouges. Wax or paint rubs deposited on the furniture can be removed by cleaning. Fixing more extensive damage to the edges and finishes may require replacement of the edge piece or refinishing. Anchor bolts may need to be tightened or replaced. Preventing future skateboard damage is essential. (See the discussion of skateboarding in Chapter 9.)

11.5

11.5 Skateboard damage along front edge of bench. Photo credit: Bill Main

Wood Replacement

Broken or cracked wood pieces should be replaced. The new piece will weather to match the color of the other pieces in a few months. Most glue breaks down in the exterior environment and is not suitable for long-term repairs.

Metal Replacement

In the early days of all-metal site furniture, steel and iron were bent and beaten into shape by hand, and every part was unique. Replacement parts weren't always available, and those that were didn't always fit. The site furniture industry has evolved, and today improved fixturing and manufacturing processes produce parts that are much more consistent and reliable, although this varies with the manufacturer. Check with the manufacturer prior to purchase about the availability of replacement parts.

Metal Fatigue

Metal has a memory and does not forget past injuries. Metal that has been bent and then bent back into its original shape is forever weakened. This is particularly significant in the case of lighter pieces such as chair legs. Site furniture parts that have been bent should be replaced.

Refinishing

Refinishing any furniture requires getting back to a clean, dry base to which the new finish will solidly bond. Refinishing wood requires scraping off loose paint and sanding off gloss to get to a good base. Wood can be refinished in place if desired.

Powder coating is done in specially designed industrial ovens. Refinishing powder-coated metal furniture requires removal from the site, disassembly, and stripping or burning off the original finish prior to applying a fresh powder coat. Because of the requirements of the process, powder coating is usually just touched up with paint in the field rather than completely refinished. Any rust or corrosion that has formed on metal surfaces should be removed or converted before the touch-up finish is applied.

Plastisol is an industrial dip process. For reasons similar to those given for powder coat, plastisol is usually just touched up with paint in the field.

When refinishing rusted steel, it is necessary to first apply a rust converter. This is a liquid that, when painted over the rust, converts the rust (iron oxide) to iron phosphate, which can be painted. Follow the instructions for the specific rust converter being used.

Because of the thickness of powder coat and plastisol finishes, touching them up with paint will not achieve a matching texture.

Repairing Versus Replacing Furniture

The time to replace site furniture is when the design or function no longer fits the current need or when the integrity of the structure is compromised. Short of this, finishes can be touched up, surfaces can be smoothed, connections can be tightened, and parts can be replaced. As long as the function and the appearance of the furniture continue to contribute to the positive experience of the space, a piece is probably worth repairing.

It is usually economical to replace parts as long as the basic structure of the site furniture is sound. Replacing bench slats, receptacle lids or liners, umbrella fabric, and even end frames can make good sense as long as the other parts and the general structure retain their integrity. It is not possible to replace embedded parts, so when embedded parts go bad, it's time to replace the entire piece.

A reasonable goal is to maintain the installed collection of furniture until the space calls for a complete renovation. At that time furniture that still has useful life can be relocated within the space or donated for use in other spaces.

12.   Sustainability

Making Sustainable Choices

Design professionals, especially architects and landscape architects, are in the vanguard of sustainable practice. Though site furniture may represent only a small part of an overall project, making sustainable choices matters. Much information is available to help in assessing the sustainability attributes of site furniture products, but a great deal still needs to be done. Many manufacturers and suppliers are trying to do the right thing—not to mention working to satisfy customers who are becoming increasingly sophisticated in their understanding and expectations. Making sustainable choices is a matter of weighing multiple factors. There are seldom any perfect answers, and often significant trade-offs. Sustainability is a journey. We use the information we have today to make the best decisions we can and use new information as it becomes available to create better solutions for the future. In the following pages we propose some broad goals, provide specific information where it is available and note where it is not, highlight complexities and trade-offs, and offer some key questions designers can ask manufacturers, suppliers, and contractors. At the end of this chapter we outline ways in which LEED® and the ASLA Sustainable Sites Initiative are helping to guide professionals in identifying and implementing sustainable practices based on the best available intelligence.

For a comprehensive discussion of materials and their role in sustainable site design we highly recommend Meg Calkins, *Materials for Sustainable Sites*.[1] We wish to acknowledge our use of this valuable resource.

The good news is that site furniture as a general category has several important sustainable characteristics:

- Site furniture is durable. A lifetime of ten to twenty years is common, and during that time it doesn't require a lot of maintenance, consume energy (except lighting), or require chemical cleaners.
- Site furniture, unlike interior furniture, is typically made of just one or two materials, so it requires minimal disassembly, making it readily recyclable.
- The most commonly used site furniture materials (metal and wood) are available with recycled content or come from renewable sources.

- Powder coat, the most common finish used on metal site furniture, is inert, so it doesn't emit VOCs (volatile organic compounds) into the environment.
- Site furniture isn't typically shipped with a lot of disposable plastic packaging.
- Site furniture may support sustainability goals through its function, as in the case of bike racks, recycling containers, and mass transit shelters. And it may help get people outdoors.

When making specific site furniture selections, the picture becomes more complex. Every product is the result of multiple inputs and outputs over its lifetime.

Major Factors in the Sustainability of Site Furniture

Function

Some site furniture products contribute to environmentally beneficial behaviors and might be said to be sustainable by function. Bike racks, for example, support an alternative form of transportation that encourages exercise, discourages automobile use, and reduces the consumption of fossil fuels. Street and park furniture encourages people to spend time outdoors, with attendant benefits to physical, social, and mental health. Transit structures encourage the use of mass transit and reduce reliance on the auto. Litter receptacles discourage littering, contributing to aesthetics and sanitation in outdoor settings. Recycling receptacles encourage postconsumer recycling of paper, bottles, and cans. Lighting and bollards powered by solar energy reduce the use of fossil fuels and limit CO_2 emissions.

Life Cycle Assessment

Life cycle assessment (LCA) is an accounting of all inputs and outputs through a product's life cycle. Sophisticated LCA tools are currently under development but not yet widely available in the site furniture industry. And even when good information is available, making sustainable choices sometimes involves trade-offs. A plus in one area may be offset by a minus in another. For example, recycled plastic lumber requires more material for support structure than wood of the same size. Composite lumber may save wood, but it can't be recycled. And while producing virgin aluminum requires large quantities of electricity, it is easily and widely recycled. The widespread availability and adoption of LCA tools will provide science-based data to help design professionals make more fully informed choices.

We propose the following principles for site furniture sustainability:

1. Conserve natural resources.
2. Reduce energy consumption.

3. Reduce ecological impacts.

4. Support sustainable strategies, such as life cycle assessment.

To choose site furniture that supports one or more of these principles, consider the following issues:

- Durability

  Longevity minimizes resource use.

- Investment in good design

  Well-designed classics are likely to be used and enjoyed longer.

- Products made from renewable resources

  Example: wood harvested using sustainable practices, with third-party certification preferred.

- Products containing recycled content

  Less energy is used in recycling materials than in their initial production.

- Products constructed from recyclable materials

  Example: steel and aluminum.

- Products made of reused materials

  Example: Great Lakes salvaged wood.

- Products manufactured in facilities that have energy conservation programs or utilize alternative energy sources

- Products made from local materials

  Example: local stone or aggregate.

- Furniture made with materials that minimize energy consumption

  Example: high-performance concrete mixes for built-in site elements.

- Products that create no or low human and environmental health risks

  Manufactured using clean technology; inert after processing; biodegradable packaging.

- Products shipped without plastic or Styrofoam packaging

- Products with functions or attributes that promote sustainable activities or outcomes

  Example: bike racks, transit shelters, recycling containers.

- Products from companies that have take-back programs

Embodied Energy

Embodied energy, which is the total energy required to produce and transform a material throughout all stages of its life, is a key input and one for which reliable data are often hard to amass. For example, the embodied energy in a steel product includes all energy expended in mining or extracting, primary processing, manufacturing, finishing, recycling, and transportation. Products made of multiple materials require calculation of embodied energy of all materials plus the energy required to assemble.

There is also the question of how the energy was generated; typically, the answer is fossil fuels, but solar, wind, hydroelectric, biofuels, and geothermal alternatives may have been used in some phases of the product life cycle, and this information would be useful. Production of recycled materials requires only a fraction of the energy required for production of the virgin material.

General information is available about the average energy required to extract and process basic materials; see *Materials for Sustainable Sites*. But the provenance of raw materials used in any particular piece of furniture may be hard to trace. And if the material is recycled, information on whether that was done regionally or the material was shipped halfway around the world, reprocessed, and returned is important for calculating reliable data on energy expended in transportation.

Emissions and Contaminants

Products vary not only in their physical properties and embodied energy but also in the amount of hazardous air emissions, water contaminants, and CO_2 released during material processing, product manufacture, and disposal. Some of the most polluting materials and processes are metal mining and processing, metal finishing, cement production, and PVC production and disposal. In the manufacturing process some hazards may be mitigated by emissions controls, wastewater treatment, and the use of less hazardous chemicals or substances. But environmental practices vary by manufacturer, and tracing the chain of what went in and what came out is a formidable task.

Materials

Metal

Steel and aluminum are the predominant metals used in site furniture manufacture. Both contain high amounts of embodied energy, much of it incurred in mining and primary processing.

Both steel and aluminum are virtually 100 percent recyclable, and there are fewer impacts associated with recycled materials than with primary materials. Aluminum contains more embodied energy than steel, but recycling aluminum uses only 5 percent of the energy used in initial manufacture. Site furniture manufacturers should be able to provide information on the recycled content of their products.

Ductile cast iron and gray cast iron are used for selected site elements. Both have a high average recycled content and are highly recyclable.

The most common metal finishing processes vary in their environment impacts:

- *Powder coating* is the most common metal site furniture finish. This sprayed-on polymer or resin powder, which adheres to metal through an electrostatic process, contains no solvents. Typically applied in a controlled factory environment, overspray is captured and reused with very little waste, and wastewater is often recycled. Once cured, powder coating is inert, so it does not off-gas. Recycling metal with powder coat finishes may require emissions control measures to protect air quality. (These controls are widely used in the United States but may not be available in offshore facilities.)

- *Galvanizing* is widely used in site furniture and related elements such as traffic light poles. It provides what is sometimes called the "fifty-year finish" because it can last from fifty to seventy-five years. The zinc used in the process is relatively nontoxic for humans, but it poses risks to aquatic organisms. Zinc coating can be removed and reclaimed during the recycling process.

- *Plastisol* is a vinyl finish that is sometimes used on metal site furniture. It is the same or similar to the soft plastic material sometimes found on hand tools such as pliers. Vinyl (and PVC) are made from chlorine (and other chemicals) that present health hazards throughout the life cycle. PVC is heavily used in the construction industry, and considerable effort is being directed at finding greener alternatives.

- *Etching* is used on stainless steel and aluminum to create a "raw" look and as an undertreatment with powder coating. The solvents employed in etching are hazardous and can pose hazards if not handled and disposed of correctly during the process.

- *Electropolishing* is widely used with stainless steel. Using large amounts of electricity and acid baths can create hazardous working conditions. No VOCs or air pollutants are emitted during processing, but wastewater can pose environmental risks if not controlled or neutralized.

- *Mechanical finishing* processes, such as polishing, bead blasting, peening, engraving, stamping, milling, and perforating, are often used in site furniture manufacture to prepare metal for other finishes. (Left unfinished, they can expose the metal to oxidation and lower the stain resistance.) Environmental and health risks are minimal, and these finishes do not impact the recycling potential of the product.

Wood

Wood is a renewable resource and a fine site furniture material under the right conditions. Wood is generally biodegradable if not treated. Wood residuals such as bark generate a majority of the energy used in wood processing (primarily kiln drying), requiring less use of fossil fuels. Most of the woods used in site furniture are hardwoods, and many of them, such as ipe, come from tropical forests. Teak is a tropical wood that is usually, but not always, plantation grown. There are few durable exterior hardwoods from temperate forests. (Jarrah and black locust are two such woods.)

Redwood and cedar, exterior softwoods from North America, are also sometimes used.

Wood forests regenerate and remove carbon from the air. They harbor enormous biodiversity, afford habitat protection, and support the livelihoods and cultural heritages of indigenous peoples. In short, they are essential to life and health on earth. Deforestation threatens all of these benefits and contributes directly to climate change by creating an imbalance in the carbon cycle.

It is critical that wood used in site furniture come from responsibly managed and monitored forests. The most reliable guarantor of sustainable wood practices is third-party certification and the Forest Stewardship Council (FSC) is the gold standard. This independent, nongovernmental, not-for-profit organization provides chain-of-custody certification that products carrying the FSC label come from forests that are managed to meet the social, economic, and ecological needs of present and future generations. (For more information, go to www.fsc.org/about-fsc.html.)

Chain-of-custody certification, in which lumber is individually tracked and tagged through the entire growth and harvesting process, typically increases material cost. Nevertheless, the demand is now sufficiently great that FSC-certified wood for site furniture is not always easy to secure. Where FSC-certified wood is not available from wood suppliers or is not offered by the site furniture manufacturer, ask about the company's internal wood policies and procedures. Some companies have established programs with requisition protocols and vendor-reporting requirements to ensure that the wood they secure comes from managed forests. SmartWood, a

12.1 Author Bill Main with old-growth cedar, British Columbia, Canada. Photo credit: Kathleen Main.

program of the Rainforest Alliance, provides verification of the legality and management of high-conservation-value forests. Its custom verification services can help companies ensure that their internal sustainable wood standards are followed and procurement policies implemented. (For more information, go to www.rainforest-alliance.org.)

Finishes on wood are problematic. Wood finishes can off-gas VOCs, and chemical treatments can limit the reuse and disposal of wood. The hardwoods typically used in site furniture do not need to be coated or finished. Left alone, the wood will wear well and weather to an attractive patina. The best environmental practice is to select a good, durable exterior wood and then leave it unfinished.

When woods not naturally resistant to decay are used, they may be pressure-treated with a preservative. Preservative treatments that involve injecting the wood with heavy metals and insecticides, such as chromated copper arsenate (CCA), can leach contaminants into landfills or release harmful chemicals if incinerated. This is an issue in site construction, but less so in furniture, as the softwoods that are pressure-treated are not often used in commercial site furniture because of their tendency to crack, check, and twist.

Plastic

Plastics are used in commercial site furniture for seating, litter receptacles, recycled plastic lumber, and small parts such as glides. On the negative side, they are made of nonrenewable fossil fuels and require the use of additional fossil fuels in their production. Hazardous wastes may be emitted in processing, with environmental and health risks varying by type. (See below.)

On the positive side, plastics can contain substantial amounts of recycled content and can sometimes be recycled. Plastic is relatively lightweight, so it uses less energy in transportation than materials such as steel. Plastic lumber is durable (typical warranties range from ten years up to the product lifetime), does not require finishing, and is resistant to insects.

The most commonly used plastics in site furniture

HDPE: High-density polyethylene is readily recyclable and can be recycled many times without significant change in properties. Its production results in fewer pollutants than is the case with PVC or ABS, and waste can be recycled during manufacturing processes. HDPE plastic lumber is used in bench slats, litter receptacles, and tree grates.

LDPE: Low-density polyethylene has recycling characteristics similar to those of HDPE and is widely recycled into plastic lumber with HDPE (the mix is less expensive than 100 percent HDPE but is also less strong, less durable, and subject to "downcycling" to a lower-grade product after multiple recycles). It is used alone in some site furniture, including benches, picnic tables, and bollards, but has lower tensile strength and density than HDPE.

LLDPE: Linear low-density polyethylene has a higher tensile strength and impact/puncture resistance than LDPE. It is often mixed with HDPE to make plastic lumber.

PVC, ABS, polystyrene: Polyvinyl chloride, acrylonitrile butadiene styrene, and polystyrene contain the most hazardous content but are not widely used in site furniture. PVC is the most common plastic used in the construction industry, and in site applications it is found in decking and fencing. At least 60 percent of its mass by weight is chlorine, posing significant health risks in manufacture and disposal. When purchasing site furniture made of composite materials, look carefully at the contents to determine whether PVC is among them.

Polycarbonate: This high-performance engineered plastic is extremely hard and tough. Although less hazardous than PVC, chemicals used in its production require worker protection and pollution controls. Polycarbonate is recyclable where programs are available.

Acrylics: Most acrylics used in site furniture are thermoset plastics, meaning they cannot be melted and remolded. However, acrylics can be reground and remolded, with limitations on the amount that can be recycled because of added color, and with the restriction that they can be remolded only into similar products. During processing the material emits acrylic acid, a skin and eye irritant, requiring worker protection. Acrylics are largely inert after processing, so off-gassing is not an issue. The most common uses of acrylic in site furniture are in making tabletops and umbrella fabrics.

Fiberglass

Fiberglass is coming under increasing regulation because styrene emissions from the resins used in its production are hazardous to human health. After processing, the material is fairly inert, so it doesn't off-gas, but fiberglass is not recyclable and ends up in the landfill.

Cement

The production of white Portland cement, which is used in the construction of seat walls, tables, planters, and other site elements, involves a high amount of embodied energy. The cement industry has the highest energy intensity per dollar value of output of any manufacturing sector, and the energy consumption per dollar value of shipment is over twice that of the second-ranked iron and steel sector.[2] It is estimated that a 30 percent reduction in the amount of Portland cement used in mixes worldwide could reverse the rise in CO_2 emissions.[3]

Concrete structures can last for thirty to forty years, but typically are in place for about twenty years. Measures can be taken to reduce the material's environmental impacts. The use of high-performance concrete (HPC) mixes can reduce the amount of energy-intensive cement, water, and/or aggregate used in concrete and result in stronger, more durable structures. And supplementary cementitious materials (SCMs) can be used to reduce the amount of cement in a concrete mixture. Recycled materials substituted for virgin aggregates in concrete reduce resource use and mining impacts and divert waste from landfills.

Concrete and brick can be crushed on-site and reused in new concrete, saving on material, landfill, and transportation costs. Recycling concrete has the added benefit that it allows steel reinforcing to be removed and sold for scrap, something that typically does not happen when concrete is landfilled.

Stone

Stone is a natural material with a significant amount of embodied energy incurred in quarrying and transporting. Transportation impacts may be high: Stone is often hauled long distances and is extremely heavy. Waste produced in cutting and shaping can be reused for other applications, such as decorative chips. Stone site elements may have potential for reuse.

Rapidly Renewable Materials

Few rapidly renewable materials are used in the manufacture of commercial furniture because products made of it are not typically robust enough to withstand active public use. Rattan is used for a limited number of products applicable in small, supervised settings such as courtyards. However, the renewable benefits of the material may be offset by its lack of durability relative to other materials. As with wood, finishes may contribute to negative environmental impacts in disposal. Bamboo also has limited application in site furniture because most bamboo materials contain glues and resins that are not suitable for outdoor use.

Fabrics

Fabrics in commercial site furniture are used primarily for umbrellas. Acrylic fiber is very durable outside and is commonly used for making umbrella fabrics. Cotton is a renewable resource used to make umbrella fabrics, though it is usually produced through industrial agriculture and is not very durable.

Manufacturing and Finishing

Manufacturing today is a complex global process. To assess environmental impacts from manufacturing and finishing, it is important to know the manufacturer and to ask questions about production practices. That said, it is often difficult to secure quantifiable information. Tracking and quantifying embodied energy and other environmental impacts through multistep processes requires sophisticated LCA infrastructure, which most site furniture manufacturers do not yet have in place.

Turning raw materials into products is energy-intensive, may involve the use of some hazardous substances, and in some cases requires large quantities of water. Manufacturing thus adds to the embodied energy in furniture. The release of hazardous air and water emissions and the disposal of hazardous solid waste from manufacturing processes are more heavily regulated and monitored in developed countries such as the United States than in the developing world.

However, most manufacturers and finishers are required to report data on emissions and contaminants to state authorities. Information about VOC emissions, solvents deposited in wastewater, and CO_2 releases can help create a profile of a manufacturer's practices. Check to see if the manufacturer has been cited for violation of state or federal environmental laws. Find out if they have earned clean manufacturing awards under programs run by many states. Inquire about energy-saving strategies (for example, co-generation) or whether the company purchases Green-E certified energy. Find out if the company uses clean technology and if it has established benchmarks against which to measure improvements. Companies that follow lean manufacturing programs, which focus on eliminating waste, are likely to a have good record in resource efficiency and waste reduction.

There is a caveat, however. Information on production practices at a manufacturer's facility may not provide a total picture of the environmental footprint of its products. Many companies outsource selected production processes, such as metal finishing, and these may have significant environmental impacts. When you consider environmental impacts, you need to consider the whole process. Complete information on sustainable practices includes supply-chain data. As in the case of in-house processes, many companies do not have the infrastructure in place to monitor and quantify data from supply chain partners. However, gathering as much information as possible on what is outsourced can help you make informed judgments about manufacturers' sustainability claims.

End of Life

What happens to a product after its useful life is over? Site furniture often has an extended life. Even after decades of use, site furniture that remains structurally sound can find a second life in less-high-profile locations. Most site furniture is made of just one or two materials, so it requires little or no disassembly for recycling. The major materials used in site furniture are, wholly or in part, recyclable:

Steel: 100 percent recyclable

Aluminum: 100 percent recyclable

Plastics: up to 100 percent recyclable (percentages vary by type and formulation)

Wood often can be reused in new products. If unfinished, it is biodegradable in the landfill.

Site furniture is quite often reused at a different site or donated to other users when it is no longer needed at its original site. Some companies have take-back programs for furniture at the end of its useful life, although this practice is not yet widespread in the site furniture industry.

LEED® and the Sustainable Sites Initiative

LEED® (Leadership in Energy and Environmental Design) and the ASLA Sustainable Sites Initiative establish standards for measuring compliance with sustainable practices across a wide range of categories. LEED® applies to projects containing built structures and specifically addresses building design and construction. The Sustainable Sites Initiative addresses landscape projects that may or may not include building construction. Both offer guidance for identifying areas in which site projects in general and site furniture in particular can support sustainability and contribute to certification for achievement.

LEED®

LEED® is a rating system developed by the US Green Building Council (USGBC), a nonprofit organization dedicated to sustainable building design and construction.

Site furniture can help projects achieve points under LEED® New 2009 rating system. To qualify for LEED® credits, the site furniture must be part of the original plan, the area(s) in which the site furniture is located must be included in the total project footprint, and the furniture must be included consistently in Materials and Resources (MR) Credit 3: Materials Reuse, through MR Credit 7: Certified Wood. Consult a LEED® AP (Accredited Professional) for guidance.

Site furniture may contribute to LEED® credits in the following categories:

Alternative Transportation: Bicycle Storage

Heat-Island Effect: Nonroof

Light Pollution Reduction

Storage and Collection of Recyclables

Recycled Content

Environmental Tobacco Smoke (ETS) Control

Onsite Renewable Energy

Regional Materials

Certified Wood

Sustainable Sites Initiative

The Sustainable Sites Initiative is a collaborative partnership, formed in 2005, between the American Society of Landscape Architects and the Lady Bird Johnson Wildflower Center, later joined by the U.S. Botanic Garden and other not-for-profit organizations. In 2007 the U.S. Green Building Council agreed to incorporate the work of the Sustainable Sites Initiative into future versions of its LEED® Green Building Rating System. The Sustainable Sites Initiative is one of the first green building rating systems to use the concept of ecosystem services as an underlying structural principle.

Site furniture may contribute to ecosystem services if it enhances human health, is made of sustainable materials, and contributes to sustainable site operation and maintenance. The Ecosystems Service Matrix contained in the 2008 Preliminary Report on Standards and Guidelines of the Sustainable Sites Initiative proposes the follow categories in which site furniture could potentially contribute to LEED® credits:

4   Site Design—Human Health Components

   4.3 Provide for optimum site accessibility, safety, and wayfinding

   4.7 Provide outdoor spaces for mental restoration

   4.8 Provide outdoor spaces for social interaction

5   Site Design—Material Selection

   5.3 Support sustainable practices in materials manufacturing

   5.4 Reuse on-site structures, hardscape, and landscape amenities

   5.5 Use salvaged and recycled-content materials

   5.6 Use certified wood

   5.7 Use products designed for reuse and recycling

   5.8 Use adhesives, sealants, paints, and coatings with reduced VOC emissions

   5.9 Conduct a life cycle assessment

7   Operation and Maintenance

   7.4 Provide for storage and collection of recyclables

   7.5 Use renewable sources for site outdoor electricity (e.g., solar lighting and bollards)

This credit-granting system, with its prerequisites, metrics-based standards, and stringent reporting requirements, is expected to be in place by 2011–12. It promises to offer design professionals structured guidance for making sustainable site furniture decisions.

Endnotes

1. Meg Calkins, *Materials for Sustainable Sites* (Hoboken, NJ: John Wiley & Sons, 2009).
2. Ibid., 104.
3. Ibid., 114.

COLOR PHOTO CREDITS

1.1 Bill Main, Beijing
1.2 Courtesy of Gustafson Guthrie Nichol, Ltd., North End Parks (Rose Kennedy Greenway), Boston, 2008
1.3 Bill Main, Old Slip Park, NYC

2.1 Copyright 2003, Project for Public Spaces
2.2 Copyright 2004, Project for Public Spaces
2.3 Copyright 2004, Project for Public Spaces
2.4 Copyright 2007, Project for Public Spaces
2.5 Copyright 2003, Project for Public Spaces
2.6 Copyright 2004, Project for Public Spaces

3.1 Courtesy of Thomas Balsley Associates, Capitol Plaza, NYC
3.2 Copyright 2003, Project for Public Spaces
3.3 Copyright 2005, Project for Public Spaces
3.4 Bill Main, British Memorial Garden at Hanover Square, NYC

4.1 Bill Main, Daley Plaza, Chicago
4.2 Copyright 2003, Project for Public Spaces
4.3 Copyright 2003, Project for Public Spaces
4.4 Copyright 2003, Project for Public Spaces

5.1 Copyright 2007, Project for Public Spaces
5.2 Bill Main, just outside Millennium Park Restroom, Chicago
5.3 Bill Main, Zihuatanejo, Mexico
5.4 Copyright 2003, Project for Public Spaces
5.5 Bill Main, Capitol Plaza, NYC

6.1 Courtesy of OLIN, Columbus Circle, NYC
6.2 Courtesy of Mithun, Photo copyright Benjamin Benschneider, Puyallup City Hall
6.3 Copyright 2003, Project for Public Spaces

6.4   Courtesy of Wallace Roberts & Todd, Scripps Institute of
       Oceanography, Pawka Green, UC San Diego
6.5   Copyright 2005, Project for Public Spaces
6.6   Courtesy of Martha Swartz Partners, Jacob Javits Plaza, NYC

7.1   Courtesy of Thomas Balsley Associates, Capitol Plaza, NYC
7.2   Courtesy of UW Memorial Union, Madison, and Wisconsin
       Department of Tourism
7.3   Courtesy of UW Memorial Union, Madison; photo by
       Connie Reeves
7.4   Courtesy of Thomas Balsley Associates, Capitol Plaza, NYC
7.5   Courtesy of PWP Landscape Architecture, Copyright 2008, Novartis
       Executive Courtyard, Basel, Switzerland

8.1   Bill Main, Mariano Park, Chicago
8.2   Copyright 2007, Project for Public Spaces
8.3   Copyright 2003, Project for Public Spaces
8.4   Bill Main, Paley Park, NYC
8.5   Bill Main, UC Berkeley
8.6   Copyright 2007, Project for Public Spaces

9.1   Bill Main, Kalamazoo
9.2   Copyright 2003, Project for Public Spaces
9.3   Bill Main, San Francisco
9.4   Copyright 2004, Project for Public Spaces
9.5   Courtesy of Bryant Park Corporation
9.6   Bill Main, Boston
9.7   Bill Main, Chicago

10.1   Copyright 2003, Project for Public Spaces
10.2   Copyright 2003, Project for Public Spaces
10.3   Bill Main, Hong Kong
10.4   Bill Main, Hong Kong
10.5   Bill Main, Chicago

11.1   Courtesy of Ken Smith, Urban logs used for communal seating in a
       schoolyard in Queens.
11.2   Bill Main, Hong Kong
11.3   Bill Main, Hong Kong, future cricket stars
11.4   Courtesy of MIG, Inc.

12.1   Bill Main, The Park at Lakeshore East, Chicago
12.2   Courtesy of Site Design Group, Ltd., Chicago Children's
       Advocacy Center
12.3   Bill Main, UW Madison

13.1   Bill Main, Daley Plaza, Chicago
13.2   Bill Main, Beijing

13.3 Courtesy of JJR—Landscape Architecture; Smith Group—
Architecture; Tom Banner—Photography, Courtyard, Providence
Saint Joseph Medical Center, Burbank

14.1 Bill Main, Crown Fountain, Chicago
14.2 Bill Main, Lurie Garden, Chicago
14.3 Bill Main, Millennium Park, Chicago

15.1 Bill Main, Buckingham Fountain, Chicago
15.2 Bill Main, Christopher Columbus Waterfront Park, Boston
15.3 Copyright 2005, Project for Public Spaces
15.4 Copyright 2007, Project for Public Spaces
15.5 Courtesy of Tom Oslund, photo by Michael Mingo, illuminated
bench at Gold Medal Park, along the Mississippi in Minneapolis

16.1 Bill Main, Roppongi Hills, Tokyo
16.2 Bill Main, Beijing
16.3 Copyright 2007, Project for Public Spaces
16.4 Bill Main, Shanghai
16.5 Bill Main, Beijing
16.6 Bill Main, Eastport Park, Boston

17.1 Courtesy of Thomas Balsley Associates, Capitol Plaza, NYC
17.2 Bill Main, Noosa Head, Australia
17.3 Copyright 2003, Project for Public Spaces
17.4 Bill Main, Christopher Columbus Waterfront Park, Boston

18.1 Copyright 2004, Project for Public Spaces
18.2 Copyright 2003, Project for Public Spaces
18.3 Bill Main, Chicago

19.1 Mayer/Reed and C. Bruce Forster, Copyright 2008, The Civic,
Portland, Oregon
19.2 Bill Main, Zihuatanejo, Mexico
19.3 Bill Main, Australia
19.4 Bill Main, Las Vegas
19.5 Bill Main, South Boston Maritime Park, Boston

20.1 Bill Main, Chicago
20.2 Bill Main, NYC
20.3 Bill Main, UC Berkeley
20.4 Copyright 2007, Project for Public Spaces
20.5 Bill Main, Madison

21.1 Bill Main, UC Berkeley
21.2 Bill Main, Madison
21.3 Copyright 2004, Project for Public Spaces

21.4   Bill Main, Hudson River Park, NYC
21.5   Bill Main, San Francisco
21.6   Bill Main, along the waterfront in Australia

22.1   Copyright 2003, Project for Public Spaces
22.2   Copyright 2003, Project for Public Spaces
22.3   Bill Main, Elevated Acre at 55 Water Street, NYC

23.1   Bill Main, Grant Park, Chicago
23.2   Copyright 2004, Project for Public Spaces
23.3   Courtesy of Thomas Balsley Associates, Capitol Plaza, NYC
23.4   Bill Main, Elevated Acre at 55 Water Street, NYC
23.5   Copyright 2003, Project for Public Spaces

24.1   Copyright 2007, Project for Public Spaces
24.2   Copyright 2007, Project for Public Spaces
24.3   Copyright 2003, Project for Public Spaces
24.4   Copyright 2007, Project for Public Spaces
24.5   Bill Main, UC Berkeley

INDEX

Page numbers followed by *p* or *t* refer to photographs and tables